Dean Worcester's Fantasy Islands

Dean Worcester's Fantasy Islands

Photography, Film,
and the
Colonial Philippines

MARK RICE

The University of Michigan Press
Ann Arbor

Published in the United States of America by
The University of Michigan Press
Printed and bound by CPI Group (UK) Ltd, Croydon, CR0 4YY
♾

2017   2016   2015   2014   4   3   2   1

A CIP catalog record for this book is available from the British Library.

Library of Congress Cataloging-in-Publication Data

Rice, Mark.
    Dean Worcester's fantasy islands : photography, film, and the colonial
Philippines / Mark Rice.
        pages   cm
    Includes bibliographical references and index.
    ISBN 978-0-472-07218-7 (hardback) — ISBN 978-0-472-05218-9
(paperback) — ISBN 978-0-472-12033-8 (e-book)
    1. Worcester, Dean C. (Dean Conant), 1866–1924.   2. Worcester, Dean
C. (Dean Conant), 1866–1924—Political and social views.   3. Colonial
administrators—Philippines—Biography.   4. Photographers—Philippines—
Biography.   5. Photography—Political aspects—Philippines—History.
6. Photography in ethnology—Philippines—History. 7. Philippines—
History—Pictorial works.   8. Philippines—Colonization—History.
9. United States—Relations—Philippines.   10. Philippines—Relations—
United States. I. Title.
E664.W83R53   2014
325'.3599092—dc23
[B]
                                                              2013048767

Contents

LIST OF ILLUSTRATIONS   vii

ACKNOWLEDGMENTS   ix

A NOTE ON TERMINOLOGY   xi

1   Establishing the Archive   1

2   Filipinos, Dressed and Undressed   40

3   Dean Worcester, *National Geographic Magazine,*
    and the Imagined Philippines   80

4   Lecturing against Philippine Independence:
    Photography, Film, and the Lyceum Circuit   118

5   Final Acts and Reactions   156

NOTES   193

BIBLIOGRAPHY   211

INDEX   217

Illustrations

Fig. 1. Dean C. Worcester, "Insurgent Prisoners on their way to Manila" (1899). 13

Fig. 2. Dean C. Worcester, "A Refugee family of Tagalogs and the little shop which they had opened on the street" (1899). 17

Fig. 3. Dean C. Worcester, "Negrito man and woman, types 3 and 4. Full length front view" (1900). 23

Fig. 4. Dean C. Worcester, "Young Tagbanua woman, type 4. Half length front view" (1902). 27

Fig. 5. Dean C. Worcester, "Negrito man, type 1, and myself, to show relative size" (1901). 43

Fig. 6. Dean C. Worcester, "Group of Negritos" (1901). 49

Fig. 7. Dean C. Worcester, "Bontoc Igorot girl, type 13. Full length front view, nude" (1904). 61

Fig. 8. "The Igorot Sequence" as it appeared in Frederick Carleton Chamberlin, *The Philippine Problem, 1898–1913*. 64

Fig. 9. Dean C. Worcester, "Bontoc Igorot man, type 1. Full length front view" (1901). 72

Fig. 10. Dean C. Worcester (attributed), "A Bontoc Constabulary soldier, without uniform" (1903). 76

Fig. 11. Dean C. Worcester (attributed), "A Bontoc Constabulary soldier in uniform" (1903). 77

Fig. 12. "The Effect of a Little Schooling." *National Geographic Magazine*, November 1913. 81

Fig. 13. "Primitive Agriculture. Tagbanua Women Harvesting
Rice, Calamianes Islands." *National Geographic Magazine*,
May 1903.   91

Fig. 14. Plate from 1903 Philippine Census. *National
Geographic Magazine*, April 1905.   94

Fig. 15. "An Igorot Gathering Lilies Near the Trail to Cervantes."
National Geographic Magazine, March 1911.   101

Fig. 16. "A Bontoc Igorot Boy Who Has Been Burrowing for Coins
in a Dish of Flour." *National Geographic Magazine*, March
1911.   106

Fig. 17. "Two Men of 'No Man's Land,' Showing Typical Dress and
Ornaments." *National Geographic Magazine*, September
1912.   111

Fig. 18. Advertisement for Dean C. Worcester's lecture series.
National Geographic Magazine, November 1913.   119

Fig. 19. Charles Martin (attributed), "Philippine Islands—N.
Luzon. Ifugao. Scene from head-hunting episode. Staged for
Dean C. Worcester. The head is papier mache. The jawbone
was formerly used for this purpose" (ca. 1912).   131

Fig. 20. Dean C. Worcester lecture brochure (1913).   144

Fig. 21. Advertisement for *Native Life in the Philippines*.
The Moving Picture World, February 28, 1914.   154

Fig. 22. "The Metamorphosis of a Bontoc Igorot." Frontispiece
to volume 2 of Dean C. Worcester, *The Philippines Past and
Present* (1914).   163

Fig. 23. Dean C. Worcester, "Blas Villamor, Bakidan, Saking,
and two other brothers of Bakidan, and myself. There are
six brothers in this family and they rule the upper Nabuagan
River valley. Bakidan is the most powerful" (1905).   167

Fig. 24. "A Possible Office-Holder." From volume 2 of Dean C.
Worcester, *The Philippines Past and Present* (1914).   169

Fig. 25. Dean C. Worcester, "Skull house ornaments with the
gentleman who took the heads from which the skulls were
obtained. Note particularly the shouldered piles of the house"
(ca. 1903).   175

Acknowledgments

———

THIS BOOK HAS BENEFITED from the support of many people. I would like to express my appreciation to the staff at the following archives: the Missouri Historical Society, the St. Louis Public Library, the National Anthropological Archives, the Thetford (Vermont) Historical Society, the Newberry Library, the Houghton Library at Harvard University, the Bentley Historical Library at the University of Michigan, the Special Collections Library at the University of Michigan, and the University of Michigan Museum of Anthropology.

Special thanks go to the following individuals whose help, encouragement, questions, and suggestions have been invaluable: Carla Sinopoli at the University of Michigan Museum of Anthropology, Kate Pourshariati at the Penn Museum, Melissa Banta at Harvard University, Pat Kervick at Harvard's Peabody Museum of Archaeology, Nina Cummings at the Field Museum, Carolyn Johnson at the University of Chicago, Ricardo Punzalan at the University of Maryland at College Park, and the film historian Nick Deocampo. I would also like to thank Tom Dwyer of the University of Michigan Press for agreeing to publish my book the way I wanted to write it.

My home institution, St. John Fisher College, has provided me with material support that allowed me to take the research trips necessary for a book such as this. I also benefited immensely from the time, energy, and commitment of two work-study students, Henry Cumoletti and Mackenzie White. I am very fortunate to work at a small college that encourages and nurtures faculty scholarship.

My interest in the Philippines stretches back to the 1980s when I served there as a Peace Corps Volunteer on the island of Siquijor. It was a wonderful and challenging experience that provided me with an understanding of the complicated relationship between the United States and the Philippines. I am indebted both to the Peace Corps as an institution and to the friends, colleagues, and host family members in the Philippines who made those two years so rewarding for me.

My family knows how important this work is for me, and my niece, Kristin Rice Sullivan, deserves special thanks for helping to shed light on several critical passages in the book. Most of all, I am forever grateful to my wife, and fellow Returned Peace Corps Volunteer, Anne Panning, and to my children, Hudson and Lily Panning, for taking an interest in what I do and for making me happy every day.

PORTIONS OF THIS BOOK have been published in different form in the following journal articles: "His Name Was Don Francisco Muro: Reconstructing an Image of American Imperialism," *American Quarterly* 62, no. 1 (2010): 49–76; "Colonial Photography across Empires and Islands," *Journal of Transnational American Studies* 3, no. 2 (2011): 1–22 (http://www.escholarship.org/uc/item/8fz4t188); "Dean Worcester's Photographs and American Perceptions of the Philippines," *Education About Asia* 16, no 2 (2011): 29–33; and "Dean Worcester's Photographs, American National Identity, and *National Geographic Magazine*," *Australasian Journal of American Studies* 31, no. 2 (2012): 42–56.

A Note on Terminology

THROUGHOUT THIS BOOK, I have chosen to use the terminology employed by Dean C. Worcester regarding the names of various groups in the Philippines. I have done so in order to simplify the reading experience and so that readers can more clearly understand Worcester's ideas about racial and ethnic identity in the Philippines. I recognize that some of the terms I include are no longer in use and, in fact, that some of them may now be considered offensive. In addition, the spelling of some groups varied over time and by user (e.g., Igorot and Igorotte, Tingian and Tinguiane). I have tried to standardize the spelling when I use the term, but I keep the varied spellings intact when quoting.

CHAPTER 1

Establishing the Archive

ONE DAY, EARLY IN 1913, Dean Conant Worcester sat down to prepare a memorandum for a lecture he was scheduled to deliver on January 20 in Manila's Grand Opera House, one of that city's most important cultural institutions. He may have been in a reflective mood when he sat down to write. The date of his lecture coincided with the fourteenth anniversary of his entry into government service as a member of the Schurman Commission, which was appointed by President William McKinley on January 20, 1899, to assess conditions in the Philippines and to recommend policies the United States should adopt in its new colony. Since 1901, Worcester had served as secretary of the interior in the U.S. colonial regime in the Philippines. Moreover, Worcester knew that the upcoming inauguration on March 4 of Woodrow Wilson as president of the United States meant that significant changes were coming to the country's colonial policies and that his days as the longest-serving colonial administrator in the Philippines were nearing their end. Worcester's lecture, which combined lantern slides and motion pictures of the Tingians, Ifugaos, and Bontoc Igorots of northern Luzon, was among the last he gave as secretary of the interior.

Although his time in government was winding down, in some ways Worcester had yet to reach the apex of his long and influential career. Over the previous two years he had published three heavily illustrated articles in *National Geographic Magazine,* and he had a fourth article scheduled for publication later that year. He was preparing to release a damning report, *Slavery and Peonage in the Philippines,* a broadside against Filipino political elites who were calling for independence. He had begun planning what would become his most important work, the two-volume book *The Philippines Past and Present* that he would fill with more than one hundred photographs that he had accumulated (some taken by Worcester, others taken by government photographers) during his long career. In addition, over the course of the previous year he had overseen the making of several short films that would result in the motion picture *Native Life in the Philippines.* By the end of the year he would be giving lectures using his films, and lantern slides made from his photographs, to large audiences in the United States, who would be enthralled by what they saw. (He had no way to know it yet, but his lecture tour would culminate with him showing his lantern slides to a committee of the United States Senate.) So, while Worcester may have been feeling reflective as he thought about his January 20 lecture, he was also looking squarely to the future.

Included in Worcester's memorandum were the lines "Camera can be made to tell the truth" and "I believe in the teaching value of pictures."[1] Although Worcester may not have paid close attention to his choice of words, it is telling that he said that the camera "can be made" to be truthful, not that the "camera tells the truth." Intentional or not, the phrasing matters. Worcester's words suggest that he recognized that the truthfulness of photography was not inherent, that the camera lens was not a transparent window onto the world. Instead, "the truth" was something that had to be coaxed out of the camera. The photographer was the one who determined the truth, and the camera had to be used in a deliberate fashion in order to reveal that truth.

Indeed, Worcester had spent more than a decade in a sustained effort to use his camera to document what he felt to be the "truth" about the Philippines. Near the end of his career, he turned to the movie camera for the same reason. The "truth" that Worcester wanted to convince his audience of was that the Philippines was incapable of self-government and that a significant population of non-Christian minority groups required a strong U.S. presence in order both to protect them and to continue guiding them toward civilization.[2] Failure to do so, Worcester repeatedly argued, would result in calamity both for the non-Christians and for the Philippines as a whole. For Worcester, cameras—both still and motion picture—were critically important for revealing that truth.[3]

To build and sustain his argument, Worcester amassed an archive of more than fifteen thousand photographs, and more than two miles of motion picture footage, taken during his years in the Philippines. Over five thousand of his original negatives and lantern slides are now housed on the fourth floor of the Ruthven Museums Building on the campus of the University of Michigan in Ann Arbor. Separated into forty-three separate categories, including thirty-one different cultural groups, roughly half of the negatives in this collection have Philippine cultural minority groups as their subject. There are also photographs that record various activities of the colonial regime itself, from the brutality of the Philippine-American War to the building of schools and roads. Housed in the University of Michigan Museum of Anthropology (UMMA), this archive is perhaps the largest collection of original negatives of officially sponsored colonial photography found in the United States.[4]

Among the many notable features of the archive is the fact that it is largely the product of a single individual. This is not to say that Worcester took all of the photographs in the archive. He did not. Among the negatives and lantern slides there are photographs taken by other men, such as Frank Bourns and Albert Jenks and, most importantly, Charles Martin, who worked as the official government photographer in the Philippines for more than a decade. Despite the different photographers included, the collection of photographs that the archive represents was conceived, collected, and organized by Worcester. In this, Worcester was similar to administrators in many European colonies in the nineteenth and early twentieth centuries. Indeed, what the historian Satadru Sen writes about Maurice Vidal Portman's archive of colonial photographs taken in the British-controlled Andaman Islands could just as easily have been written about Worcester's photography in the U.S.-controlled Philippines. Like Portman, Worcester was "the major editor of the archive, having played a decisive role in selecting, labeling, organizing, and preserving what exists."[5]

Also like Portman, and other colonial ethnological photographers, many (though by no means all) of the photographs in the Worcester archive conform to what Sen calls the "established idioms of colonial photography and anthropology" as they developed through the course of the nineteenth century.[6] Anthropology and photography both emerged as part of a dominant strand of European positivism in the nineteenth century, and both were deployed as strategies for ordering a world increasingly enmeshed in the networks of a nascent global capitalism. In Europe and in the United States, photographs of colonial subjects frequently were organized in such a way as to categorize the cultures of those subjects. The ordering of culture was done in order to make difference visible when such difference suited the colonizing nation. At other times the ordering was done in order to erase difference, grouping together people who, on their own, did not recognize their commonality. Photography helped make anthropological subjects "fully legible . . . for inspection," as Christopher Pinney puts it, and such inspection was a routine aspect of the consolidation of colonial power.[7]

The political and cultural ideologies that undergird the construction of ethnographic archives such as Portman's and Worcester's didn't come under close scrutiny by historians until several decades after the establishment of such archives, a point made by Eleanor Hight and Gary Sampson in the introduction to their 2002 book *Colonialist Photography: Imag(in)ing Race and Place:*

> Many of the photographs taken and acquired by the colonial governments of Britain and other countries were gathered together in official archives. In the "scientific" documentation of the indigenous populations of Africa, Asia, Oceania, the Americas, and the Middle East, entire archives of photographs were assembled for the study and subsequent ordering of the world's populations. At first glance these photographs might appear to have been conceived with an apparent artlessness or scientific candor to bring familiarity and classification to a great variety of ethnic groups and cultures. Only within the past two decades, however, have scholars begun to shatter this façade of objectivity.[8]

While it may be true that scholars were relative latecomers in questioning the objectivity of colonial archives, many people both in the United States and the Philippines vocally and angrily denounced Worcester's photographic representations of Filipinos as gross misrepresentations, a fact I will return to later.

DEAN WORCESTER DID NOT initially set out to build an archive of ethnographic photographs, in part because he was trained neither as a photographer nor as an anthropologist. Born in Thetford, Vermont, in 1866, he studied zoology at the University of Michigan, graduating in 1889. His first exposure to the Philippines came during his undergraduate years. In 1887 and 1888 Worcester was part of a zoological expedition to the Philippines, then a Spanish colony, led by his professor, James B. Steere. Worcester's classmate Frank Bourns was another member of the expedition. Seeking more adventure and believing that there was much more scientific exploration to do in the islands, Worcester and Bourns secured money for a return trip to the Philippines as the sole members of the Menage Expedition, which lasted from 1890 to 1893 and gained enough attention that an article about it was published in the *New York Times* in 1896.[9] Although Worcester and Bourns encountered several different cultural groups while on these expeditions, their efforts were directed primarily toward the gathering of zoological specimens, not ethnological information.[10] In time, however, Worcester grew to recognize that both photography and ethnology could prove useful to him, and he spent a great deal of energy on both during his career in the Philippines.

In fact, this shift in his interests began a few years before his 1901 appointment as secretary of the interior, when he emerged as one of the nation's leading experts on the Philippines. When the Spanish-American War began on April 25, 1898, Worcester knew more about the Philippines than most Americans. While teaching zoology at the University of Michigan, he established himself as an authority on the Philippines in an article he coauthored with Bourns that appeared in the October 1897 issue of *The Cosmopolitan* magazine. Titled "Spanish Rule in the Philippines," the article was illustrated with several photographs taken during the Menage Expedition. The article mentioned linguistic and cultural variability in the Philippines, but its main point was to condemn Spain for how it administered the islands.[11]

In the months following the publication of that article, Worcester found himself in demand as a lecturer and as an author, and he wrote several articles about the Philippines for popular magazines. As Rodney Sullivan writes in *Exemplar of Americanism,* the only full-length biography of Worcester, "Between April and October of 1898 widely circulating American journals carried six new Worcester articles on the Philippines." Among the prominent magazines he wrote for were *The Independent, The Century,* and *National Geographic.* Sullivan points out that Worcester's reach extended beyond the readers of those magazines, "as major newspapers reprinted and further circulated the material."[12] Many Americans were deeply curious to know more about a place they had never heard about before on the other side of the globe where the United States was engaged in a war.

In addition to these articles, Worcester wrote a highly successful book, *The Philippine Islands and Their People,* that he based partly on the letters he had written home during his earlier expeditions to the Philippines. Worcester's book was reprinted four times between October 1898 and January 1899, and it earned positive reviews in popular magazines as well as in academic journals. One review noted in particular the book's "descriptions of the people, that enable us to judge for ourselves how far they are capable of organizing and maintaining self-government or any other kind of government; shrewd glimpses into the workings of the minds of savage Tagbanuas and Mangyans, barbarian Moros and semi-civilized Visayans and Tagalogs."[13] Worcester included several photographs of representatives of different culture groups in the Philippines, photographs that he believed would help drive home his argument that even "the civilized natives are utterly unfit for self-government."[14] This was an argument that he would continue to hammer home for the next fifteen years, and an argument for which he found photography to be very useful.

As it turns out, Bourns shot most of the photographs included in Worcester's book, and it appears that he was the chief photographer on the Menage Expedition. In photographs in which both men appear, it is Bourns who holds the shutter release. Based both on the book's text and its images, it seems clear that when the men separated, Bourns would take the camera with him. For example, at one point in the book Worcester writes about a large snake that he had killed on Palawan and his wish that he could have photographed it prior to skinning it: "I have always regretted that I did not have the camera with me. When Bourns brought it, a few days later, we got a photograph of the skin."[15] In the coming years, Worcester would be sure to have his camera ready as much as possible.

By the end of 1898, Worcester's reputation helped to secure him a meeting with President William McKinley to discuss tensions rising in the Philippines between Filipino revolutionaries who were eager to establish the Philippines as a sovereign republic and the U.S. military, which was acting under McKinley's policy of "benevolent assimilation" and was unwilling to accept Philippine independence.[16] Worcester offered his services if the president felt that he could be of use to the country. A short time later Worcester obtained a leave of absence from his teaching position at the University of Michigan in order to accept an appointment to the Schurman Commission. Though he was the youngest member of the Commission, Worcester had far more experience in the Philippines than any other member. On January 30, 1899, less than two weeks after his appointment, Worcester, Commission head Jacob Schurman, and their staff set off across the rough waters of the northern Pacific Ocean aboard the Canadian ocean liner RMS *Empress of Japan*, headed to Yokohama, Japan. From there they sailed to Nagasaki, Shanghai, and Hong Kong before finally heading to Manila.

During the two-week trip to Yokohama, Worcester spent time developing his skills as a photographer. Aiding him was his secretary, Penoyer L. Sherman, a chemist who left his position at the University of Michigan in order to accompany Worcester to the Philippines. Although Worcester had worked in photomicrography while on the staff of the University of Michigan, the view camera apparently was a new piece of equipment for him. He revealed in a letter to Douglas Flattery of the Loews Theatres Company, dated November 13, 1912, that "photography has been my recreation during the past fourteen years."[17] In other words, Worcester's interest in photography coincided with his emergence as one of the country's foremost experts on the Philippines. He may have bought the camera in order to secure new photographs for the writing and lecturing he no doubt imagined he'd be doing once he returned to the United States.

In a February 11, 1899, letter he wrote to his wife, Nanon, Worcester reported that he was getting his camera prepared to take photos: "Day before yesterday Sherman and I got together and fixed up a focusing cloth which would button right onto the camera. This morning all of us have been marshalled on deck while the first and second officers took shots at us, and if they get negatives that are any good I will try to get prints to send you. I have not taken any pictures myself, yet, but shall load plate-holders to-day and keep on the watch for snap-shots running down the coast of Japan."[18] Several photographs from the voyage can be found in the UMMA archive in series number 59. They are mostly unremarkable and consist of group portraits of the ship's crew and of the commission contingent, along with views of harbors, coastlines, and ships shot from onboard the *Empress*.

Sullivan downplays the significance of Worcester's photographic activities during this trip, saying only that Worcester "tinkered with his camera between bouts of seasickness, taking group photographs on the deck."[19] In actuality, Worcester was quite serious about mastering the intricacies of working with a view camera and learning the chemistry used to develop his negatives and to make prints. He was committed to documenting his work while on the Commission, and the camera was one tool for keeping records of what he saw. Given the recent success of his public lectures, his articles, and his book, Worcester was fully aware of the fact that upon his expected return to the United States he would once again have the opportunity to capitalize on his experiences in the

Philippines. At that point he had no way to foresee how long his career in the Philippines would last.

In addition to his camera, Worcester used his letters to keep track of his activities while a member of the Commission. In one letter written aboard the *Empress,* he mentioned to his wife that he had forgotten to number the letters he mailed home the way he had intended, "but will call this one *nine,* and hereafter will keep a list."[20] It wasn't simply that Worcester was a passionate cataloger and collector, though he certainly was both, writing on the very first page of his 1914 book, *The Philippines Past and Present:* "As a boy I went through several of the successive stages of collector's fever from which the young commonly suffer."[21] It was also that Worcester used his letters to draft sections of potential future articles, speeches, or books.

Indeed, several of Worcester's original typed letters found in the Thetford (Vermont) Historical Society have sections bracketed on them (including the section quoted above about his desire to keep track of his letters.) The Worcester manuscript collection at the University of Michigan's Bentley Historical Library has typed manuscript pages that were taken from many of the same letters, but with the bracketed sections omitted, a clear indication that the letters were more than just family letters in Worcester's mind. In a related way, the photographs, many of which he mailed home to his wife and mother, weren't sent just to show his family what he saw; Worcester most likely imagined he would be able to make use of them at some later point.

THE SCHURMAN COMMISSION departed from the United States hoping to find a relatively calm, though undoubtedly tense, situation in the Philippines. The recently signed Treaty of Paris ending the Spanish-American War and President McKinley's famous "benevolent assimilation" speech signaled to Filipino political leaders that the United States was unwilling to recognize Philippine sovereignty, but the precise nature of the future relationship between the United States and the Philippines was not yet clear. Despite the Commission's hopes, the Philippine-American War erupted while Worcester and Schurman were crossing the Pacific. In his February 14 letter to Nanon, Worcester wrote: "We anchored inside the breakwater [of Yokohama] about nine o'clock, and were at once met by one of the secretaries from the American Legation, at Tokio, who informed us that he had important and *private* news for us. We had already obtained papers from the pilot, and had learned of the report of fighting at Manila, in which 1900 insurgents were said to have been killed, as well as of the passage [by Congress] of the Peace Treaty [ending hostilities between Spain and the United States], by a very narrow margin. The latter event greatly pleased us, and the former, while undesirable in itself, was, I fear, one of the inevitable things."[22]

Even with the deteriorating situation in Philippines and the uncertainty of what his work as a commissioner would actually entail, Worcester continued to focus much of his attention on photography. Walking around Yokohama, he noticed a new photographic technique that impressed him enough to go into detail about it in his letter:

> They have gotten up a new process since I was here, and now take, or rather *print* photographs directly on lacquer, producing most beautiful effects. They use them for album-covers etc., and they are entirely permanent, and so more satisfactory than the sort of covers that I brought home before. I wanted to get one large fifty page album, and three or four small ones in which I could mount photographs which I take out here, and give to friends. I got the large one and it is a perfect beauty. The small ones I could not find in stock, and there was no time to get them made. We looked over colored photographs, and took in the town generally.[23]

His letter continues in a similarly enthusiastic vein, revealing his excitement about being in Japan and on his way back to the Philippines.

Two days later, Worcester wrote to Nanon that he had established a darkroom aboard the *Empress,* and that he had been taking photographs during the voyage down the Japanese coast. Indeed, his desire to take photographs prompted him to cut short his letter: "I want to be out taking photographs as we run in, so will only write a note. There is little enough to write in any event. I have been taking a few 'snap-shots' of objects along the shores, and every one of them has turned out fairly well. Sherman and I were developing negatives yesterday."[24] (That his chosen camera used $5'' \times 7''$ glass-plate negatives instead of a much lighter and more portable Kodak camera suggests that he wanted his photographs to be more than just "snap-shots.")

In his next letter, written on February 18 while they were approaching Shanghai, Worcester presented himself to Nanon as a worldly traveler who knew how to open doors for his fellow commissioners. For example, he writes that the commission's disbursing officer, "Major [James E.] Sawyer[,] was very much taken with the carved bamboo canes that I had purchased at Kobe, and was anxious to get some for himself. The whole crowd insisted on going with us, and as a natural result, the advent of our extensive cavalcade caused a big rise in prices. I finally persuaded the Major quietly to leave the crowd with me, and we then got what we wanted at a reasonable cost."[25]

Worcester immediately followed this anecdote with one about Schurman's desire "to see geisha girls dance." Worcester says that his initial inquiry into the matter suggested that there were no "respectable" teahouses in town, but he was able to find someplace to bring Schurman through his rickshaw driver:

> We had to sit on the floor and were promptly provided with refreshments, consisting of fish served in several ways, pickled mushrooms, oranges, *saki* and something which looked like bars of soap. I did not get up courage enough to tackle it. Our entertainers appeared in due time—two samisen players and three dancers, the latter little girls of eight to twelve years. One of them was very clever, but the other two were no good. They all managed to keep their clothes on, though some of the dancing was decidedly suggestive. . . . We had a good deal of fun, but judged from the standpoint of artistic merit I fear the "show" could not be very highly recommended.[26]

Although he told Nanon that it was Schurman's idea to watch the dancing, Worcester would later reveal his own interest in the bodies of young Filipinas.

In the same letter, Worcester gave Nanon additional details about his photographic activities: "I spent quite a part of the day in developing a few negatives which I had taken. Our dark room here on board is very small and steam pipes run through it, so that it heats up at once when closed, and we are obliged to stop after developing a plate, and open things up, cool off ourselves, and move all our chemicals out into the air until they get down to a proper temperature again." He went on to tell her that he planned to make some contact prints using "solio paper" (a type of printing paper that didn't require a chemical bath for the image to appear) that he would mail to her once they reached Hong Kong.[27]

While in Hong Kong, Worcester and Schurman learned more about the fighting in the Philippines, but Worcester believed that the war would not last long. He knew that many Americans would oppose the United States fighting the Filipino revolutionaries, but his own opinion was clearly in favor of a strong U.S. military strike: "All in all things are looking promising. I imagine the country is howling over the fighting, but it was bound to come, and once at it, the best way to end it is to hit them *hard*." He also blustered about his own martial vigor, saying that any "Tagalog that tries to monkey around me with a bolo [a type of machete] will be gathered to his fathers," before relaying to Nanon his love of comfort: "It is time for me to get my bath and go to breakfast. During the trip across the Pacific I missed my salt-water bath only one morning. You see I am quite luxurious when I have time to be!" [28]

Worcester continued his letter the next day, after learning "that there were very extensive fires in Manila and the suburbs, set by organized incendiaries, and accompanied by more or less skirmishing." One result of this escalation in fighting was that the commission's departure for the Philippines was delayed. Thus, Worcester was able to turn once again to his photography:

> I must purchase or take some photographs here before leaving. Sherman developed my negatives yesterday. I was using the mixed lot of plates with which Goodyear brought my number from twenty to thirty dozen, and had unfortunately just struck a new kind, which were slower than the others, so that most of the negatives proved to have been under-exposed. As I feared, I was too far from many of the ships to get the best results, but shall at least get something to give you an idea of how things looked when we came in. Unfortunately it is cloudy to-day [*sic*], and I fear I shall not get on very fast with printing this afternoon, but will do my best, or rather have Sherman do his while I am dictating letters to the stenographer.[29]

Also while in Hong Kong, Worcester learned that word of *The Philippine Islands and Their People* had preceded him across the ocean. At breakfast on the morning of February 24, Lady Blake, the wife of Hong Kong governor Sir Henry Blake, remarked "that an American 'savant' had just published a book on the Philippines which she was anxious to get," without, it seems, recognizing that Worcester "was the fellow in question." In appreciation of her kind words, Worcester brought Lady Blake a copy of his book. He then lamented to Nanon: "I ought to have brought a trunkfull, more or less. I have only four copies left I believe."[30]

ON MARCH 4, Worcester and Schurman landed in Manila and Worcester soon made the acquaintance of Admiral George Dewey and General Elwell Otis, two other members of the commission who were already in the country. Almost immediately, Worcester began to photograph aspects of the Philippine-American War, including portraits of the admiral. On March 11, he wrote to Nanon: "In a few days I shall photograph fort San Antonio Abad where the Insurgents made their strong stand, and also the house where [General Francis] Green[e] and his staff passed the night, before the attack. It has since been occupied by the insurgents, and has been shelled by the fleet and shot to pieces generally."[31] Six days later, he wrote that the U.S. Army had taken control of Pasig, and that he went there to photograph: "The spot was rather picturesque, and we took a photograph of some of the men as they stowed away their grub."[32] He told her that he would send a package of photographs showing her scenes of war.

Worcester did not put himself in the line of fire and his photographs do little to reveal the ferocity of the fighting. As the above passages suggest, he typically went places after the fighting was over, photographing scenes of the aftermath, such as resting soldiers, trenches, damaged buildings, and Filipino fighters dead, wounded, or captured, such as this photograph (fig. 1) of captive Filipinos being guarded by American soldiers. This photograph was taken near the town of Polo in the province of Bulacan, north of Manila.

In the photograph, a line of prisoners stretches almost across the frame of the photograph, their guards spread out between them and the camera. There are equal amounts of sky above the prisoners and ground below them, dividing the image into three roughly equal horizontal bands. We cannot see any of their faces clearly due to the distance from which it was shot. Worcester was more interested in showing the number of prisoners than he was in showing any particular details about either the prisoners or the American soldiers guarding them. The photograph suggests the capacity of the U.S. military to subdue a numerically superior opponent. Perhaps the most interesting detail in the photograph is the shadow at bottom left showing Worcester, his camera, and one other figure—probably Sherman. (Worcester seems to have been particularly proud of this photograph; in an April 17 letter to his mother, he mentioned "a beautiful picture" he took of Filipino prisoners being taken to Manila,[33] and he included the image in his 1914 book, *The Philippines Past and Present.*)

In his first weeks in Manila, Worcester had no official work to do. He kept busy taking photographs, getting to know Dewey and Otis, and meeting with acquaintances old and new. In a letter dated just four days after he arrived in Manila, Worcester wrote to his mother about renewing relationships that he had established during the Menage Expedition:

Fig. 1. Dean C. Worcester, "Insurgent prisoners on their way to Manila," near Polo, Bulacan (1899). (Courtesy of the University of Michigan Museum of Anthropology, UMMA 58-B-036.)

"The first day we were on shore Don Pedro [Sanz] and Felix Fanlo came to Bourns's house looking for me, but I was down by the river. Yesterday I found myself near the address they had left, and ran in to see them. I struck Felix Fanlo and his brother down stairs, and they were delighted to see me." Walking upstairs, Worcester ran into other members of the family, and then Don Pedro himself, and he wrote, "I have not been so much delighted for a long time."[34]

The origins of Worcester's relationship with Sanz and Fanlo are recounted in *The Philippine Islands and Their People*. While on the Menage Expedition, Worcester met Sanz on the island of Romblon, where Sanz was one of the wealthiest and most powerful residents. According to Worcester, "The majority of the inhabitants of the place are dependent on" Sanz.[35] Worcester admired Sanz, writing, "His native helpers were everywhere contented and prosperous, and the results accomplished during his thirty-nine years of residence in the Philippines served to show what might have been brought about in the colony at large had the conquering nation contained more men like him."[36] According to Rodney Sullivan, Sanz, a Spaniard, provided Worcester with "a model of what could be done in the Philippines given efficient, paternal supervision."[37]

Worcester was thrilled to renew his acquaintance with Sanz, even if the circumstances weren't ideal for Sanz or his family. In his 1898 book, Worcester nostalgically recalled Fanlo's generosity while Worcester convalesced at his house after surviving a bout with typhoid fever: "Sõr Fanlo, a Spaniard on whom I had no earthly claim, watched with me night after night, and treated me as if I had been his brother. He did everything for my comfort that kindness could dictate or ingenuity devise."[38] Having mostly recovered from his illness, but too sick to continue his expedition in the Philippines, Worcester left for the United States: "As I bade good-by to the friends who had made it possible for me to come safely through the most trying of all my experiences, words failed me to express what was in my heart, and I could only grip their hands." He continues: "At ten o'clock that evening the lights of Manila sank into the bay as we steamed toward Corregidor, and when I awoke the next day nothing was visible save gray mist and the ever-restless waters of the China Sea. I had seen my last of the Philippine Islands and their people."[39] When he wrote those—the last words in his book—Worcester had no way of knowing that he would be back in the Philippines in less than a year and that he would renew his acquaintance with Fanlo and Sanz six years after he took his leave of the Philippines.

Worcester's admiration for the Spanish landowner and his family is reflected in the fact that the UMMA archive has six photographs showing Sanz. Five of the photographs show Sanz with members of his family, while one shows him sitting in a carriage with Worcester (48-B-006).[40] Two photographs (48-B-001 and 48-B-002) show Sanz with Fanlo and Sebastian Felice, his sons-in-law. Sanz sits in a chair while the two younger men stand behind him; all three are surrounded by potted plants on plant stands. Like much of Worcester's early photography, there is nothing exceptional about these images—their contrast is high and there is little attention paid to the details, which seem jumbled and hastily composed. Although he doubtless recalled the kindness of Sanz and Fanlo when he took their photograph, there is little sign of fraternity in either the posing or the looks on the men's faces. The photographs are stiff and formal, and do little to reveal a warm relationship between the photographer and his subjects.

The solemnity of the photographs may well have reflected the circumstances they found themselves in when they reunited with Worcester, who wrote to his mother that Sanz had to flee Romblon after his plantation was attacked by "some five-hundred Tagalogs" from Luzon and Mindoro. Sanz's family "brought absolutely nothing with them except a little extra clothing. They are living here now in a hand-to-mouth sort of way." Worcester was optimistic that he could "do the old man a good turn" through his position as a commissioner.[41] In a letter to Nanon he hinted at how he might be able to aid Sanz: "Old Don Pedro was full of information as to where Insurgent steamers were likely to be taken, as well as to the number of Tagalog soldiers in Tablas, Romblon, and Sibuyan." Worcester passed this information along to Dewey, who "was very much interested, and asked me to get full data. This I did, and in a day or two I shall present him with them. I fancy he will send a gun-boat to recapture Romblon."[42]

The Schurman Commission scheduled its first meeting for March 20, having been waiting for the arrival of the last commissioner, Charles Denby, before they commenced their official duties. The scheduling of that meeting prompted Worcester to lament to Nanon that his photography was being disrupted: "I did not send the photographs as I promised because just as I had them ready Admiral Dewey came in, and wanted some of them, which I was of course glad to give him, but it broke my set for you. I have more made, but they are not yet toned, and I fear that I cannot get them done this morning, as we are to have our first meeting at nine."[43] (As it turned out, Denby didn't arrive when the other commissioners had expected him to, preventing them from commencing their official business until his arrival on April 2.)

Even after the Commission began its official work, Worcester continued to photograph regularly. His subjects included both the war and the daily life around Manila. The UMMA archive contains more than two hundred of these photographs, thirty-one in category 57 (Native Industries), and 207 in category 58 (Current History). Nearly one hundred are photographs of what Worcester labeled the "insurrection against the United States." By contrast, he took very few photographs that he categorized as being ethnological in their purpose. It seems that Worcester was not yet thinking about his photographs in the same kind of politically strategic way that he later would. After all, it wasn't yet clear that the Philippine resistance to U.S. occupation would last as long as it did. In addition, Worcester had not yet fixed on a method for using his photographs to advance an argument for U.S. control of the Philippines.

Even more significantly, given their prominence in the archive as a whole, there is not a single photograph in the UMMA of non-Christian Filipinos taken in 1899. There are only four photographs that he catego-

rized as being of Tagalogs, all of which are family portraits. Three of the
Tagalog photographs were taken in August in Bacoor, Cavite, located
just to the southwest of Manila. One (43-D-001) is an outdoor portrait of
a man named Felix Quenca along with his wife and three children standing in a grove of bananas. All are immaculately dressed for the occasion
and they stand facing the camera directly, uncertain looks on their faces.
The other two (43-D-002 and 43-D-003) show women and girls of a Tagalog family standing on what appears to be the courtyard or balcony of a
large home. They, too, stand directly facing the camera and are dressed
in formal clothing. In the accompanying descriptions for both photographs in the UMMA archive, Worcester wrote: "Several girls show white
blood."

The fourth photograph, taken on April 13, 1899, shows a refugee
family standing by their small shop on a street in Manila (fig. 2). Shot
from middle distance and from a slightly oblique angle, Worcester
placed the family and their shop in the direct center of the frame. For a
street scene, the photograph is oddly static. The family stands stiffly looking at the camera, and there is little activity going on around the shop,
which is constructed of tree limbs and blankets. Worcester doesn't allow
the viewer to see what kinds of merchandise are being sold. The likely
intent of the photograph was to serve as visual evidence of the presence
of people displaced by the Philippine-American War. Worcester would
have placed the blame for this family's deprivations at the feet of the
"insurgents." However, given the isolation of the people in this scene,
the photograph does little to suggest that there were large numbers of
refugees in the city.

This photograph also appears in an index of photographs that
Worcester prepared in 1905, which will be discussed in detail below.
However, in that index, the photograph was not classified as being about
Tagalogs. Instead, it was included in a series of photographs about the
recent history of Manila. Moreover, the description of the photograph
did not refer to the people shown as refugees, saying only that they were
a "group of Tagalogs about a street vendor's shop." As will be discussed
in greater detail below, Worcester regularly wrote different captions for
individual photographs, allowing them to tell different "truths" depending on the context in which he used them.

AFTER THE SCHURMAN COMMISSION completed its fact-finding mission in the Philippines, Worcester returned to the United States in October 1899 to aid in the writing of the official Commission report. He also

Fig. 2. Dean C. Worcester, "A refugee family of Tagalogs and the little shop which they had opened on the street," Manila (April 13, 1899). (Courtesy of the University of Michigan Museum of Anthropology, UMMA 43-A-098.)

resumed lecturing about the Philippines. Audience expectations had changed since the previous year, the general curiosity that many Americans had about the Philippines having given way to intense debates about the role of the United States as a colonial power. In a lecture given before Chicago's Hamilton Club on November 15, 1899, Worcester criticized those who would make a political issue of U.S. control of the Philippines and he claimed for himself "emotional detachment, practicality, and respect for 'facts.'"[44]

Worcester made a distinction in his speech between what he called "the Filipino people" and "their Tagalog masters," and claimed that the United States was fighting the latter in order to protect the former. In this way he denied the legitimacy of the leadership of the Philippine Republic, many of whom came from Tagalog families. He also argued that the Philippines was uncivilized, but that "under our guidance they will make rapid progress in civilization, and will eventually be able to take an important share in the government of their country." He finished by quoting from Rudyard Kipling's recently published poem, "The White Man's Burden," telling his audience: "There is work for us to do. The future of ten millions of human beings, no less than the honor of a great nation, are in our keeping. The eyes of the world are upon us."[45]

Worcester also gave two lectures on "The Peoples of the Philippines" before the National Geographic Society in Washington, D.C. He told his mother that he "had some fifty new lantern slides made, and spent a large amount of time in translating a Spanish monograph on the manners and customs of many of the wild tribes with which I never came in contact." It isn't clear what photographs he had lantern slides made from but if any were used to illustrate those "tribes" he never encountered, then he had to secure such photographs from other sources.[46] His first lecture was on "the pagan tribes," and the second on "the Mohammedan and Christian tribes," and both lectures attracted large audiences. He told her that for the first lecture, all twelve hundred seats in the auditorium were full, "with a hundred people standing downstairs, and a hundred and fifty in the gallery.[47] As Sullivan points out about these lectures: "The disproportionate attention paid to the ethnic and Muslim minorities revealed that his contacts with sophisticated, urban Filipinos during 1899 had not shaken his belief that the 'real' Filipino dwelt close to nature in remote, unexplored hinterlands."[48]

It might be more accurate to say that Worcester did not actually believe that "real" Filipinos even existed. In a section of the Schurman Commission's final report, titled, "The Native People of the Philippines," Worcester wrote that the inhabitants of the Philippines are "*at present* collectively known as 'Filipinos'" (emphasis added), indicating his belief that such a designation was both misleading and temporary. He went on to say that there were "three sharply distinct races" inhabiting the Philippines, "the Negrito race, the Indonesian race, and the Malayan race." The Negritos he felt to be "incapable of any considerable degree of civilization or advancement." According to Worcester, the Indonesians—who, he said, lived exclusively on the island of Mindanao—were "physically superior" both to the Negritos and to the majority Malayan people. Each of these racial groups was further divided into many different "tribes" that he listed in an accompanying table giving an air of scientific authority and detachment to his central argument that "the Filipinos do not constitute 'a nation,' or 'a people.'"[49] As Paul Kramer writes in his book *The Blood of Government,* Worcester's "argument of tribal anarchy . . . became the centerpiece of arguments against Filipino self-government."[50]

Establishing a pattern that he would maintain throughout his Philippine career, Worcester contributed several photographs to the Commission's report. Some were photographs taken in 1899 and showed various examples of "native industries" in the Philippines. Other photographs showed representatives of different Philippine cultures. Most of those photographs were either studio photographs or photographs that he and Bourns had taken years earlier. Some of those same photographs may have been made into the lantern slides that he used in his National Geographic Society lectures. It wasn't until he returned to the Philippines as part of the Second Philippine Commission that Worcester began in earnest to take his own ethnological photographs, photographs that he would use repeatedly in an effort to reveal what he claimed was the "truth" about the racial and cultural heterogeneity in the Philippines, and the importance of the U.S. maintaining control of the islands.

WHATEVER WORCESTER'S LONG-TERM PLANS may have been when he joined the Schurman Commission, by the time he was appointed in March 1900 to the Second Philippine Commission (also known as the Taft Commission), he apparently had decided that he was done with academia. According to a brief article in the *New York Times,* Worcester notified the University of Michigan on March 14 that he was resigning his position as a professor of zoology: "It is generally understood by his former faculty colleagues that Prof. Worcester will not teach again. They state that he has his eye on some business enterprises that will keep him in the Philippines when his duties on the commission are over."[51]

In *The Philippine Islands and Their People,* Worcester told readers that "great opportunities will open before the capitalist" if the Philippines were to "come under the control of some progressive nation," and if the capitalist had "patience and enterprise enough to familiarize himself thoroughly with existing conditions, and to overcome the obstacles which they present."[52] Worcester may well have imagined himself to be one such capitalist, one who would be able to take advantage of his familiarity with the Philippines to become a prosperous businessman in the islands. In order to do so, however, he would first need to help guarantee that the United States would be the "progressive nation" controlling the Philippines.

During his time in Washington between his commission appointments, Worcester made the acquaintance of William Henry Holmes, the head curator of the United States National Museum at the Smithsonian Institution. In the course of one of their conversations, Worcester agreed to provide Holmes with copies of some of the photographs he planned to take upon his return to the Philippines. More than two years later, Holmes received a letter from Worcester reminding him of their conversation. Apologizing, and expressing his concern that Holmes may have "long before this reached the conclusion that I have forgotten my promise," Worcester delivered a list of 279 photographs "secured by me during the past two years."[53] Worcester informed Holmes that the photographs were being sent under separate cover.

Worcester donated the photographs to the National Museum with the understanding that "they will not be published or reproduced without" his consent. He pointed out that many of the photographs "were secured in the face of serious obstacles, and at the cost of no little time and labor" and that he "may eventually desire to reserve certain of them for my personal use,"[54] in lectures or publications. The accompanying list of photographs shows a variety of individuals from more than a dozen different cultural groups, ranging from Negritos to Igorots to Moros to Tagalogs. The photographs were organized roughly by geography, moving from central and northern Luzon down to Mindanao. This is significantly different from the organizational scheme that Worcester would later develop, one based on a perceived racial and cultural hierarchy existing in the Philippines.

The photographs began with eighty-five images of Negritos from Pampanga, Mariveles, and Rizal, followed by twenty-five photographs of "Igorrotes of Benguet," twenty-nine photographs of "Igorottes of Bontoc," eighteen photographs of "Tinguianes of Abra Province," six photographs of "Kalingas of the Cagayan Valley," twenty-nine photographs of "Gad-Danes of the Cagayan Valley," seven photographs of "Remontado Type," twenty photographs of "Tagalog Types from the Vicinity of Manila," five photographs listed as "Miscellaneous," sixteen photographs of "Moros of Sulu, Cotabato and Davao," two photographs of "Tirurayes of Cotabato" from the Davao region, thirteen photographs of the "Bagobos," four of "Samales," two photographs each of the "Tagacaolos" and "Bilanes," four of the "Atás," two of the "Kalaganes," and two of the "Guiángas." Finally, from the Calamianes island group, he included nine photographs of the "Tagbanúas."

Worcester's 1902 donation to the National Museum was the first of several distributions of his photographs. In 1904, he "presented a series of nearly 600 photographs representing the different tribes inhabiting the islands of the Philippine group" to the American Museum of Natural History."[55] Over the course of the next two years, Worcester sold three much larger sets of prints. While there is a great deal of overlap among and between these sets of prints, no two of them are exactly alike. To date there has been no exact count of how many Worcester photographs exist, and nobody has determined the precise degree of overlap between them.[56] According to the website of the UMMA, "he and his staff took nearly 16,000 photographs between 1890 and 1913."[57] Worcester himself put the number even higher. In a 1914 letter, Worcester wrote that he had in his possession over a thousand lantern slides "carefully selected from the Government collection of negatives and my own totalling approximately 22,000."[58]

Besides the UMMA archive in Ann Arbor, the three biggest collections of Worcester photographs are at the Newberry Library in Chicago, the Peabody Museum at Harvard University in Cambridge, Massachusetts, and the Rautenstrauch-Joest Museum in Cologne, Germany. All three of these came about through sales of prints that Worcester made in 1905 and 1906. The UMMA archive, on the other hand, consists of negatives and lantern slides that Worcester's family donated after his death in 1924. One way to look at these archives, then, is to keep in mind that the archives that came into being during Worcester's lifetime were created with Worcester's explicit approval and through his own selecting of images—either in consultation with the buyers or else on his own. By contrast, Worcester did not edit his photographs for the UMMA archive. Though it is possible that his family members sorted through his negatives prior to donating them, Worcester himself had no hand in determining which images would be included in that donation.

The years between 1900 and 1905 saw a number of significant events contributing to the development of Worcester's archive of photographs. The first was Worcester's own efforts to travel widely throughout the country taking photographs of different non-Christian Filipino groups. These trips were a regular part of his activities as secretary of the interior, and he apparently relished taking them. In his 1914 book, *The Philippines Past and Present*, Worcester wrote: "The only thing that kept me in the Philippine service for so long a time was my interest in the work for the non-Christian tribes,"[59] and much of that work entailed his annual "inspection trips" to visit those tribes. Worcester felt that these trips were of great importance in the civilizing mission of the colonial regime. However, a more skeptical view of Worcester's inspection trips can be found in a journal kept by Governor-General Cameron Forbes, who wrote in his entry of May 21, 1911: "I had two days with Worcester before he left for his annual trip. It is his great spree of the year, and he's off now with his beads and his bits of cloth, and I hope he'll stop before he gets his wards in a condition of pauperism. It is well enough to begin with, but not a good plan to carry too far."[60]

Worcester's 1911 trip to northern Luzon was one of his last. His first was in 1900, when he went as far as the town of Baguio in Benguet Province, more than 150 miles north of Manila. During this trip, he made photographs of Negritos near the town of Dolores, Pampanga, and of Igorots in Baguio. The UMMA archive has nineteen of the Negrito photographs (series 01-H) and more than forty of the Igorot photographs (included in series 10-A and series 10-C). In them we can see Worcester's efforts to develop a consistent photographic style for documenting non-Christian Filipinos.

The photographs in the Negrito series can be broken down into three categories: full-length portraits of men and women standing in front of a white sheet used to isolate them from their environment, close up frontal and profile portraits of men and women in front of the sheet, and photographs that show the Negritos using their bows and arrows in an attempt to document them in their "natural" life. The photograph seen in figure 3 combines the first and third kind of photograph seen in the series. Captioned "Negrito man and woman, types 3 and 4. Full length front view," it shows a man and woman standing in front of the white sheet, with the man holding his bow and a single arrow. The sheet does not block out the entire background, and we can see the leaves of banana trees behind them. The incomplete blockage of the natural background unintentionally emphasizes the constructed nature of the photograph by revealing the line and clips holding the sheet in place. It shows viewers that the photograph was taken outdoors and highlights the artificiality of the backdrop. In time, Worcester would make sure that the white backdrop covered the entire frame of the photograph, rendering the constructed nature of the scene less obvious.

In the series of photographs that he made of Igorots, Worcester chose to shoot in a more naturalistic vein. Many of these photographs show people dancing during a festival or sitting together in groups. Others show different kinds of houses around Baguio. Only two photographs in the series show the kind of frontal and side portraits that Worcester would commonly make in the coming years. One of the most striking feature of this particular series is the poor quality of the photographs. Few of the photographs have the right exposure and many of them have serious flaking on the negatives, making it difficult to see details in the images. In these early photographs made outside of the more controllable conditions in Manila, Worcester's photographic struggles are evident.

Fig. 3. Dean C. Worcester, "Negrito man and woman, types 3 and 4. Full length front view," Dolores, Pampanga (1900). (Courtesy of the University of Michigan Museum of Anthropology, UMMA 01-H-006.)

The second major event in Worcester's early tenure as a government administrator was the formation of the Bureau of Non-Christian Tribes. With the establishment of a civil government on July 4, 1901, Worcester was appointed secretary of the interior of the Philippines, the position he held until 1913. As secretary, he oversaw a variety of bureaus, including those of "forestry, mining, agriculture, fisheries, public lands, government laboratories, patents and copyrights, and non-Christian tribes."[61] In the first annual report of the Philippine Commission (illustrated with dozens of photographs Worcester took of non-Christian Filipinos), Worcester wrote: "There is at present a lamentable lack of accurate information as to the non-Christian tribes of the Philippines." He acknowledged that the previous estimates of the number of such tribes—estimates that he had relied on in the report of the Schurman Commission—were inaccurate and that "any attempt to make a statement" as to the population and distribution of non-Christian Filipinos "is at present to a very large extent guesswork."[62]

In order to gain information that Worcester believed would result in appropriate laws, legislation was passed on October 15, 1901, that created the Bureau of Non-Christian Tribes with David P. Barrows appointed to direct the Bureau. Barrows had originally gone to the Philippines as superintendent of schools in Manila. However, his background in anthropology and his study of Native Americans made him appear to be more qualified than any other candidate to serve in the position. To facilitate the work of the Bureau, Worcester and Barrows relied on volunteers to conduct ethnological surveys in different areas around the country. To aid in this, Barrows prepared a pamphlet giving instructions on how to conduct those surveys. The pamphlet said that the Bureau's objectives were "the investigation of the little known pagan and Mohammedan tribes of the Archipelago, the conduct of systematic work in the anthropology of the Philippines, and the recommendation of legislation in behalf of these uncivilized peoples."[63]

Barrows began with the same assumption as Worcester—that there was no "single homogenous race"[64] that allowed for the designation of a Filipino national identity. Also like Worcester, he based many of his assumptions about Filipino diversity on the scholarship of Ferdinand Blumentritt, an Austro-Hungarian scientist who had never been to the Philippines. In order to appropriately classify the different cultures, Barrows provided a number of guidelines that largely conformed to the practices of physical anthropology and ethnology at that time. As Mary

Jane Rodriguez notes in her article, "Reading a Colonial Bureau," the data that Barrows was seeking was intended to "'determine the truth of the propositions' concerning the highly debatable racial classifications of the peoples of the archipelago," classifications formulated by Blumentritt (based on Spanish reports coming out of the Philippines) and initially embraced by Worcester and Barrows.[65]

Barrows's pamphlet provided instructions for how to get precise measurements of the head and face of the subjects. Other physical features that he wanted recorded included tattooing, scarring, teeth filing, hairstyles, dress, and ornamentation. As an adjunct to the written notes taken by the volunteers, Barrows added: "If photographs can be taken, get two bust views of each individual, one full face showing both ears, and the other an exact, sharp profile of the left side of the head." He went on: "Frequently in the same tribe there will be found to be more than one type. Do not try to *average* the characteristics of these, but describe each type separately and with care, and notice if the different types occupy any different social position, or appear to differ in intelligence."[66]

The notion of "types" is significant here. As Rodriguez writes, within the Bureau of Non-Christian Tribes "there was much preoccupation with phenotypes or the observable physical characteristics of people because these would be used eventually to argue for the alleged 'savagery' of these groups."[67] Many of the portraits in Worcester's archive conform to the front and profile views suggested by Barrows, and Worcester routinely classified his subjects by what "type" they were in the tribe they belonged to. In many instances, Worcester listed each individual as a different "type." It is unclear if he deliberately sought individuals who he felt represented different types within a culture group, or whether he used the word "type" as a synonym for "example."

The third major event in these early years of Worcester's tenure as secretary of the interior was the hiring of Charles Martin as the official government photographer. The exact circumstances surrounding the hiring of Martin are unclear. As an employee of the colonial regime, Martin's name first appears in the 1902 report of the Bureau of Government Laboratories. Paul Freer, the superintendent of the Government Laboratories, wrote that the laboratory added space "to accommodate the government photographer,"[68] and he named Martin as the photographer who had been hired that year at a salary of $1,200 (roughly $30,000 in 2012 dollars). Martin was put to work immediately, as noted at the end of Freer's report:

During the fiscal year the bureau of government laboratories purchased a complete equipment for the government photographer, Mr.
Charles Martin. The work undertaken was varied. During the year
three trips were made outside of Manila, one to Bangued, Abra, where
the photographer joined the governor of the province, and the others
with the chief of the mining bureau to the region near Angat, Bulacan.
Two hundred and eighty-six views were taken. In Manila work has been
done for the board of health, bureau of architecture, bureau of non-
Christian tribes, bureau of forestry, and the honorable the secretary of
the interior. In all about 2,200 prints have been made.[69]

Martin is also mentioned in Barrows's 1902 "Report of the Chief of
the Bureau of Nonchristian Tribes," in which Barrows stated that Martin was to accompany Barrows and Dr. Albert Ernest Jenks, the assistant
director of the Bureau of Non-Christian Tribes, on a 1902 ethnological survey of the Cordillera region of northern Luzon. (This may have
been the trip to Bangued that Freer mentioned.) Barrows wrote that
the equipment that they were bringing with them included "instruments
for photographical surveys, anthropometric instruments, photographic
supplies, etc. Most of this equipment was purchased by the chief of the
bureau in the United States and was made on plans especially designed
for use in this work. Its general adaptability for mountain exploration
has been proven by its use in the past two months."[70]
Accompanying Barrows's report were five photographs selected to
represent the work of the Bureau. Curiously, though, Martin did not take
any of the photographs. Based on his own records of travel, four of the
photographs were without question made by Worcester—a photograph
of Worcester standing next to a Negrito woman taken in February 1901
(01-A-041), photographs of a Tagbanua man (04-A-001) and woman
(04-A-005) taken in December 1902, and a photograph of a Remontado
man taken sometime in 1902 (37-A-002). The fifth photograph, taken
of an Ata man of Mindanao in May 1901 (17-A-001), was almost certainly taken by Worcester as well, as Worcester had traveled to that region in
1901. However, even if Worcester wasn't the photographer, it was taken a
year before the hiring of Martin as the government photographer.
The Tagbanua photograph is seen in figure 4, a half-length portrait
of a woman positioned in front of a white sheet. In its posing and use of
a white backdrop, it was precisely the type of portrait that Barrows wanted for the Bureau of Non-Christian Tribes. In keeping with Barrows's
instructions, the frontal portrait is followed in the UMMA archive by a

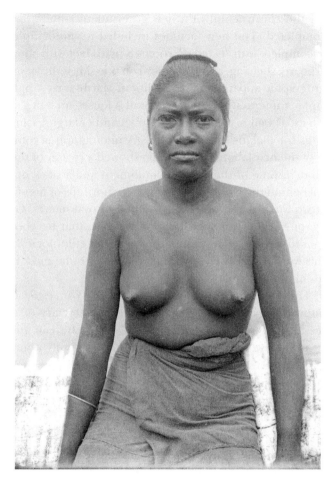

Fig. 4. Dean C. Worcester, "Young Tagbanua woman, type 4. Half length front view," Calamianes Islands (December 1902). (Courtesy of the University of Michigan Museum of Anthropology, UMMA 04-A-005.)

profile of the left side of her face. Worcester cataloged the photograph as "04-A-005 Young Tagbanua woman, type 4. Half length front view." In Worcester's alphanumeric cataloging system, the "04" indicated that she was Tagbanua, and the "A" designated that the photograph was taken in the Calamianes islands. The "005" indicated that this photograph was the fifth in that particular sequence of photographs. Both the cataloging and the listing of the woman as a "type" of Tagbanua clearly ground this Worcester photograph in the ethnological agenda of the Bureau of Non-Christian Tribes.

In 1904 the construction of a new government laboratories building was completed. The new facilities included a photography studio
for Martin complete with "two dark rooms 8 by 10 feet with large leaded
sinks, drip board, shelving, and tables, and on one side is the stand for the
photomicrographic apparatus."[71] In addition, Martin was "supplied with
5 by 7 Graphic cameras with Zeiss series and A lenses, an 8 by 10 camera
with Zeiss lens, as well as a Goertz anastigmat and enlarging camera and
an apparatus for making lantern slides." A photograph accompanying
the report of the new laboratory building showed a corner of the studio,
which included some of the camera equipment and a stack of albums.
On the wall behind the equipment hung three portraits of non-Christian
Filipinos (two women and one man) framed in oval mattes. Given the
wide range of Martin's photographic obligations, that he chose these
photographs to display suggests the prominence of ethnological photography in his work. Like Worcester, Martin seemed to be most proud of
those kinds of photographs.

As Karl Hutterer notes in his article, "Dean C. Worcester and Philippine Anthropology," throughout his career as secretary of the interior, Worcester gave his "undivided interest" to the Bureau and to the
Ethnological Survey, even after multiple reorganizations removed the
survey from Worcester's direct control and, ultimately, resulted in the
survey losing its position of prominence within the colonial regime.[72] For
more than a decade Worcester actively participated in the surveying of
non-Christian Filipinos as part of his annual inspection trips to different
provinces. Martin, too, traveled widely throughout the Philippines taking such photographs. Both men contributed extensively to the growing
body of ethnological photography made in the country.

Worcester's annual reports as secretary of the interior, many of which
were illustrated with his photographs, provide details of such travels. For
example, in his report of 1904, Worcester wrote that during that reporting year (July 1, 1903 to June 30, 1904), Martin "made two expeditions
into the provinces. During the first of these he secured 126 negatives
showing the work on the Benguet road. During the second he visited the
provinces of Abra, Lepanto-Bontoc, Isabela, and Nueva Viscaya, in order
to secure for the ethnological survey photographs showing types of the
less known non-Christian tribes of this region and illustrating their houses, methods of industry, religious rites, amusements, etc. Seven hundred
and fifty excellent negatives were taken, of which 500 were developed
in the field under very trying conditions."[73] These reports can be used
to ground individual photographs to specific geographic and historical

contexts, allowing us to better understand the ongoing construction of Worcester's archive.

Similarly, in a 1906 article that he published in the *Philippine Journal of Science,* "The Non-Christian Tribes of Northern Luzon," Worcester detailed his own trips to northern Luzon in the years from 1900 to 1906. For his trip of 1903 Worcester reported that he traveled from

> Manila to Bangued, the capital of Abra, from which point numerous *Tingian* settlements were visited; thence to Cervantes in Lepanto, by way of the *Tingian* settlements of Kayan and Bagnan, and the Bontoc *Igorot* settlement of Sagada; thence to the Bontoc *Igorot* settlement of Mayinit and return; thence to the Bontoc *Igorot* settlements of Talubin and Amboan; thence through the mountain range to the *Ifugao* settlement of Banaue, in Nueva Vizcaya, returning to Bontoc; and thence by another route through the Bontoc and Lepanto *Igorot* settlements to Kayan; thence by the route previously traveled to Cervantes, and through Benguet to Baguio and Manila.[74]

It should be noted that in addition to these trips, Worcester and Martin also traveled extensively through the Visayan region and the southern Philippines, where they also made hundreds of photographs.

The collection of photographs amassed by Worcester is weighted disproportionately toward images of non-Christian Filipinos. Of the roughly forty-five hundred negatives in the UMMA archive, more than twenty-six hundred are catalogued as being of cultural groups. Of those, fewer than three hundred show "civilized," Christian Filipinos as defined by Worcester (i.e., Ilocanos, Pangasinans, Pampangans, Tagalogs, Visayans, Zamboanguenos, Spaniards, and Spanish or German Mestizos). The other twenty-three hundred or so are of non-Christian Filipinos. In other words, over half of the total photographs (and nearly 90 percent of the photographs of people) in the UMMA archive are of non-Christian Filipinos. Comparing the number of photographs that Worcester included in the *Index* that he prepared in 1905 with the populations of different culture groups in the 1903 census yields some startling results indicating just how skewed toward non-Christian Filipinos Worcester's photography was. For example, the most populous group—the Visayans, with a population of 3,219,030—are represented by only forty-four photographs. By way of contrast, there are five times as many photographs of Negritos, despite the fact that the Negritos had a population less than 1 percent the size of the Visayans.

As Worcester's archive grew, his interest expanded beyond gathering photographs to finding multiple ways to get his photographs into the hands of people he believed shared his vision of the Philippines. It is one thing to make photographs and to collect them in an archive, but it is something else entirely to circulate those photographs. After all, it is in the public performance of photographs that their work is most effective. Although Worcester regularly included photographs in his annual reports as secretary of the interior, those reports had a limited audience. So, too, did the published reports of the Ethnological Survey. Loaning his photographs for inclusion in books and articles written by people who were not part of the colonial government in the Philippines, and selling editions of his prints to collectors, allowed him to widen his reach into the public arena.

The years 1905 and 1906 were pivotal both in the construction and in the dissemination of the Worcester archive. Nearly five hundred of the photographs in the UMMA archive were made in 1905, more than in any other year. However, that year, and the following year, saw major changes to the Ethnological Survey. As Hutterer writes, in 1905 "the Survey was transformed into the 'Division of Ethnology,' attached to the Bureau of Education," which "removed the Survey from Worcester's control."[75] Cameron Forbes, then serving as the secretary of commerce, commented in his journal entry of September 20, 1905, that he "expected some hostility from [Worcester], for we laid pretty violent hands on some of his favorite measures and institutions," most likely a reference to the reorganization of the Survey. Two days later, Forbes hinted that his fellow commissioners did not hold Worcester's work in very high esteem: "Worcester is figuring the cuts by departments and finds himself the worst injured. He'll be heard from presently. It is naturally so, as much of his work is optional—ours necessary."[76]

Worcester was not one to back down from a fight, and the following year "the Division of Ethnology was taken out of the Bureau of Education and transferred to the Bureau of Science,"[77] which once again brought it under Worcester's control. As Worcester wrote at the start of his 1907 annual report:

> The transfer [of the Ethnological Survey] to the bureau of education left the secretary of the interior in a somewhat anomalous position. He had executive control over five provinces organized under the special provincial government act, and largely populated by non-Christians . . . but was left without agents to make such investigations

as he might deem necessary, and was thus forced to depend upon the courtesy of another department for assistance which was essential to the proper performance of his duty. This fact . . . led to the transfer of the division of ethnology from the bureau of education to the bureau of science. This change places it where it logically belongs, in view of the fact that one part of its work is strictly scientific while the other part is necessarily carried on at the request, and usually under the direction, of the secretary of the interior.[78]

However, as Hutterer points out, even though he was able to regain control of the Survey, "government-sponsored ethnological work in the Philippines never again regained the degree of prominence and support it had enjoyed during the years when the Survey had the rank of an independent government bureau."[79]

While fighting for the future of the Survey, Worcester became increasingly determined to get the Survey photographs into the hands of other people, perhaps in part to demonstrate the value of the work he had been undertaking. The sale of his photographs to three collectors was arranged against the backdrop of this reorganization struggle. The first was to the American timber magnate Edward Ayer, who agreed to pay for a set of prints from Worcester for the sum of four thousand dollars (around $100,000 in 2012 dollars). These photographs, along with additional prints provided to Ayer in 1910, are now archived in Chicago's Newberry Library, with a duplicate set in Chicago's Field Museum. As Charles C. Lockwood wrote in his 1929 biography of Ayer, *The Life of Edward E. Ayer*: "Just as rapidly as he received from Mr. Worcester the pictures and their accompanying descriptions, he sent them to the Museum and had them copied there; so now there is in the Field Museum one of the most complete and useful Philippine collections in the world."[80]

The circumstances surrounding this sale are recounted in detail in Lockwood's book: "A good many years after the Philippines came into our possession, Mr. Ayer visited the Islands and saw much of Mr. Worcester. One day the scientist was showing the collector his photographs of the primitive people." After viewing "one or two hundred of these pictures," Ayer "grew tired" and asked Worcester how many photographs he had in total. Worcester informed him that he had eight thousand photographs representing thirty-six different "linguistic groups."[81] In the end, Worcester sold him 5,340 photographs, followed in 1909 or 1910 by a supplemental sale of more than two thousand additional photographs.

Ayer took credit—although how fairly isn't clear—for the alphanumeric categories that are distinctive of how Worcester's photographs are organized. According to Lockwood, Ayer told Worcester: "I should want you to take the first photograph you have of the Tagalogs and mark it 'Number 1, Series 1, Tagalog' and describe it. The next oldest photograph would be 'Number 2,' and so on through all the photographs you have of the Tagalog Nation. What I should desire would be to have you indicate how each group differs from other linguistic groups, with a description of each race, and a long list of photographs to illustrate each group, by individual examples."[82] It's impossible to say whether Ayer had any impact on Worcester's classifications. Certainly there are similarities, in that Worcester's *Index* has an alphanumeric system that classifies groups by cultural categories (e.g., "10" indicates Benguet Igorots) as well as by geography ("10-A" means Benguet Igorots from the town of Baguio) and then series of photographs made in that location. (Thus, photograph 10-A-062, a photograph of a group of Igorots standing in front of a house, captioned an Igorot house "of the better class," is the sixty-second photograph in that series.) Critically, however, Worcester didn't start with the Tagalogs. Instead, he put the Negritos (the group he felt to be the least civilized) as number 1, and he worked upward through the chain of perceived civilization until he arrived at series 32 (mestizos) and 32 1/2 (mixed populations) before shifting away from ethnology to topics such as zoology, geography, and history.

Worcester did not provide Ayer with copies of all of his photographs, though neither Worcester nor Ayer said why that was the case. As noted above, of the eight thousand photographs that Worcester told Ayer that he had, Worcester ultimately sold him only 5,340, leaving more than twenty-five hundred unaccounted for. According to Worcester's breakdown of the provenance of the photographs he sold Ayer, Worcester made 1,889 of them, while an additional 3,451 were selected from the government library in Manila. Of those, Martin made the overwhelming majority. Some of the series can be attributed specifically to one man or the other, but other series contain contributions by both men. Critically, though, there are no major differences in style that would allow a viewer to tell who the photographer was for any give photograph just by looking at it.

Worcester took the lead on organizing and cataloging the photographs in his archive, with Martin assisting him. In his 1907 annual report, Freer recounted the work of Martin in that reporting period: "The number of prints made during the last fiscal year was very much greater than in any similar preceding period, the total being well over

20,000." In addition, "One class of work was undertaken for which there had previously not been much demand, for during the year we made 319 lantern slides." Martin took photographs on "two expeditions, one to Mindanao, where he photographed a good series of Subanos, taking about five weeks, and another to Mayon, where he obtained collections from the volcano, having ascended the summit of the mountain during the expedition." Then, Freer continued: "The work of replacing the old negative envelopes, of cataloguing and classifying all negatives, and of completing the catalogue begun by the honorable the secretary of the interior occupied about six weeks toward the end of the fiscal year. In order to make the work at all possible four temporary employees were engaged, who spent all their time on our negatives. The result is that at the present time all the envelopes have been typewritten, the negatives have been classified and numbered, both in the regular album and catalogue, and only a few varied subjects remain to be adjusted."[83]

Working from his extensive notes and catalog of images, Worcester prepared a four-volume *Index* for Ayer that not only provided brief descriptions for every photograph included in the sale but also included narratives about each culture group represented. These narratives provide good insight into Worcester's ideas about race, culture, and civilization in the Philippines and they reflect then-popular theories of cultural evolution that Barrows articulated in his 1903 report: "We have tribes representing the whole scale of culture from savagery to civilization."[84] The *Index* opens with a discussion of the Negritos, the most "savage" of all the peoples in the Philippines: "To the anthropologist the Negritos are the most interesting tribe in the Philippine Islands. . . . They are dwarfish in stature, with very dark skins and closely curling hair. They come practically at the bottom of the human series, being on a level with the Bushmen of South Africa and the Blacks of Australia."[85] Worcester went on to assert his opinion that the Negritos likely were incapable of civilization, and that their numbers were declining, an assertion he kept making for years, despite there being little evidence to support it.

Reading through the descriptions of other culture groups reveals Worcester's language shifts as he sees increasing degrees of civilization in succeeding groups. Thus, the Ilongots (series 2) are a "quite savage tribe"[86] and the lowland Mangyans (series 3) "are a lazy, filthy, and degenerate set."[87] By contrast, the Bontoc Igorots (series 8) are "industrious" and "a kindly, jovial people,"[88] and the Buquidnon [*sic*] (series 11) "are said to be a pacific and industrious people."[89] At the upper end are the Tagalogs (series 28), "one of the most important, if not the most important, of the civilized tribes of the Philippine Islands,"[90] and the Visayans, "numerically the most important civilized or uncivilized tribe in the Philippine Islands."[91] Despite their importance, neither the Tagalogs nor the Visayans were well represented in the sale of photographs to Ayer, with only forty-four photographs of the latter and thirty-eight of the former. By contrast, Worcester sold to Ayer nearly three hundred photographs of Negritos, and over four hundred photographs of Bontoc Igorots.

The 1905 *Index* that Worcester prepared for Ayer also has an important shift from the organizational scheme that Worcester employed in his 1902 donation of photographs to the National Museum, a shift that remained more or less intact through Worcester's death in 1924. As noted above, the early organization was based more on geography than on perceived hierarchies of racial or ethnic identity. The table below shows the original nineteen categories as Worcester organized them in 1902, and the positions of those same categories in the 1905 *Index* and in the UMMA archive, both of which contained far more categories than Worcester included in 1902:

Culture Group	1902 list of photos	1905 Index	UMMA
Negritos	1	1	1
Benguet Igorots	2	10	10
Bontoc Igorots	3	8	8
Tinguians	4	6	6
Kalingas	5	5	5
Gad-Danes	6	24	38
Remontados	7	23	37
Tagalogs	8	28	43
Miscellaneous	9	n/a	n/a
Moros	10	22	23
Tirurayes	11	12	12
Bagobos	12	15	15
Samales	13	n/a	n/a
Tagakaolos	14	19	19
Bilanes	15	16	16
Atás	16	17	17
Kalaganes	17	20	20
Guiángas	18	18	18
Tagbanúas	19	4	4

In addition to being recounted in Lockwood's book, Worcester's sale of photographs to Ayer was well documented in the records of the colonial government. Paul Freer reported their sale in his 1906 annual report: "During the past year the library, through the honorable, the secretary of the interior, received P2,906.80 as its portion of the payment by Mr. E.E. Ayer, of Chicago, for a set of the photographs of the Philippine government. The catalogue accompanying this set was prepared by Mr. Worcester, and the sum thus made available represents the difference between the authorized sale price of the prints and the amount paid by Mr. Ayer for the prints and catalogue. The thanks of the bureau are due both to Mr. Ayer and Mr. Worcester for their efforts in behalf of the library."[92]

Worcester also mentioned the sale of the photographs in his report for that year, providing additional details about his efforts to distribute the photographs that he controlled in the government archive. Writing about the developments in the scientific library that fell under his purview as secretary of the interior, Worcester reported:

> The library fund was increased during the year to the extent of some 3,000 pesos by the sale of a series of photographic prints from the very valuable collection of negatives owned by the government. These prints, which are ordinarily sold without descriptions for P0.20 each, brought P1 each as a result of the preparation by the undersigned of a full series of descriptions to accompany them, and the amount in excess of the usual charge for making the prints was converted into a special fund for the purchase of books for the scientific library. The sale of two additional sets of photographs on similar terms has now been arranged for, and a corresponding increase in the amount available for the purchase of books during the present year will result.[93]

The two other sets of prints that Worcester sold were bought by Cameron Forbes and by Georg Küppers-Loosen. Forbes, an 1892 graduate of Harvard University, was appointed commissioner of commerce and police in the Philippines in 1904. The following year he received a letter from Frederic Ward Putnam, the director of Harvard's Peabody Museum, in which Putnam requested that Forbes "make a special effort to secure for the Museum a collection illustrative of the life and customs of the native peoples of the Philippine Islands."[94] Despite his belief that Worcester's work was "optional" and thus a deserving target of budget cuts, Forbes nevertheless seemed impressed by the results of Worcester's ethnological activities. On October 12, 1906, Forbes wrote in his journal: "Took the automobile this morning to Worcester's and had a long talk with him. He is giving me a complete set of his Philippine and the

Government Philippine photographs, some five or six thousand, nicely classified, and I believe a volume of some 600 pages of description. This will be one of three existent and should be priceless later. I am paying him a good round sum for it, all of which goes to the Philippine Scientific Library."[95] Forbes delivered the photographs to the Peabody in 1912.

The other sale—to Küppers-Loosen—also took place in 1906. When Küppers-Loosen died in 1910, the photographs were transferred to the Rautenstrauch-Joest Museum in Cologne, Germany.[96] In addition to purchasing photographs from Worcester, Küppers-Loosen accompanied Worcester on trips to make photographs, including a trip to Mindoro in June 1906, where they photographed Mangyans, apparently making the Mangyan people nervous by their activities. R. S. Offley, the governor of Mindoro, reported on the visit by the two men:

> Shortly after the visit of Commissioner Worcester and party to this settlement [Lalauigan], last June, several of its people died from eating poisoned fish, but to Commissioner Worcester's camera was attributed all the trouble. A large bonfire was built at one end of town and every living thing had to jump through the flames on its way out to drive off the evil spirit. The president of the town attributes their bad luck to the "Evil Eye" of a German scientist who accompanied Commissioner Worcester. This gentleman, who had a birth scald or mark over one eye, had a camera focused as is sighted a rifle, and his antics while trying for a picture would tend to make an enlightened Christian somewhat nervous.[97]

In addition to selling the photographs to Ayer, Forbes, and Küppers-Loosen, another effort on Worcester's part to get his photographs before a wider audience came in the 1906 article that he published in the *Philippine Journal of Science*. In this article Worcester provided elaborate descriptions of seven non-Christian tribes of northern Luzon. After several years of adjusting the presumed numbers of such tribes, by 1906 Worcester had decided that seven was the right number. More than fifty plates accompanied the article, most of which included multiple photographs so viewers could compare representative "types" of the different tribes. Worcester told readers that the "halftone illustrations which accompany this paper are all from absolutely authentic photographs. Of these, four were taken by Mr. [William] Reed, formerly of the Ethnological Survey, or by a photographer working under his directions; two were taken by Dr. Albert E. Jenks, formerly Chief of the Ethnological Survey; two by Dr.

M. L. Miller, present Chief of the Division of Ethnology of the Bureau of Education; ninety-one by the Government photographer, Mr. Charles Martin; and ninety-nine by myself." [98] Worcester does not indicate which photographs were taken by which photographer, however. His point was not to make such a distinction; rather, he seemed more interested in demonstrating to readers that the authenticity of the photographs could be guaranteed by noting the scientific and governmental credentials of the photographers.

Worcester's 1906 article garnered some attention in the United States when Jenks, by then a professor of anthropology at the University of Minnesota, published a positive review of it in 1907 in *American Anthropologist.* In the review's first paragraph, Jenks wrote that Worcester's article "shows ethnologists in the United States that the scientific study of ethnology has sympathetic and strong support in the Philippine Government. In fact, it is to Secretary Worcester that the beginning of Philippine ethnologic study by Government support owes its origins, and his paternal care has more than once since given the work new lease of life."[99]

Jenks stated that the strongest contribution that Worcester made in his article was to skillfully combine photographs and text in order to delineate the different culture groups found in northern Luzon. He echoed many of Worcester's claims about the levels of civilization, the attractiveness of the physique, and the details of the clothing of the different tribes. He appreciated the fact that Worcester provided an effective corrective to earlier classificatory systems dividing the non-Christians of northern Luzon into as many as thirty-six different groups. Jenks also defended Worcester's use of the word "tribe" and how it was applied to these different groups. In order to help bolster Worcester's reputation to readers who might have been skeptical of the anthropological credentials of a zoologist turned colonial administrator, Jenks wrote: "Mr. Worcester is acquainted with groups of each of the seven tribes he presents in this study, and most of the data presented in regard to the Ilongots, Kalingas, Ifugaos, Benguet-Lepanto Igorots, and Tingians are of his personal observation."[100]

Jenks had a few words to say about the photographs that Worcester included with his article: "Such pictures as are shown in plates IX, LX, and LXI are of the greatest value in presenting clearly the cultural differences in the several tribes of people; they show, respectively, different typical methods of man's headdress, different typical war weapons, and different typical war shields." However, Jenks was less impressed with Worcester's use of portraits: "Plate II, showing a full-length picture of a typical man of the Negrito, Ilongot, Kalinga, and Ifugao tribes, is unfortunately very misleading. As reproduced, the Ifugao man is only four-fifths as tall as the Negrito (shown as the tallest man on the page), whereas in reality the typical Negrito is only four-fifths as tall as the typical Ifugao or other pagan Malayan of northern Luzon. If definite measurements are not at hand to publish with such comparative illustrations, better scientific results will follow if pictures published for their scientific value are reproduced as near as possible in a natural scale."[101]

In other words, Jenks was not critical about Worcester's belief that ethnological portraits were useful for helping to describe and comparative different groups, nor was he critical of Worcester's photography per se. Rather, Jenks believed that Worcester and Martin were not rigorous enough in their use of anthropometric techniques, and Jenks wished that the photographs were taken with some kind of scale so that viewers could quickly measure the bodies of the subjects through a standardized metric. Jenks likely would have been happy if Worcester had adhered to the proposal put forth by J. H. Lamprey in 1869 "that anthropologists photograph their subjects against a background grid of 5-cm (2-inch) squares formed by hanging silk threads on a large wooden frame," a proposal that Christopher Pinney says "was designed to surmount difficulties in the 'questions of comparison' that anthropologists had to confront when uniquely embodied individuals were represented in diverse ways."[102] Pinney also tells us that anthropologists working in many parts of the British Empire adopted Lamprey's system. Worcester was almost certainly aware of this system. However, like many other ethnological photographers working in various parts of the globe, neither he nor Martin adhered to it, adopting a less rigorous approach to photographing their subjects.

When Jenks reported his frustration that Worcester's portraits were misleading in terms of the scale of the human bodies presented for visual examination, he echoed Lamprey's own belief that, as Pinney puts it, "individual variation was an obstacle in the way of . . . a complete visual knowledge that would assimilate bodies as data in a vast system of comparison."[103] On the other hand, Jenks was enthusiastic about two other photographs, neither of which made a pretense of adhering to standards of ethnological photography: "Figure 3 of plate L, and figure 2 of plate LXIII present two of the rarest photographs taken in the Philippine islands; they are, respectively, a Tingian fisherman throwing a casting-net, and a beheaded body of an Ifugao warrior."[104] Jenks appreciated the Tingian photograph (06-J-017) for Worcester's ability to capture the net clearly in midflight, and he appreciated the Ifugao photograph (07-B-081)—which Worcester reproduced multiple times, and which will be discussed in chapter 3—for its visceral details.

Worcester continued to add photographs to his archive for several more years, but as he moved into the later stages of his political career he was increasingly interested in making use of his photographs to argue for the prolonged retention of the Philippines by the United States, an argument based at least in part on his own commercial interests in the Philippines, such as cattle ranching and coconut growing.[105] Critically examining both the contents of the Worcester archive and the circulation of its images is important in order to better understand not only how his photographs fit into the conventions of ethnological photography at that time period but also the political uses of those photographs. It is also important to understand what kinds of photographs he withheld from public scrutiny, and how the inclusion of those photographs in the analysis of Worcester's photographic career can deepen our understanding of the archive as a whole. Indeed, it is possible to reveal a wide variety of manipulations and misrepresentations of Filipinos in the Worcester archive, and it is to those that we now turn our attention.

CHAPTER 2

Filipinos, Dressed and Undressed

———

DEAN WORCESTER, ALONG WITH several other colonial administrators in the Philippines, socialized from time to time in an informal fraternal organization that they called the Buccaneers. Their name probably wasn't chosen to suggest any kind of piratical pillaging of the Philippines; it is more likely that they called themselves Buccaneers in order to suggest a certain esprit de corps that real buccaneers were reported to have held. Casting off their official roles, and gathering at vacation homes in places such as the mountain retreat at Baguio or the bayside town of Pasay, Worcester and the other men felt free to engage in a degree of revelry beyond what might otherwise be deemed appropriate for men conducting the serious business of running a colony. Temporarily erasing the power hierarchy in the colonial bureaucracy, their Buccaneer "sprees" allowed them to relax together and to poke good-natured fun at themselves and at each other.

One such spree was held on March 3, 1909. Worcester was the featured guest, and his fellow commissioners took great pleasure in gently mocking Worcester's photography. Cameron Forbes, at that point the vice-governor of the Philippines, wrote about the spree in detail in his journal:

> Wednesday night we had a Buccaneer spree at Pasay. I gave a lecture
> on non-Christian Tribes. . . . We had lantern slides prepared with most
> absurd pictures, Worcester seated on Mayon Volcano, the Governor's

and Worcester's faces photographed on to children and Igorots and other savages. I made my story just as far-fetched and absurd as it could be. Then dinner, songs, and general poking of jokes. We all came as Igorots. . . . Each had one of the little basket hats, a shield, a spear, a red gee string over our trousers, and generally we found ways of roasting Worcester, our guest of the evening, and incidentally poked fun at the Governor whose appreciation of it all was noisy and whole souled. Through by 10.30.[1]

Forbes's description of the evening is revealing. Worcester's position as secretary of the interior made him responsible for a wide variety of bureaus in the Philippines, including the Bureau of Agriculture, the Weather Bureau, the Bureau of Lands, the Bureau of Science, and the Bureau of Health. Nevertheless, for a night of good-natured ribbing, his friends and colleagues were able to boil down the essence of Worcester's personality to his work with the Bureau of Non-Christian Tribes. For Forbes and the other Buccaneers, Worcester could best be understood through the intersection of three elements—photography, lecturing, and the non-Christian population of the Philippines.

In addition, Forbes's detailed account of the costumes that the men wore draws attention to the symbolic uses of clothing as markers of savagery and civilization in the colonial Philippines. While Forbes was careful to point out that all the men wore their trousers, his reference to the Igorot clothing, particularly the "red gee string," suggests the near-nudity that Worcester frequently described as being the "authentic" clothing of many non-Christian Filipinos. The clothing of the Buccaneers while on their "spree," coupled with the merging of Worcester and Governor-General James Smith with "children and Igorots and other savages," indicates the degree to which the men enjoyed playing with savagery in order to confirm their own sense of power and civilization as white American men.

Forbes's journal recounts another episode that further reveals the complicated role of clothing in the Philippines and Worcester's attempts to use clothing as markers of civilization. A few months after his November 24, 1909, inauguration as the new governor-general in the Philippines, Forbes took his first trip through the mountains of northern Luzon, accompanying Worcester on Worcester's annual inspection trip through the region. On May 11, 1910, Forbes and Worcester entered the town of Kalinga and the following morning there apparently was a bit of a kerfuffle surrounding a question of diplomatic protocol: "One request they preferred was that of the presidentes [the Kalinga leaders meeting with Worcester and Forbes] having the privilege of wearing a coat but Worcester doesn't like their appearance in coats, and wouldn't grant them that." In a footnote, Forbes expanded: "Here Worcester's love of ethnology, his admiration for the beauty of the naked savage, and his hopes of keeping them in their primitive state outdid his good sense and administrative judgment. This was the sort of request, reasonable and dignified, which should have been granted."[2]

THE JUXTAPOSING OF "savage" and "civilized" and of "naked" and "clothed" was integral to Worcester's strategy of using photography to advance his political aim of long-term U.S. control of the Philippines. These juxtapositions took many different forms; one form can be seen in a 1901 image showing Worcester standing next to a Negrito man named Ibag (or Ybag)[3] (fig. 5). Taken in the year that a civilian government was established in the Philippines, this photograph plays a critical role in Worcester's archive of images. In fact, the photograph served as the cornerstone of the set of prints that Worcester sold to Edward Ayer, having been assigned the number 01-A-001.[4] At the end of his government career in 1913, Worcester used the photograph to advertise a series of lectures he was prepared to give about the Philippines. Worcester also included the photograph in his 1906 article in the *Philippine Journal of Science* and in a 1912 article he wrote for *National Geographic*. Clearly then, this photograph was one that Worcester believed had particular power and resonance to convey the "truth" that he said photographs could be made to tell.

This photograph was one of at least ten that Worcester took of Ibag (whose name Worcester didn't mention), including one showing him standing alone in the same spot, and several profile views with Ibag's head tilted in a variety of poses. Of all of the photographs, Worcester apparently felt that the one seen here was the strongest image. On the surface, the photograph is a straightforward image of two men standing next to each in a clearing. The day is sunny and both men look directly into the camera. They are far enough away from the camera that no part of their bodies is cut off by the photograph's edge, but close enough that we can see their facial features distinctly. Although both men are positioned almost exactly in the center of the frame, it is clear that the camera operator—most likely Worcester's assistant, referred to only as "Serrano" in a journal that Worcester kept—used Worcester's body to frame the image. Worcester, more than the man next to him, is centered

Fig. 5. Dean C. Worcester, "Negrito man, type 1, and myself, to show relative size," Mariveles, Bataan (1901). (Courtesy of the University of Michigan Museum of Anthropology, UMMA 01-A-002.)

vertically in the photograph. His body, and not that of Ibag, was the measure used to set up this photograph.

Worcester's body was the measure in other ways, too. One reason why Worcester made this photograph was to display the size of the Negrito man standing next to him. (In the Newberry *Index*, the photograph is captioned, "Full-grown Negrito man and myself, showing relative size."[5]) That Worcester was over six feet tall and weighed more than two hundred pounds, and thus was not a representative of the average height of American men, goes unmentioned. In addition, it is unknown whether Ibag was of average height. The photograph, though, asks viewers to assume that both men are, in fact, "typical" representatives of the groups they represent here, and it made that insistence in multiple venues for more than a decade after it was taken.

It isn't only Worcester's size that is used as a measure against which to view the Negrito man. Contrasts in skin tone, facial expression, clothing, and posture are also crucial to the way this photograph functions. Taken at a time when racial segregation was hardening in the United States, the racial dichotomy that the photograph depicts could be seen by viewers as representing both the new imperial context of the Philippines and the long-standing realities of segregation within the United States. As Vernadette Vicuña Gonzalez writes in her article, "Headhunter Itineraries: The Philippines as America's Dream Jungle": "The visual tropes of empire were rehearsed in the space of the U.S. South, which was hospitable to such racial taxonomies."[6] In a similar fashion, Bonnie M. Miller argues in *From Liberation to Conquest* that the "'Africanization' of the Filipino" in the cartoons during the Spanish-American War and the Philippine-American War "turned the imperial project into an extension of domestic conversations about race relations."[7]

Any presumed linkages between African Americans and Filipinos could well have been heightened by this photograph and by the scores of other photographs of Negritos that Worcester made in early 1901. However, it is difficult to know for certain to what degree white Americans viewed this particular photograph in terms of domestic racial politics. Indeed, it seems possible that the Negritos were not viewed within the same prism of "Africanization" as other Filipinos. For example, in one Charleston, South Carolina, newspaper article about the Negritos that appeared in 1900, titled "Uncle Sam's Ape-Men," there is no mention of Africans or African Americans as a point of connection for understanding the Negritos. Rather, the Negritos were referred as "curious black dwarfs . . . who are the most monkey-like people in the world."[8]

The idea of Negritos as a missing link was frequently commented on by Worcester and by many other people. As it turned out, Ibag later became part of the Negrito delegation that traveled to St. Louis in 1904 for the World's Fair. While there, he was photographed repeatedly, both with other people and individually. He appeared as "The Filipino of Yesterday" in an article published in *World's Work* in August 1904, alongside a portrait of a Filipino Army Scout (a member of the U.S. organized and led military force) labeled "And of Today," an effort to promote both the idea of "a bifurcated racial formation" in the Philippines and the promise of civilization under American tutelage.[9] The Gerhard Sisters, two of the more prominent photographers at the fair, also photographed him, labeling him "The Missing Link" in studio portraits they made of him, one a profile view of the man, shirtless, shot from midtorso up, and another showing him standing and holding his bow and arrows. Laura Wexler has argued that this photograph would have been seen as part of the "mystery of ethnological transformation" at an exposition in which racial hierarchies and theories of social evolution were placed firmly in the foreground.[10] Although such theories placed African Americans far below white Americans, they were nevertheless above the status of such a "missing link."

If photographs such as the one in figure five linked U.S. colonialism in the Philippines to the legacy of the American South, they also linked colonialism with the American West, particularly through the body of Worcester, who stands erect, hands straight down at his sides, pale eyes staring directly into the camera from the shadow cast by his roughrider hat. His beard is trimmed, his hair cut short. His coat is bright, clean and buttoned to the throat, a watch chain conspicuous on his chest. His shoes are clean. He is the very model of "masculine strength and self-determination" that many Americans yearned for at the turn of the century.[11] His imposing figure could reassure viewers that he—a white American man—is firmly in control of this new colonial frontier. He is an exemplar of rugged individualism, a white man willing to bear the burden of uplifting a supposedly inferior people. Indeed, he is, as Rodney Sullivan titled his biography of Worcester, the "exemplar of Americanism."

If Worcester was shown in this photograph to be the standard of American civilization, viewers could easily enumerate the ways in which Ibag was Worcester's inferior. He comes up only as far as Worcester's chest and his posture can be read as an insolent slouch. His heavy-lidded eyes appear lethargic and nearly closed. (He may have suffered from a condition called ptosis, as no other Negritos photographed by Worcester had eyelids as heavy as his. Moreover, in the photographs taken at the World's Fair his eyes remained heavy-lidded.) His loincloth would barely have qualified as clothing for most American viewers, rendering him practically naked and indisputably savage and primitive. Indeed, the only visible sign of recognizable civilization in this man is a dark, new-looking bandana tied around his throat, most likely given to him by Worcester as a gesture of goodwill. In his journal entry for January 27, 1901, the day that this photograph was made, Worcester wrote: "Semilla had sent ahead a man with the cloth, necklaces, etc., that I had left with him, to show them to the Negritos and say that these things would be distributed on our arrival."[12]

Worcester took photographs of several other Negrito men and women in the same spot, and Worcester himself appeared in at least two other photographs. This encounter—which resulted in one of his first extended series of ethnological portraits—made an impact on Worcester, and he wrote about it in some detail in his journal. The photographs were made in Mariveles, on the southern tip of the peninsular province of Bataan, located across the bay from Manila. It appears that the primary reason for the journey to Mariveles was to obtain photographs. As Worcester wrote: "There were some thirty Negritos, all of whom were very much dressed up for the occasion. Most of the men had old hats and cast-off European clothes. . . . We passed around the *anisado* [a type of wine] and the cigars, and I then began photographic operations. Had great difficulty in getting a good light and was forced to choose between bright sunshine and shade so deep that I was afraid of under-exposure if I made the time short enough to catch people who do not know how to keep still."[13]

It is unlikely that the men and women he was interacting with did not "know how to keep still," but it is very possible that they may not have been photographed previously and didn't recognize the technological limitations of photography that required them to stay still for the duration of the exposure. Seen in this way, the photographic encounter between Worcester and this community of Negritos went beyond the simple making of photographs. It also introduced the Negritos to one facet of their incorporation into a modern colonial regime. Not only was photography used to visually record and identify the different cultural groups inhabiting the Philippines, but the very act of being photographed—selecting where to place the subject in relation to the camera, what the subject was to wear, how many exposures to make, and so forth—entailed controlling the bodies of colonial subjects.

Worcester was not interested in photographing Negritos in the Western clothing that many of them were wearing upon his arrival. Much like his later disapproval of Kalinga leaders wearing jackets to a formal conference with Governor Forbes, Worcester believed that the Negritos were more authentic without such clothing: "There was no difficulty whatever in getting the women to assume their normal costume, which consists simply of a piece of cloth wound about the waist and reaching to the knees."[14] He went on to write about the session in which the photographs were made: "Took a number of full-length pictures of men and women and one of the smallest developed Negrita in the crowd standing by myself, in order to show comparative sizes. She did not look more than ten years old, but she had a child. Impossible to find out what her real age was; they guessed it at eighteen."[15] That photograph (01-A-041) was another that Worcester repeatedly used in publications and lectures, including the 1902 Report of the Bureau of Non-Christian Tribes discussed in chapter 1.

Worcester's desire to have the Negritos remove their Western-style clothing reveals one the problems inherent in photography's search for authentic ethnological images: Who decides what is authentic? For Worcester, the answer clearly was himself. In this he illustrates a point made by the historian Philippa Levine in her article, "States of Undress: Nakedness and the Colonial Imagination": "When indigenous people were shown or described as clothed, the emphasis was as often on their misappropriation of clothing as it was on the civilizing effects and functions of dress."[16] Had the Negritos been consulted about the matter, they may well have said that the appropriate (and, hence, perhaps more authentic) way for them to dress was by wearing pants, shirts, dresses, and so on. For Worcester, however, "authenticity" required the Negritos to dress as he wanted them to appear, and both the logic of contemporary anthropology and the coercive power of the colonial regime guaranteed that Worcester's vision of authenticity would win out. As Levine observes, many anthropologists, as well as commercial photographers, "posed natives in what the photographers thought was their natural state on the grounds that this state would soon cease to exist, either because a people was doomed to extinction or because of the inexorability of modernization."[17]

Because Worcester had a great deal of control over the circulation of his images, his notion of authenticity was the one that American viewers would be exposed to. For example, there are two photographs in the UMMA archive whose index numbers are successive. (They are successive in the 1905 *Index,* too.) The two photographs share superficial similarities, in that they both show groups of Negritos posed for the camera in outdoor settings. However, while Worcester selected one of the photographs for publication, there is no indication that the other photograph was ever published. More important, the two photographs present very different readings of Negritos. In the unpublished photograph (fig. 6) most of the people wear Western-style clothing. They stand in an open field with a stone structure and hills in the background. About half of the subjects look directly at the camera. Given what Worcester said about the way the Negritos were dressed when he arrived in Mariveles, this was likely one of the first photographs that Worcester took that day. In addition, his description of the photograph in the 1905 *Index* suggests that Worcester felt the need to explain the clothing seen in the photograph, going so far as to indicate that, while the people in the photograph were from Mariveles, the photograph was not actually made in Mariveles: "Group of Mariveles Negritos in civilized dress on the occasion of a visit to the Island of Corregidor to pay their respects to the Philippine Commission."[18] It seems that Worcester wanted the photograph to be understood as showing the Negritos in atypical clothing.

By contrast, the other photograph (UMMA 01-A-111) shows a smaller group of five Negritos (three men and two women) posed on a rock in a stream with no Western clothing—the men wearing nothing but loincloths, the women's breasts bared. That photograph showed the Negritos in what Worcester argued was their more natural state, and he wanted to promote that vision of them. Including this photograph in lectures and publications, Worcester was able to deflect attention away from the possible perception of Negritos as rural residents who wore recognizable clothing and were adjusting to modern civilization. He was able to steer Americans toward a perception of Negritos as savage forest dwellers whose near nakedness marked them as uncivilized and whose numbers were in inevitable (and, possibly, welcome) decline.

THE CONTRAST BETWEEN being clothed and being naked is woven throughout the Worcester archive. This element of his photographs helps ground Worcester's work in particular historical contexts. As Philippa Levine notes, in the view of many colonial scientists "[p]hotography managed scientifically could reveal authenticity and truth, and the literal uncovering of the body facilitated that aim."[19] In addition to revealing the "truth" of colonial subjects, the contrast between the "naked" native and "clothed" Westerner helped demarcate the line between what it meant to be savage and what it meant to be

Fig. 6. Dean C. Worcester, "Group of Negritos," Mariveles, Bataan (1901). (Courtesy of the University of Michigan Museum of Anthropology, UMMA 01-A-112.)

civilized. As Ruth Barcan writes in *Nudity: A Cultural Anatomy*, "the uncultivated nakedness of the 'savage' . . . is understood as both a symptom and a problem to be fixed."[20] Photography's concurrent emergence with the social sciences perhaps inevitably led to the former being adopted by the latter in order to better understand human variability and evolution, whether in monogenetic or polygenetic theories.

As William Ewing writes in his book, *The Body*, "since photography was seen as the purveyor of absolute truth, it was inevitable that it should be used to provide objective records of a people and their culture, aiding in measurement, analysis and classification. Although the general theoretical framework was centered on social evolution, on the hierarchies this suggested, and on race, in practice this meant close scrutiny of the human body, since an understanding of the body was considered to be the key to an understanding of race and culture."[21] For Worcester, this understanding was as much political as it was scientific. Having committed himself to a strategy that used the non-Christian Filipinos as the primary rationale for long-term control of the Philippines by the United

States, he needed to do his best to assure that the photographs he circulated reinforced that rationale.

It is precisely this close scrutiny of the human body—particularly the undressing of female bodies—that has led to some of the most intense criticism leveled at U.S. colonial photography in the Philippines. As with photography emanating from other colonial systems, Worcester's photographs of Filipinos can be viewed as part of "an enduring Western fascination with representing native peoples, a fascination conventionalized through the tropes of performance . . . exotic mise-en-scène, and the spectacle of nudity."[22] Ewing points to the scientific motives that undergird such photography, but many other critics see motives other than science at work. For example, Elizabeth Mary Holt discusses "the long western tradition in which the tropics—the Philippines in this case—furnishes the site for European sexual or pornographic fantasies" in her analysis of a single photograph, "Wealthy Young Tagalog Lady and Her Maid," that was reproduced in the 1905 book, *Our Islands and Their People*.[23]

Although it is difficult to know for certain what Worcester's thoughts were when he made any particular photograph, there are numerous examples in the Worcester archive of "exotic mise-en-scène" that can easily be interpreted as having been made to feed his sexual fantasies. This is particularly true of a number of photographs taken in northern Luzon. There, he photographed many young Igorot women and girls in the process of undressing, and sometimes posed completely naked, in deeply shaded forest settings, by mountain streams, and, on at least one instance, on a bed with an ornately carved headboard, frequently in sensual poses reminiscent of Paul Gauguin's paintings in Tahiti. These photographs have none of the more formal posing found in his ethnological portraits and seem to have been made with artistic (or erotic) intent in mind.

It doesn't necessarily follow, however, that all photographs showing Filipina breasts were "signs of conquest" as Nerissa Balce declares at the beginning of her provocatively titled essay, "The Filipina's Breast." Balce argues that "the bare brown bosoms of indigenous women were markers of savagery, colonial desire, and a justification for Western imperial rule."[24] In contrast to the breasts, Balce says that "the Filipina native's scowl" reveals the resistance to the U.S. imperial project in the Philippines.[25] Through a reading of the bodies of Filipinas in turn-of-the-century travel books, she argues that the "Filipina photographs we view today are indexical and iconic signs of the U.S. Empire. . . . Photography as a technology of empire embodies the figurative and literal effects of American colonization for Filipina subjects."[26]

It is tempting to try to interpret the meaning of the facial expressions found in colonial photographs, but it is risky to draw firm conclusions about what those expressions mean, particularly when only one photograph of a given person is examined. This is not to deny that there was a great deal of resistance to American colonialism in the Philippines. However, if we assert that a scowl reveals resistance, we must also accept that a smile signals a willing and congenial photographic encounter. It is often impossible to know definitively the circumstances surrounding the making of a photograph, or whether a facial expression seen in an image was fleeting or fixed. Moreover, conventions of posing and preparing one's face for the camera are both historical and cultural, making it even more difficult to know precisely how to "read" the face of a photographed subject.

Having said that, it is beyond dispute that colonial photography was rife with voyeurism and coercion. As Barcan writes, "The invention of photography provided a new vehicle" for a voyeurism that was already part "the colonial encounters."[27] Likewise, Vicente Rafael notes the "relentless voyeurism that animated late imperial projects" in his discussion of U.S. colonial photography in the Philippines.[28] If voyeurism is understood simply as the desire to look at other people, then all photographs of people can be considered voyeuristic. However, if voyeurism is understood as an erotic attraction to the witnessing of the private activities of others, then not all photographs showing such things as female breasts are necessarily voyeuristic. As Barcan writes, "Clothing constitutes a highly complex continuum or matrix; there is no simple opposition between being clothed and being naked."[29] In the context of the Philippines, different culture groups had different ways of being dressed, and Worcester was highly attuned to those different kinds of clothing. Put quite simply, there was no single way to be naked in the Philippines and oversimplifying what bare breasts signify in these photographs may do more to obscure than to illuminate Worcester's photographic practices.

WORCESTER, TRAINED AS A ZOOLOGIST, frequently commented on the clothing of the people he encountered. He looked at the cut, color, and fabric in much the same way as he looked at the plumage of birds: as a way to categorize and classify people. For example, in his copiously illustrated 1906 article in the *Philippine Journal of Science*, Worcester set out to classify and describe what he said were the seven "Non-Christian Tribes of Northern Luzon." In addition to the names used by, or ascribed to each group, and their "habitat," his article reflected David Barrows's guidelines for ethnological surveys in the Philippines by including a "brief description of the physical characteristics of its members; of their dress and ornaments, including ornamentation of the skin by scarring or tattooing."[30] For Worcester, physical features were a more useful means of classifying people than were "folklore, or religious beliefs," neither of which he described in the article "except in so far as they are directly related to the subjects above mentioned."[31]

Barcan notes that for Europeans (and for Americans), "only certain forms of dress counted as 'clothing.' It was Europeans who defined whether body paint, feathers, ornaments, skins and so on constituted nakedness or dress, before ever they went on to determine that nakedness noble or wretched."[32] Worcester frequently went into great detail describing the clothing of the people he photographed, and made fine distinctions between clothing that he determined was actually clothing and clothing that he determined was ornamental and, thus, not actually clothing. In order to reveal the dress of people on the one hand, and their ornamentation on the other, he variously had to dress or undress individuals for the camera. Their bodies, for this purpose, were sometimes little more than the armature for what he wanted to show his Western readers.

For example, in his description of the Negritos in his 1906 article, Worcester wrote, "as many of the groups of the *Negritos* frequently come in contact with civilized natives, they often acquire from the latter articles of civilized dress of which they are very proud. Many of the women habitually wear *camisas* or upper garments, which the ones who are unmarried are very reluctant to remove."[33] In contrast to what Worcester wrote, none of the Negrito women shown in the photographs included with the article wear any such upper garments. Instead, Worcester drew attention to details such as bark skirts and to the ritual or ornamental scarification on the torsos of the women. For Worcester, these were more authentically Negrito than was the adoption of Western clothing, which he viewed as "inappropriate" clothing for the Negritos.[34]

By way of contrast, a photograph of a Kalinga woman in the same article (UMMA 05-D-020) was presented to viewers with attention drawn specifically to the elaborate clothing she was wearing. Included as one of four photographs of women (three Kalinga and one Ilongot) that Worcester selected to show different kinds of ornamentations, the caption for this photograph reads: "A very wealthy *Kalinga* woman of Took-took, Cagayan, showing elaborate dress and ornaments. Note the great mass of dead hair, the scarlet and yellow feather hair ornaments, the bead collar, the typical ear ornaments, and the necklace of agate beads.

When first seen this woman was wearing only a very abbreviated skirt, but before being photographed she adorned herself as shown."[35] Because Worcester was interested in showing the "elaborate" clothing and accessories that the woman wore, he did not have her remove her clothing before photographing her. Indeed, it is possible that he requested that she dress herself in her most elaborate clothing for the purposes of documenting what he said was typical Kalinga clothing. If so, it again raises the question of authenticity, but this time reversing the terms of that seen in his photographs of Negritos: Which is more "authentic," Kalinga women wearing elaborate clothing or Kalinga women wearing no upper garments?

Worcester suggests that the woman put on those clothes specifically because she was going to be photographed. He doesn't say whether the decision was the woman's or his own. If it was the woman's decision, it is unlikely that Worcester would have recognized that decision as a sign of her modesty. Indeed, one justification that Worcester gave for compelling men and women to dress less modestly than they would want to dress in his presence was his assumption that, for many non-Christians, clothing was more about display than about modesty. Regarding the Kalingas, he wrote: "The women wear skirts reaching from the waist to the knees, or in rare instances, even to the ankles; also *camisas* of brightly colored and large-figured cloth of European manufacture, or of the handsome striped cloth which they themselves weave. . . . That the habitual wearing of so many clothes by the women is a matter of display rather than of modesty is shown by the fact that they discard their *camisas* when at work, and if they have occasion to cross deep streams, strip naked, regardless of the presence of men."[36] That the woman seen in this figure may have chosen to put on those clothes prior to being photographed—an act of individual agency based on her own conceptions of modesty and what it meant to dress appropriately for the camera—seems not to have occurred to Worcester.

In order to provide a more nuanced critique of Worcester's practice of photographing naked Filipinos and Filipinas, it is important to acknowledge the complexity of what it meant to be dressed and what it meant to be undressed, both to the people he photographed and to the viewers that Worcester had in mind for his photographs. Of course, such an understanding is not always achievable. For one, Worcester had in mind multiple audiences for his photographs—and his own interests slid uneasily along the intersections of science, politics, and prurience. His intended audiences included himself, his colleagues in the Philippine

Commission, members of the wider scientific community, politicians in the United States, and general readers of his books and articles. Then, too, there is the difficulty of knowing what his photographic subjects thought about being dressed versus being undressed, or how they felt in general about being photographed. (Recall the discomfort of the Mangyans discussed in chapter 1.)

Nevertheless, when working with the Worcester archive it is possible to see the ways that many of his published photographs operate when paired with other photographs of the same subject; the addition of text can further complicate what his photographs reveal. For example, when he made the set of photographs of Negritos in Mariveles in late January 1901, Worcester wanted to do more than photograph them in their "authentic," non-Western clothing. He also wanted to get photographs of the Negritos without any clothing at all. The section from his journal detailing this desire is worth quoting at length:

> Having been told by Lieut. Long that he had repeatedly seen Negritos absolutely naked in the forests and that they commonly wore only a clout, I was anxious to find out if this was the case and if possible to secure a photograph. Nothing could be done in the presence of the crowd, so I had the camera removed to a protected spot, and asked Semilla to talk with the chief and with the husband of one of the women, so that there might be no mistake as to my intentions and offering to pay. I suggested a photograph in a clout, but Semilla said it would be easy to secure a photograph in "cueros" [i.e., *en cueros*, Spanish for naked], which I assured him would be still more satisfactory. He shortly returned, saying the matter could not be arranged. He had been foolish enough to speak to the chief about it in the presence of the crowd, and the old man, who was greatly taken with the idea, had made a public announcement, which was enough in itself to spoil the project. The women all objected, though their husbands were all anxious not to lose this chance to make money and one of them even went so far as to pick up his wife and try to carry her, whereupon she wept. Semilla said the women all declared they would not indulge in such a disreputable project. I had him bring the chief and one of the men and discussed the matter with them, but was unable to accomplish anything. They agreed the ladies would not consent. The chief said the statement that the women were ever naked or only in a clout was untrue.[37]

Despite the reluctance of the Negritos to pose *en cueros,* Worcester was able to secure more than a dozen photographs of naked Negrito men and women a couple of weeks later when he returned to Mariveles on February 10 and took more photographs. His journal entry for that date includes the sentence: "Took measurements of a number of men and women and tried the experiment of having one of the men photograph his wife, in order to get picture for the National Museum."[38] In 1902, Worcester sent several of those photographs to William Henry Holmes, and he also included many photographs of nude Negritos in his sale to Georg Küppers-Loosen as well as to Forbes. However, he apparently did not sell any such photographs to Ayer. The UMMA archive has more than a dozen such photographs.

In the list of photographs that he sent to Holmes, Worcester went into more detail about the nude photographs, as well as about Negrito attitudes toward nudity more generally:

> In spite of their scanty clothing, the Negrito women are modest, as are the men. The nude pictures were secured in every instance by first focussing the individual, drawing slide of plate holder [i.e., inserting the film plate], setting the shutter, and retiring while a wife sprung the shutter on her husband, or the husband on his wife as the case might be. Pictures of unmarried individuals nude could not be secured by me, and it was only with the greatest difficulty that a young unmarried girl could be persuaded to expose her bust, although married women habitually go naked from the waist up.[39]

This is a remarkably revealing passage. Not only does Worcester admit to the lengths to which he was willing to go in order to obtain photographs of nude Negritos, it also reveals the sensitivities of the Negritos to issues of nudity and modesty, sensitivities that Worcester did not seem to take very seriously. In addition, it helps illustrate the differences between what it meant to be dressed or undressed in the Negrito context in comparison to the American context. For married Negrito women, there was no contradiction between modesty and the wearing of clothing that Worcester and other Americans considered to be "scanty." Like American viewers, Negritos found bare breasts to be immodest, but only if a woman was unmarried.

Although the majority of Worcester's nude photographs have non-Christian Filipinos as their subject, his archive also contains photographs of naked Tagalogs, classified by Worcester as "civilized" and described by him as being very modest in their dress. Indeed, Worcester pointed out the modesty of their dress in one photograph that he included in his 1898 book *The Philippine Islands and Their People*, the caption of which reads, "Spanish Mestizas Showing Tagalog Dress (Without Tapis)— Manila."[40] The skirts of the two women in the photograph reach to the floor, and their blouses have high necklines and provide full coverage of their arms and torsos. Worcester also emphasized both the civilized nature and the importance of the Tagalogs in the 1905 *Index* he prepared for Ayer.

Despite his acknowledgment of Tagalog modesty, there is a series of more than thirty images in the UMMA archive showing Tagalog women in various states of undress and in a variety of poses.[41] Though undated, the photographs were most likely made in 1900 or 1901, as several of them were sent to Holmes in 1902. Gaps in the cataloging numbers assigned to them suggest that originally there were perhaps as many as eighty of these photographs, which are included in series 43-A at the UMMA. Some of the women stand facing the camera, while others sit on chairs. Some women were photographed both with their hair up in elaborate buns, then with their hair released. There are also sequences showing some of women disrobing for the camera, removing articles of clothing one at a time. None of the women are named, and it is impossible to know what the relationship was between the women and the photographer—in all likelihood, Worcester himself.

The photographs were taken in what appears to be a large wooden house, complete with sliding doors, shutters, and a canopied bed. The very fact that the photographs were made indoors immediately distances them from photographs made in places like forest clearings or rice fields. In photographs of non-Christian Filipinos taken outdoors, the seminakedness of the subjects could be presented as evidence of their supposedly savage existence close to nature. Photographs taken indoors, however, especially in modern houses such as the one in the Tagalog photographs, make their subjects' nakedness appear less "natural." That is, viewers of photographs of naked Tagalog women in a house likely would assume that the women generally were not naked, which would disrupt attempts to present the photographs as neutral, scientific documentation. A further complication to viewing these as ethnological stems from the fact that in his 1906 sale of photographs to Küppers-Loosen, Worcester placed the photographs in category 38-X (History—The City of Manila and Municipal Improvements) instead of in with other photographs of Tagalogs (category 28).[42] For Worcester, then, these photographs seem to have been less about people and culture than they were about place and time.

The presence of a bed adds an overtly sexualized element to several of the photographs, most disturbingly in five photographs of a fourteen-year-old girl, four of them showing her naked. In the UMMA archive, Worcester has designated her as "young Tagalog woman, type 3," providing a scientific veneer to the photographs. In two of the images the girl stands in front of the bed looking directly into the camera, her face impassive. In one, she gazes at the camera, her hands down at her side, a slight movement of her head blurring her face. In the second standing photograph, she continues to gaze directly into the camera but she is turned slightly to the side, one palm held firmly against her thigh while her other hand is held behind her head, accentuating her breast. In both photographs, her stomach bears the imprint of a waistband from the clothing that has been removed, and the tonal contrast between her hands, feet, and face and the lighter skin of her arms, legs, and torso tells us that she is in a state of undress that is not typical for her.

Other photographs of her are even more troubling. In one, the girl sits on a chair, her legs spread, with her hands resting on the seat on the outside of her thighs. As in all of the photographs in which she appears, she stares straight into the camera. In another, she lies on top of a desk that has been covered with a white sheet. Her head and her left arm are on a pillow and her body is slightly twisted in order to turn her torso toward the viewer. She is posed as though sexually available, the bed in the background accentuating the erotics of the image.

Although it can be difficult to read emotions in photographed subjects, in the majority of the photographs in this sequence the Tagalog women do not appear to be uncomfortable about having their photographs taken while naked. Their faces are impassive and they make no effort to shield their bodies from the camera. Although this can only be speculation, it is possible that these women were prostitutes who Worcester paid to pose for him. Records indicate that Worcester kept track of prostitution in Manila. His 1901 journal contains copies of cablegrams and a memorandum prepared for the secretary of war, Elihu Root, detailing alcohol use and prostitution in the city. According to the memorandum, "Houses of prostitution are not licensed, but as a sanitary measure which was found to be necessary in order to maintain the efficiency of the army by minimizing venereal disease, all persons known to be prostitutes are examined weekly," examinations that the prostitutes were required to pay for. The memorandum noted that the "large collection of soldiers now in Manila would unquestionably seek such satisfaction" regardless of whether or not brothels were allowed. Thus, "Prostitutes are not prosecuted for being prostitutes or forbidden to ply their business so long as no complaint is made of them for disorderly conduct."[43] Houses of prostitution would have provided Worcester with the ability to photograph naked Tagalog women without causing undue scandal.

Worcester did not make all of his photographs of naked Filipinos available to other people, seemingly preferring to keep some of them private. Archival evidence suggests that he shared more such photographs with Küppers-Loosen than he did with the either Ayer or Forbes, for reasons that are unknown.[44] Take, for example, the five photographs in the Newberry collection of Bontoc Igorots made in March 1903 at Kanu, that have a catalog designation of 08-P. The *Index* indicates that Worcester himself made the photographs. As it turns out, he made at least seventeen additional photographs during that visit to Kanu. Those other photographs are present in the UMMA collection, but were not included in the set that Worcester sold to Ayer. However, Worcester did sell at least three of those additional photographs to Küppers-Loosen.

None of the Kanu photographs at the Newberry show fully naked Bontocs. However, six of the Kanu photographs at the UMMA show women fully, or nearly, naked, including the three that he sold to the German collector. Intriguingly, while the database of images at the Rautenstrauch-Joest Museum acknowledges that the five photographs that Worcester sold both to Küppers-Loosen and to Ayer were made by Worcester, the other three photographs are listed as "*fraglich*" (the German term for items of uncertain origin). This suggests that Worcester may have wanted to distance himself from those photographs, despite the fact that all of the photographs were made during the same visit to Kanu.

One sequence of three photographs in that series shows different Bontoc women in successive stages of undressing. In the first photograph in this sequence (08-P-020), the woman stands facing roughly 45 degrees to the viewer's left. The photograph's caption at UMMA reads: "Bontoc Igorot woman from Kanu, type 14. With head basket on her back. Full length front view, standing." In *The Bontoc Igorot*, the first book to be published from the work of the Ethnological Survey, Albert Jenks wrote that such baskets were "used for carrying food, blankets, anything, on the trail."[45] In addition to the basket, the woman wears a skirt reaching to her knees, a necklace, beaded hair band, earrings, and bracelets.

She also holds a walking stick. She stands on a box covered with a white sheet that extends seamlessly up and behind her, all attention focused on her, her clothing, and the basket. The photograph is a fairly conventional ethnological photograph showing details of the material culture of the Bontocs.

In the second photograph (08-P-021), a different woman sits on the covered box wearing a skirt almost identical to the one in the previous photograph. The photograph's caption reads, "Bontoc Igorot woman from Kanu, type 15. 3/4 length front view." She looks directly into the camera, her head tilted slightly to her right, her hands resting on her lap. Again, this photograph fit into the conventions of ethnological photography from that time period. Indeed, Worcester included this photograph in the set of images he sold Ayer in 1905, a good indication that he felt comfortable with the public circulation of this image.

The third image (08-P-022), of yet another woman, complicates the scientific readings of the first two images, not simply because of what it shows but also because of the fact that Worcester felt the need to withhold the photograph from some viewers. The photograph is captioned, "Bontoc Igorot woman from Kanu, type 16. Full length front view, nude." She stands facing the camera directly, all clothing removed, wearing only earrings and a hair band. Her hands are positioned straight down the fronts of her legs and her shoulders are held slightly high, her body language perhaps suggesting that she was uncomfortable being photographed in this way. Her eyes do not look directly into the camera, but gaze slightly past the viewer's head. It is significant that he withheld this photograph and other photographs of fully naked women from his sale to Ayer. It suggests that at least one of the two men recognized that such photographs had potentially troubling implications that could disrupt their supposedly scientific intent.

There are several other examples of Worcester making, and then withholding, photographs of naked men and women. One additional example, however, may suffice to suggest both the complicated layers of meaning in such photographs and the degree of coercion found in Worcester's photographic archive. This one revolves around photographs made in preparation for the 1904 World's Fair held in St. Louis at which Filipinos figured prominently. In his 1904 report to Worcester, Mertin Miller, then serving as the acting chief of the Ethnological Survey, wrote: "Throughout the past year all field work which has been carried on has had direct reference to the preparation of the exhibit for the exposition at St. Louis."[46] This suggests that the photographic activities for the Ethnological Survey that year were also in preparation for the St. Louis exposition.

The popularity of the exhibit of the 114 Bontoc Igorot men, women, and children who were on display at the St. Louis is well known. In his highly regarded book, *All the World's a Fair,* Robert Rydell writes:

> From the start of the fair, the Igorot and Negrito villages, especially the former, caught the fancy of fairgoers and of the nation to a degree unsurpassed since the summer of 1893. . . . The perceived simplicity of Igorot life doubtless accounted for part of their appeal and made some fairgoers long for less complicated way of living than that represented by the monuments to industrialization contained in the White City palaces. But the immediate impetus to see the Igorot exhibit stemmed less from preindustrial longings than from a powerful mixture of white supremacist sexual stereotypes and voyeurism.[47]

The Igorot exhibit was regularly featured in newspaper and magazine articles, and both professional and amateur photographers were drawn to that exhibit more than perhaps any other at the fair.

For the organizers of the Philippine Exposition at the fair, however, the Negritos and Igorots represented something other than preindustrial simplicity. Describing the selection of non-Christian Filipinos sent to the fair, Miller said of the Negritos: "They are probably at as low a stage of culture as any people in the islands," and he may have shared Worcester's oft-repeated assertion that the Negritos were destined for extinction. As for the Igorots, Miller wrote: "The Igorot from Bontoc are as good an example as the islands afford of the primitive mountain agriculturalist of Luzon. There is probably none of the pagan population of the islands further advanced in general culture than they, and probably no people in the islands, pagan, Christian, or Mohammedan, as far advanced in agriculture."[48] Of course, the agricultural achievements of the Igorots were not on display in St. Louis. Instead, their "scanty" clothing, dancing, and diet are what attracted many fairgoers.

Worcester made many photographs of the Bontocs as they prepared to depart for St. Louis, including this photo (fig. 7) of a young Bontoc Igorot woman. Like many other photographs in the Worcester archive, this photograph complicates the supposedly neutral photographic encounters that helped build Worcester's ethnographic archive. Taken in Manila in 1904, its caption in the UMMA archive reads "Bontoc Igorot girl, type 13. Full length front view, nude." The photograph is one of

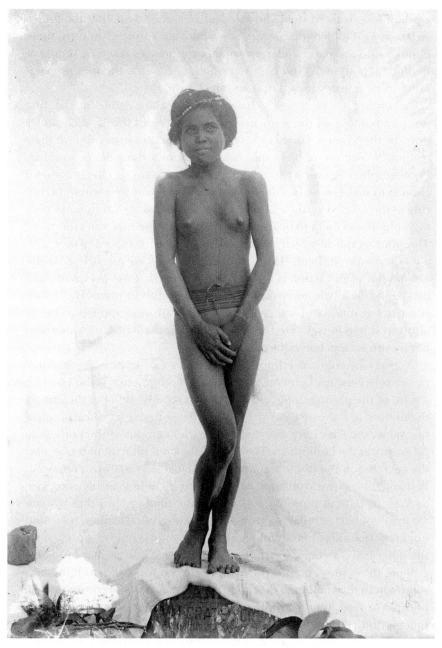

Fig. 7. Dean C. Worcester, "Bontoc Igorot girl, type 13. Full length front view, nude," Manila (1904). (Courtesy of the University of Michigan Museum of Anthropology, UMMA 08-A-075.)

three taken in sequence. The first two read, "Bontoc Igorot girl, type 13. Full length front view, showing leaf costume," and "Bontoc Igorot girl, type 13. Full length side view, showing leaf costume." In turn, these photographs are part of a larger sequence of images taken in Manila of Bontoc men, women, and children who had traveled there in preparation for the journey to St. Louis and the World's Fair.

According to Worcester's *Index,* the leaf skirt visible in the first two photographs of the sequence is an example of the "leaf costumes worn by the women when engaged in dirty work, in order to save their clothes."[49] Neither photograph, however, shows the woman working. Photographed against a white backdrop, there is no specific situational context to make sense of why she was wearing those leaves without referring to the text. Nevertheless, the presence of the leaf skirt in those photographs allows them to be discussed within the discourses of ethnology. The photograph in which the leaf skirt has been removed makes such a reading more difficult. Here, Worcester reveals his voyeurism. At the bottom left of the frame is the cluster of leaves that she previously had tucked into her belt, where one small leaf remains in place. Her hands cover her genitals and she crosses her knees in what appears to be an effort to shield herself. Her eyes look away from the photographer and her mouth is clenched tightly.

Viewers of colonial ethnographic images can ignore the unequal power relationships between subject and photographer if the coercive nature of the photographic encounter isn't readily visible in the images themselves, or if the images can be construed as having practical or scientific value, such as Miller asserted for the photographs of the Ethnological Survey in the Philippines. Having said that, it is difficult to see beyond the coercion in the photograph where the leaf skirt has been removed. Perhaps this is why Worcester chose not to include it in his 1905 sale to Ayer. If we limit ourselves to studying the photographs that Worcester made publicly available through the Newberry collection, we would not know that this photograph existed. We would, however, know about the other two photographs from the sequence. While we may justifiably critique those photographs for treating the woman in them more as a specimen than as a human deserving her dignity, it would continue to be possible to read them as ethnological photographs not atypical of their time period, allowing their surface calm to remain largely untroubled. Not only does the photograph in figure 7 resist such reading, it compels us to rethink the other two photographs as well. Placing the photographs that Worcester withheld alongside those he made public compels us to rethink the gaps and overlaps between the multiple archives holding his images.

One other troubling detail regarding this photograph bears mentioning: the contrast in skin tones between the woman's hand and her arm. In the *Index*, Worcester wrote of the Bontoc Igorots: "The dress of the adult women consists of a narrow piece of cloth, woven of twisted bark fiber, secured at the waist by a belt of similar substance ornamented at one end by strings of the seeds commonly known as 'Job's tears.' The skirt is very scanty."[50] However, a close examination of the woman's wrist reveals a clear tan line, and the skin of her hands and her lower legs show the effects of long-term exposure to the sun, effects not seen on her arms or torso. What this suggests, then, is that this particular woman did not conform to the image promoted by Worcester that Igorot women routinely went about bare-breasted. Indeed, she may never before had worn a leaf skirt like the one she wore in this sequence.

IT IS POSSIBLE TO TRACK some of the manipulations and misrepresentations in Worcester's photographs on the simple basis of what photographs were made and how they entered or were withheld from the different archives where they either do or do not exist. Other manipulations can be seen in the ways that Worcester used the photographs in his lectures, reports, articles, and books. Close, skeptical readings of such photographs can yield surprising insights that can help us better understand Worcester's political uses of photography. Indeed, one of the best known and most widely reproduced series of photographs taken by Worcester is also one of the most problematic. Analyzing the photographs alongside other photographs in the archive and Worcester's written records reveals a significant degree of misrepresentation embedded in the photographs. This series is a sequence of three photographs that purportedly show the transformation of a Bontoc Igorot man from abject savagery into martial civilization through his enlistment into the Philippine Constabulary, a paramilitary police force organized by the American colonial government (fig. 8).

Worcester included the Igorot sequence (as I will refer to it) in many of the lectures that he gave after leaving his position in 1913, including his 1914 testimony before a Senate committee debating Philippine independence. He did not, however, include the sequence in his 1914 book, *The Philippines Past and Present*, or in any of the articles that he wrote for *National Geographic Magazine*. In fact, it seems that the only time that Worcester himself used the sequence in print was in his 1910 annual

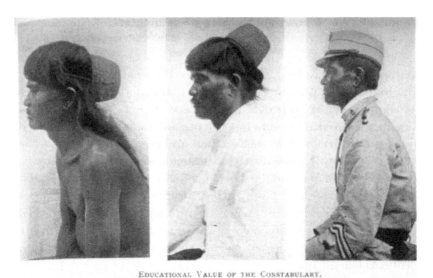

EDUCATIONAL VALUE OF THE CONSTABULARY.

1. Bontoc Igorot on entering the service, 1901.   2. After a year's service, 1902.
3. After two years' service, 1903

Fig. 8. "The Igorot Sequence," reprinted from Frederick Carleton Chamberlin, *The Philippine Problem, 1898–1913*. (UMMA 08-A-026, 08-A-028, and 08-A-029.)

report as secretary of the interior. The fact that he did not include it in any other publication is surprising, given the rhetorical power of the sequence and Worcester's penchant for reusing his photographs in multiple contexts. Frederick Carleton Chamberlin's 1913 book, *The Philippine Problem, 1898–1913*, may have been the only general interest publication in which the sequence appeared during Worcester's lifetime. However, the sequence has been reproduced and discussed in more than a half dozen books and in several articles since the 1990s, a clear indication of the enduring power of the sequence to pique the interest of scholars.

Worcester began piecing together the Igorot sequence as early as 1902. He sent the first two photographs to William Henry Holmes with captions that hinted toward what he would say about the sequence years later. In 1902 the caption for the first photograph read: "Type A. Head man of the settlement at Bontoc, as he appeared at the time of the American occupation; half length; side." The caption for the second photograph read: "Type A. In American dress; half length; side." Worcester also sent an accompanying frontal portrait, the caption for which had a bit more detail: "Type A. In American dress; half length; front. This man is now a sergeant in a Company of Insular Constabulary, and is doing efficient work."[51] Note that the caption doesn't say that the clothing the man was wearing was part of the Constabulary uniform, only that it was "American dress." However, it would be easy to assume that the clothing was, in fact, related to his work in the Constabulary, and that assumption later helped guide how the sequence was viewed. The third photograph in the Igorot sequence was not included in the collection that Worcester sent to Holmes.

By 1905, Worcester had assembled the entire sequence and included it in his sale to Ayer. They were placed in a longer series of photographs showing Bontoc members of the Philippine Constabulary. In the *Index,* Worcester went into some detail about the series: "These three pictures tell a most instructive tale in three chapters. The first shows Francisco, a very influential Bontoc Igorotte, as he was in 1901. At that time he was absolutely wild and was a successful and celebrated head-hunter. 38-q 8 shows him about a year later after a years' contact with Americans. 38-q 9 shows him in the month of March, 1903. At this time he was the first sergeant of the Constabulary at Bontoc, and was a well disciplined and well-trained soldier."[52] Note that, here, Worcester doesn't say that the second photograph shows him as a member of the Constabulary; only the third photograph is captioned such. Other details in his descriptions of the photographs merit skepticism, particularly the claim that Francisco was "absolutely wild" and the claim that the first two photographs were made "about a year" apart.

In his 1910 annual report, Worcester used essentially the same text for the captions of the photographs, which he printed on three successive pages (instead of on one page as seen in Chamberlin's book). In the report, the photographs were included in a longer series of photographs intended to show the benefits of American control for the non-Christian Filipinos. Other photographs in the series show Benguet Igorot women working with a weaving loom, a group of Bontoc Igorot Constabulary soldiers standing in formation, and Benguet Igorot schoolchildren standing in front of a new school they had helped build. In his biography of Worcester, Rodney Sullivan says that the 1910 report "must rank as one of the most divisive and impolitic public documents in the history of colonial administration. It was subversive of Philippine national and territorial integrity and grossly exaggerated the division between lowlanders and mountain dwellers."[53]

Among the more inflammatory arguments Worcester made in his

report was that "[t]he average hill man hates the Filipinos on account of the abuses which his people have suffered at their hands, and despises them because of their inferior physical development and their comparatively peaceful disposition, while the average Filipino who has ever come in close contact with the wild man despises them on account of their low social development and, in the case of the more warlike tribes, fears them because of their past record for taking sudden and bloody vengeance for real or fancied wrongs."[54] The core of Worcester's argument was that whatever degree of civilization had come to the non-Christian Filipinos (such as the transformation of a savage Igorot into a disciplined Constabulary sergeant) was the direct result of American actions. If the United States were to cede control of the non-Christian Filipinos to the Christian Filipinos, further development in the region would likely grind to a halt, and violence inevitably would erupt between the two groups.

Modern historians who have included the Igorot sequence in their books overwhelmingly denounce the imperialist argument embedded in the sequence. However, they have been inclined to accept that the Igorot sequence shows what Worcester said it shows, ironically reinforcing Worcester's arguments about the efficacy of the U.S. colonial regime in transforming the non-Christian Filipinos. One of the first books that revealed a renewed interest in the Igorot sequence was Benito Vergara's 1995 book, *Displaying Filipinos*. Reproducing the sequence as it appeared in Chamberlin's book, Vergara also includes Chamberlin's original caption: "Educational Value of the Constabulary: 1. Bontoc Igorot on entering the service, 1901. 2. After a year's service, 1902. 3. After two years' service, 1903."[55]

Vergara points out that the Igorot sequence shows "civilization as primarily a cosmetic change. There is no real 'educational value' the reader can see despite what the caption says; only in the cutting of hair and change of clothes is the civilizing process supposed to be manifested." Vergara asks pointed questions of the photographs: "[W]hy were they taken in the first place? Were they part of the standard bureaucratic procedure for the constabulary?"[56] However, he doesn't provide answers to the questions. For Vergara, the Igorot sequence is fundamentally an example of a colonialist assumption about "a certain visuality in civilization that photography could unerringly reproduce on its own."[57]

In the years following the publication of Vergara's book, many other historians have seen in the Igorot sequence a classic example of American imperialist thought about the Philippines. Eric Breitbart included the sequence in his 1997 book, *A World On Display*, mistakenly believing that the sequence was made at the 1904 St. Louis World's Fair: "Using techniques pioneered by the nineteenth-century French photographer Alphonse Bertillon, many St. Louis World's Fair photographs show front and side-view close-ups to identify ethnic groups, or, in some cases, supposedly showing the transformation of an Igorot into a civilized member of the Philippine Constabulary, to perpetuate racist stereotypes."[58] In *Tender Violence*, Laura Wexler repeats Breitbart's assumption that the identity of the sequence's photographer is unknown, and she states directly that the sequence was "taken at the fair."[59] Although the message of the Igorot sequence likely would have found a receptive audience in St. Louis, given the fair's emphasis on racial hierarchies and social evolution, the photographs were not made there. However, it is entirely possible (though as yet undetermined) that the Igorot sequence was on display in St. Louis.

Vicente L. Rafael also writes about the Igorot sequence in his 2000 book, *White Love and Other Events in Filipino History:* "Government reports, travel accounts, and historical narratives were generously illustrated with photographs of the natives' inevitable transformation under U.S. tutelage. For example, there were pictures of savages turned into soldiers."[60] Rafael reproduced the images and their captions as Worcester presented them in his 1910 report: each image having its own caption. For the first, the caption reads, "Evolution of a Bontoc Igorot constabulary soldier—1901, when he was a head-hunting savage." The caption for the second image reads: "Evolution of a Bontoc Igorot constabulary soldier—1902, after he had been for a year in contact with Americans." The caption for the third image reads: "Evolution of a Bontoc Igorot constabulary soldier—1903, when he was a well disciplined and competent sergeant of a company of Philippine constabulary made up of his fellow tribesmen."[61]

By 2006, the Igorot sequence had become enough of an icon of American imperialism in the Philippines that it was printed on the front cover of Paul Kramer's justly acclaimed and award-winning book, *The Blood of Government*. The sequence appears again inside the book. Like Vergara, Kramer includes the caption supplied by Chamberlin in 1913. In a critical discussion of the image and its function in Chamberlin's book, Kramer writes:

> Narratives of upbuilding, capacity, and homogenization within Filipino military units were enfolded in a much-reproduced photographic series generated by Dean Worcester, probably in the early 1910s.

Drawing on familiar before-and-after genres common to U.S. reform literature, it featured three successive shots of the same Igorot man at progressive stages. In the first, leftmost image, the man slouches shirtless, wearing only a small woven hat on the back of his head. In the second, he sits further upright, dressed in the white cotton uniform of a low-ranking Constabulary officer, ostensibly two years later. In the third, an additional two years later, he sits fully erect in a lieutenant's uniform. The series vividly brought together in a single cartoon the overlapping definitions of imperial progress.[62]

Accepting the veracity of the sequence, Kramer states that the individual in the second photograph is wearing a "low-ranking" officer's uniform, and that he is wearing a "lieutenant's uniform" in the third image. Kramer seems to look past the images and into the sequence's intended message when he writes that the individual sits the most erect in the final image of the sequence. The individual in the middle image of the sequence is just as erect—if not more erect—than the individual in the third image.

The UMMA archive includes the negatives for the Igorot sequence and two other photographs of the same man in different poses, with all of the photographs dated to 1901. If correct, the dating of the three photographs immediately disrupts Worcester's assertion that they were taken in three successive years. In addition, the original description of the third photograph reads "Bontoc Igorot Man, type 5. After a year in jail. 1/2 length profile. Bontoc, Bontoc. '01." For now, the most important thing to note from this description is that it says that the photograph shows an individual after spending a year in jail, not after spending two years in the Constabulary. Both the Constabulary and the penal system were instruments of colonial authority and control and were used to impose American-style discipline on Filipinos. Moreover, it would not be surprising if some Constabulary soldiers had their first exposure to American martial order in jail, and became collaborators with American officials upon their release.

Nevertheless, the function of jails is different from the function of military barracks, and Worcester's audience likely would have seen the sequence in a different light if they viewed the person in the sequence as a released (and potentially recidivist) criminal rather than as a police officer gradually gaining authority and power along with civilization. The circumstances surrounding the change from "jail" to "Constabulary" are unclear, but by 1905 Worcester found it useful to omit the part about the man having been in jail. (If, indeed, he ever had been in jail. If the negative sleeve was inaccurate about the date, it may have been inaccurate in this regard, too.)

Worcester's journal provides some insights into the origins of the first two photographs of the sequence, revealing some of the deception built into it. On February 6, 1901 (less than two weeks after his first photographic encounter with the Negritos in Mariveles) Worcester wrote about a delegation of Igorots who had traveled from Bontoc to Manila to see the city and to meet with Worcester and other members of the Philippine Commission. The delegation wanted to air their grievances about political and economic corruption taking place in Bontoc: "Name of the old fellow who headed the party (who had been to Spain for the former Exposition), Don Francisco Muro."[63] In this, and in subsequent entries in Worcester's journal, Muro—the man depicted in the Igorot sequence—comes across as a respected Bontoc leader who had traveled to Europe and who was savvy enough to know how to seek redress for the problems in Bontoc.

This is a far cry from being simply a "head-hunting savage," as Worcester called him in the 1910 report, or an inexperienced recruit into the Constabulary, as Chamberlin would have had his readers believe. Even his name suggests the level of esteem to which he was held, with "Don" being a Spanish honorific and not Muro's first name. Accompanying Muro to Manila were four other Bontoc men, including Antonio Sevilla, who later traveled to St. Louis as the leader of the Igorots at the 1904 World's Fair. Truman K. Hunt, a gold prospector living in Bontoc, who served as the lieutenant governor of Bontoc Province in 1902 and 1903, and who also served as the manager of the Igorot Village at the St. Louis World's Fair, also accompanied the Bontoc men.

When he wrote that Muro "had been to Spain," Worcester likely was referring to the 1887 Exposition of Philippines Islands. Eight Igorots, in addition to around thirty other members of cultural minority groups in the Philippines, were brought to Spain for the exposition in order to illustrate "Philippine backwardness," much to the dismay of many educated, Hispanicized Filipinos.[64] Kramer notes that the exhibition of Igorots at the 1904 World's Fair drew comparisons with the Madrid Exposition, particularly among Filipino critics: "Just like the Spaniards they had displaced, the Americans were using the islands' non-Christian peoples to cynically misrepresent Filipinos on the whole as savages requiring indefinite colonial rule."[65] Kramer also points out the misleading representation of Igorots in 1887, quoting one observer of the Exposition: "'The Igorots are neither savage nor irrational, as an historian of those provinces told us.' They were 'susceptible to modern civilization,' some being 'somewhat enlightened' and others 'of notable intelligence,' such as the party's leader, who 'speaks Spanish correctly, has a vast knowledge of geography and commerce, [and] knows Latin, Ilocano, and other dialects.'"[66]

Revealing these elements of Muro's past—the fact that he had traveled to Spain and may have spoken Spanish, his Spanish name and honorific, and the political astuteness that led him to seek out Worcester on the behalf of his people—would have disrupted the simple reading of transformation that Worcester and Chamberlin wanted people to see. The power of the Igorot sequence resides in the apparent transparency about what is going on: in a sequence of three photographs, an anonymous man, a metonym for all "head-hunting savages," visibly rises out of his primitive nature, pulls on clothes, and becomes a civilized man that Americans could be proud of. Complexity interferes with propaganda, and the Igorot sequence was constructed as propaganda by and for the supporters of American colonialism in the Philippines.

In addition to his Spanish name, other evidence within the photographs suggests that Muro had adopted some Western customs, further disrupting any reading of him as a symbol of primitive backwardness. Although American viewers in the early twentieth century may well have read the clean-shaven face in the third image of the sequence as an indication of the success of civilizing the Igorots, the mustache seen in the first two photographs of the sequence was not the norm for the Bontocs. Very few mustaches are seen on men in any of the other photographs of Bontocs in the UMMA collection, and Albert Jenks noted in *The Bontoc Igorot* that the "scant growth of hair on the face of the Bontoc man is pulled out. A small pebble and the thumb nail or the blade of the battleax and the bulb of the thumb are frequently used as forceps; they never cut the hair of the face."[67] The fact that Muro not only grew his mustache but apparently trimmed and groomed it suggests that he had already become somewhat acculturated to Western bodily aesthetics prior to his encounter with Worcester that February.

On the morning of February 6, Worcester took the Bontoc delegation "to meet the Commission informally" and to arrange for a more official meeting with his fellow commissioners the next day. Worcester then wrote about the technical challenges of photographing them:

Took the Igorrotes home, fed them up and photographed them. The tattoo marks barely visible in best negatives and quite invisible in the prints when negatives are made without ray filter. Experimented with rapid plates, wide-open diaphragm and with ray filter and got results sufficient to convince me that the tattooing can be photographed in this way. Gave nine second exposure with wide-open diaphragm and still had under-exposure, using ray filter, when one-half second with the same plates and 32 diaphragm was ample time without ray filter.[68]

This entry is significant both for its revelation that Worcester's skills as a photographer had developed far beyond what they had been in 1899 and for its revelation that Worcester felt that the tattoos were important details that he worked hard to pick up in his photographs. It adds potential significance to the fact that in the first photograph of the Igorot sequence as well as in a frontal portrait made of Muro at the same time (UMMA 08-A-025), no tattoos are visible.[69]

Given Worcester's difficulties in capturing tattoos in his first attempt at photographing the Bontocs, it is possible that Muro had tattoos that were not recorded in the photograph. However, it is also possible that Muro did not have himself tattooed, a possibility reinforced by the fact that Worcester eventually was able to make negatives and prints that showed tattoos on many of the men who accompanied Muro to Manila. Worcester photographed all five of the Bontoc men on February 6, most of whose names he did not record in his journal. Some photographs show men standing, some sitting, some in profile, and some looking straight into the camera. In many of the photographs, the men clearly were wearing pants. In other photographs such as the one in figure 9 piles of clothing can be seen at the edge of the frame, a detail that is particularly revealing. It suggests that the Bontoc men had traveled to Manila wearing Western-style clothing, apparently aware of, and conforming to, Western conventions of attire while on their political mission, and that Worcester had the men remove their clothing in order to make more "authentic" portraits of them.

On February 7, Worcester wrote: "Made one print from each negative before breakfast in order to show them to the Igorrotes." Later that morning, Worcester met with the other commissioners "in regard to matters in Bontoc and Lepanto." After lunch, Worcester "[s]pent most of the afternoon getting pictures with an extremely trying light, which changed constantly. Finally succeeded in getting some especially fine negatives, which I developed as I went along."[70] Presumably, those pictures were additional photographs of the Igorots. The entry for February 8 reads: "Made prints of negatives before breakfast, so as to give them to

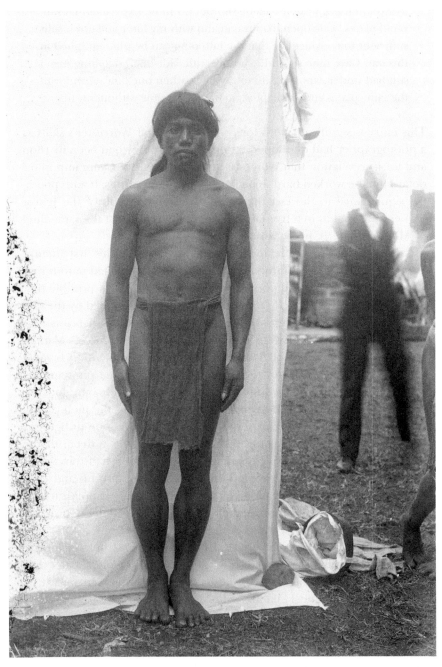

Fig. 9. Dean C. Worcester, "Bontoc Igorot man, type 1. Full length front view," Manila (1901). (Courtesy of the University of Michigan Museum of Anthropology, UMMA 08-A-004.)

the Igorrotes, who were much pleased with them." Later that afternoon, Worcester "made memorandum as to selling of Government property by the ex-Presidente of Bontoc and gave the Igorrotes all canes and Francisco an army blanket. Brought them all down to the Ayuntamiento [city hall], where I got from Branagan twenty-five dollars gold to turn over to Hunt for the purchase of arms and other products of the Igorrotes."[71] Having completed their business in Manila, Muro and his companions returned to Bontoc.

Muro encountered Worcester again about four months later and it is almost certain that the second image in the Igorot sequence was made during this meeting. On June 6, 1901, Worcester embarked on a trip from Manila to northern Luzon, what Worcester referred to in his journal as the "Igorrote trip."[72] Worcester's June 11 entry notes that a group of Igorot men had met their party in order to carry Worcester's photography supplies—cameras, negative plates, and so forth. On June 17, while in the Benguet region, "the forenoon was spent in looking about the Agno valley . . . seeing how the Igorrotes live in this town, in photographing them, their houses, their methods of cultivation, the town, the valley, etc."[73] Worcester next traveled from Benguet to Lepanto where he met with local Igorot leaders to discuss the possibility of forming a provincial government in the area. Worcester noted that "[m]ost of the Igorrote headmen had coats of white or blue or other color (frequently a khaki coat they had got off a soldier) and some of them also wore trousers of remarkable patterns."[74]

Worcester intended to continue from Lepanto to Bontoc, but news of the imminent inauguration of William Howard Taft as governor-general of the Philippines forced a change of plans and he had to return to Manila. Before doing so, however, Worcester met with Muro, who had traveled to Lepanto in order to escort Worcester's delegation to Bontoc. Worcester's journal entry for June 21 records the meeting: "Dr. Hunt . . . had brought with him from Bontoc the day before the Igorrote Francisco and the President of Bontoc, the former having been one of the Bontoc Igorrotes who visited Manila last February. They had come to escort the Commissioners back to their country, where the people were all being assembled and headmen had proclaimed a holiday. Francisco had on a full rig of clothes—white coat, trousers made out of a pair of miner's Alaska drawers, army leggings and American shoes."[75] Worcester's entry goes on to note the disappointment expressed by Muro at the cancellation of Worcester's planned visit to Bontoc.

(In *The Philippines Past and Present*, Worcester also briefly mentions this episode, aggrandizing his importance in the eyes of Muro for the benefit of his readers: "At Cervantes we were met by a delegation of Bontoc Igorots, who begged us to visit their country, and we were just preparing to do so when we received a telegram recalling us to Manila to be present at the inauguration of Mr. Taft as civil governor."[76] In this telling, Worcester puts a different spin on the story. Assuming that his journal provides a more accurate, dispassionate account of the events, Worcester already intended to travel to Bontoc and the Bontocs did not beg him to favor them with his presence.)

Although Worcester's journal does not specifically mention photographing Muro while in Cervantes, journal entries written when Worcester returned to Manila discuss the developing of negatives and the making of prints from exposures made while on his trip. Moreover, the description of Muro's clothing in the June 21 journal entry matches the clothing seen in the middle image of the Igorot sequence, seen more clearly in a frontal portrait of Muro made at the same time (UMMA 08-A-027). In addition, information from the negative sleeves at UMMA for both images note that the photographs were made in 1901 in Cervantes.

When viewed in the context of Worcester's other meeting with Igorot leaders who wore jackets and trousers, and in the context of the clothing that can be seen in the photographs taken in February 1901, we can see that the clothing Muro wears in the second photograph of the Igorot sequence had nothing to do with the Constabulary, and that such clothing was often worn by Igorot men when they met with American officials. Worcester's photographs and journal entries reveal that many Igorots, including Muro, owned Western-style clothing and wore them when they felt the situation warranted it. Thus, although the Igorot sequence asks viewers to see the clothing as evidence of the civilizing effects of the American presence, it may be more accurate to say that Muro's undressed torso in the first photograph of the sequence was actually the effect of Worcester's desire to document Worcester's own perception of the "authentic" bodies of Igorot men. In other words, Worcester himself created the "savage body" of the first photograph in the sequence, and later contrasted it with the "civilized body" seen in the other photographs of the sequence.

There can be little doubt that the first two photographs in the sequence are of Don Francisco Muro, that both photographs were taken in 1901, and that the second photograph has nothing to do with Muro serving in the Constabulary. It is important to also stress that Muro was an active agent in the making of the first two photographs, and that he wasn't being photographed as part of a bureaucratic routine of photographing Constabulary recruits. Had Muro not initiated their first meeting in February 1901, and had Muro not traveled to meet Worcester in June, Worcester would not have been able to construct the Igorot sequence and insert it into the public debates about U.S. control of the Philippines. Beyond these facts, however, things become more problematic, particularly in regards to the identity of the individual in the third photograph of the sequence. Worcester and Chamberlin would have us believe that the third photograph also shows Muro, but if the sequence's caption was fabricated, and if the circumstances surrounding the making of the first two photographs intentionally misled readers, then it is possible that the sequence's assertion that all three photographs show the same man is also misleading.

Close visual analysis of the photographs in the Igorot sequence raises doubts about the identity of the man in the third photograph. To be sure, he bears close resemblance to the two confirmed photographs of Muro in the sequence. On the other hand, certain details that are easily seen in the first two photographs—lines by Muro's eye, a small scar on his upper cheek—are not visible in the third photograph. The vagaries of lighting and camera angle may account for these differences, and the photograph may—indeed, most likely does—show Muro.[77] However, it is also possible—however remotely—that when Worcester assembled the sequence sometime between 1902 and 1905 (perhaps for the 1904 St. Louis World's Fair) he selected a photograph of a similar-looking individual in order to create a visual argument about the benefits of American colonialism in the Philippines. Without the third photograph, the sequence's message was tenuous at best; with it, a story of radical transformation under American tutelage could easily be read into the images.

In addition to discrepancies in certain details found in the photographs, the attribution of the third photograph in the UMMA archive also raises questions about the identity of the individual in that photograph. Like the other two photographs in the sequence, the third photograph has an attributed date of 1901 and is listed as having been taken in Bontoc. The Constabulary was established in 1901; however, Worcester did not travel to Bontoc in 1901. His first trip there was in 1903, and no other photographs at UMMA taken in Bontoc are dated earlier than 1903.

Given each of these facts, the origin of the third photograph remains unclear. It probably is a photograph of Muro as a Bontoc Constabulary soldier taken in 1903 as Worcester wrote in his 1905 *Index*. The

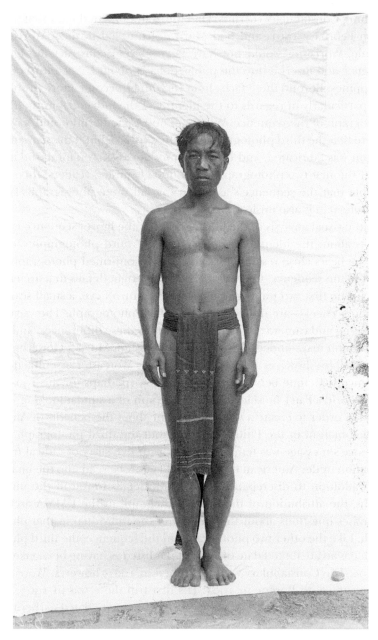

Fig. 10. Dean C. Worcester (attributed), "A Bontoc Constabulary soldier, without uniform," Bontoc, Bontoc (1903). (Courtesy of the University of Michigan Museum of Anthropology, UMMA 08-A-055.)

Fig. 11. Dean C. Worcester (attributed), "A Bontoc Constabulary soldier in uniform," Bontoc, Bontoc (1903). (Courtesy of the University of Michigan Museum of Anthropology, UMMA 08-A-054.)

uniform matches those worn by Constabulary soldiers in other photo-graphs taken in that year. For example, figure 10 and figure 11 show a Bontoc member of the Constabulary taken in 1903 with the captions as they appear in the UMMA archive. These photographs reveal that several years before the Igorot sequence was published, Worcester was interested in creating before-and-after sequences showing—at the very minimum—the sartorial transformation of Igorots when they put on their Constabulary uniforms. The photos were part of a sequence of photographs, perhaps made for display at the St. Louis World's Fair, that also show groups of Bontoc Igorots in Constabulary uniforms and in traditional clothing, what Worcester termed "warriors of the new school" and "warriors of the old school."

Though conjectural, it would make sense that the third photograph of the Igorot sequence was taken at the same time as these photographs. Like the Igorot sequence, Worcester argued that these photographs demonstrated the civilizing function of the Constabulary. In the 1905 *Index,* Worcester described the two photographs in figures 10 and 11, "38-q 3 and 4. A Bontoc Constabulary soldier before and after enlist-ment," and they are followed by another pairing of photographs with a very similar description.[78] However, even casual analysis of the two photo-graphs reveals that they were made at the same time, weakening Worces-ter's argument about the success of the Constabulary at bringing civiliza-tion to the Igorots. If the two photographs were, in fact, taken "before and after enlistment," there was no real passage of time allowing the supposedly civilizing effects of the Constabulary to do its work. As much as Worcester may have wanted it to be so, clothing alone isn't enough to indicate civilization. After all, these Constabulary soldiers could—and undoubtedly did—take off their uniforms as easily as they put them on.

Given the evidence that Muro was a respected Bontoc leader with a long history of interactions with Western imperial powers, it does not seem unreasonable that he might have joined the Constabulary in an effort to adjust his leadership position to new political realities, one of his final acts as a Bontoc leader.[79] Whatever reasons Muro may have had for doing so, Worcester did not record them. Worcester had other sto-ries to tell, stories embedded in political debates about the future of the United States in the Philippines. What mattered to Worcester and to his supporters such as Chamberlin was that their audiences believed that the sequence was a coherent visual representation of one man's transforma-tion under the guidance of American colonial authority. As long as view-ers accepted what the captions told them, the sequence could effectively convey the message that Worcester intended.

In his lectures and in many of the articles that he published for general audiences in the United States, Worcester turned to some of his favorite photographs in order to persuade his readers that the Philippines still desperately needed the guiding hand of the United States to continue up the path of social and cultural evolution. Sequences such as the one of Muro, or the other before-and-after pairings of Igorot Constabulary soldiers, helped Worcester promote the idea that a strong American hand was both necessary and effective for the racial uplift of Filipinos. They showed that non-Christian minority groups had the potential to become civilized if there was a steady hand to guide them. The images that he found to be the most compelling he returned to repeatedly in his lectures and publications. There were particular photographs that he believed had the most power to tell the "truth" to the multiple audiences that he wanted to reach. After 1910, when political shifts in the United States made him less certain about the future of his policies, Worcester intensified his effort to use his photographs to convince his fellow Americans that the policies he advocated were the right ones for the country to follow.

CHAPTER 3

Dean Worcester, *National Geographic Magazine,* and the Imagined Philippines

FOR SUPPORTERS OF U.S. COLONIALISM, one of the most straightforward ways to demonstrate the benefits of American rule in the Philippines was to offer visual contrasts between the Philippines at the time of the U.S. arrival and the Philippines after a few years of American control. That kind of contrast is what makes the Igorot sequence so powerful. In his study of American colonial photography in the Philippines, Benito Vergara says that the "clearest 'evidence' of America's success in the civilizing process were presented in the constant use of 'before and after' pictures."[1] Nevertheless, although he did use it in his public lectures, Worcester chose not to include the Igorot sequence in his magazine articles or his 1914 book, *The Philippines Past and Present.*

He did, however, publish this pairing of two photographs of young Ilongot women that appeared in the November 1913 issue of *National Geographic* (fig. 12). Worcester had previously used the photograph on the left side of the pair in his 1906 article in the *Philippine Journal of Science,* though not as part of a sequence. In that publication, the photograph was one of the other three images included with the photograph of the Kalinga woman discussed in the previous chapter. In that publication, the caption for the photograph of the Ilongot woman read: "Ilongot woman of Dumabato, Isabela, showing physical characteristics and

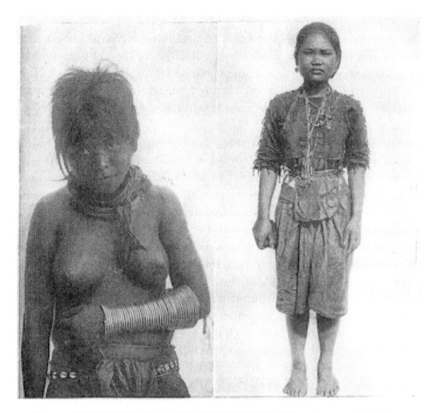

Fig. 12. THE EFFECT OF A LITTLE SCHOOLING. "The picture to the left shows a typical Ilongot girl as we found her. The picture to the right shows an Ilongot girl who has attended school for a time." *National Geographic Magazine*, November 1913. (Photo on the left, UMMA 02-D-017. Photo on the right is not part of the UMMA collection, nor is it in the Newberry archive.)

typical ornaments. Note especially the shell girdle, the heavy wire orna-ment on the left forearm, and the fine, braided rattan cord about the neck."[2] While both the caption and the photograph can be criticized as another example of objectification typical of ethnological photography from that era, Worcester does not specifically ask readers to view the woman disparagingly. Instead, he wanted readers to see her as a good representation of Ilongot women in general.

His use of the photograph changed markedly, however, in his *Nation-al Geographic* article. There, the photograph was transformed into the before image in a sequence titled "The Effect of a Little Schooling." The caption reads: "The picture to the left shows a typical Ilongot girl as we found her. The picture to the right shows an Ilongot girl who has attended school for a time."[3] Though still portraying her as "typical," the significance of that designation changed, becoming more judgmental. Worcester does not explicitly state that the second photograph shows the same individual as the first, but the caption allowed casual readers to assume that they do, in fact, show the same person.

At a minimum, readers were presented with a stark contrast between the two women (rendered "girls" by the caption). The juxtaposition works through posture and clothing, with the "before" image showing her bare-breasted and slightly hunched, her arm held awkwardly in front of her, her face cast down as she rolls her eyes up to look at the camera. The "after" photograph shows another young woman standing erect, fully clothed, her arms held straight down at her sides. Her presentation is one of self-confidence and modesty, the implied results of enrolling in a school established by the American colonial government. Readers were asked to contemplate which woman was a better representative of what the Ilongots could be. The expected answer, of course, was the second "girl," the one who had gone to an American school.

ALTHOUGH HE ISN'T OFTEN MENTIONED in published histories of *National Geographic Magazine,* Worcester was anything but a marginal figure in that magazine's emergence as a major publication in the early twentieth century. Indeed, Worcester's photographs were at the very center of the entwined histories of *National Geographic* and American colonialism. That the magazine's success was linked to U.S. control of the Philippines has been well documented by historians. Worcester's centrality in that relation has not been, however. This is surprising given that Worcester contributed five lengthy articles to the magazine between 1898 and 1913, and that his photographs appeared in many other articles that he did not write. In fact, Worcester's photographs helped create and popularize the magazine's ethnographic aesthetic, and his photographs in *National Geographic* influenced the ways that many Americans thought about and envisioned the Philippines. Although he wrote for other magazines as well, with no other popular publication did Worcester have as deep or long-lasting of a relationship as he had with *National Geographic.*

In her analysis of the thirty articles about the Philippines that appeared in *National Geographic* between 1898 and 1908, Julie A. Tuason argues that the magazine's pages reveal a rhetoric of imperialism that was "new, [and] distinctly American," an imperialism that Tuason says "assumed that commercial development and moral tutelage were twin imperatives" of the United States within the Philippines.[4] This rhetoric of imperialism reflected back to Americans both the expanding role of the United States in global capitalism and its supposedly benign civilizing mission in the Philippines. Tuason says that the prestige of the National Geographic Society, the magazine's parent organization, "lent credence to a view of the world—and America's role within it—that readers could unquestioningly accept as truth, thereby permitting the ethical assumptions that were so thoroughly embedded within it to remain unchallenged."[5]

Of course, Americans did not universally support U.S. imperialism in the Philippines, and Tuason may have overstated readers' unquestioning acceptance of the magazine's rhetoric. Nevertheless, it is true that *National Geographic* was a respected, influential, and increasingly popular magazine in the early years of the twentieth century, and it undoubtedly had a hand in shaping the attitudes of many Americans toward their government's imperial agenda. Given its global orientation, the magazine played a critical role in helping American readers learn about the country's new colonies. As a measure of its interest in the Philippines, the magazine published over forty articles about that particular U.S. colony between 1898 and 1913. (The outbreak of World War I in 1914 turned the magazine's focus elsewhere, and the next article about the Philippines didn't appear until 1930.)

Worcester wrote the final four articles about the Philippines published in *National Geographic* before the war. Three of these articles focused on the non-Christian population of the Philippines and were written in the midst of a pivotal moment in the political debates surrounding the future of the United States in the Philippines. Unsurprisingly, given his politics, Worcester used those articles to argue for U.S. retention of the islands. (The fourth article he wrote was about the 1911 eruption of the Taal Volcano, located thirty miles south of Manila.) As he had been doing for more than a decade, Worcester used the non-Christian Filipinos as a foil to argue for U.S. control of the Philippines. The United States was needed, he argued, to continue to facilitate a shift from savagery to civilization, and in order to protect the non-Christians from the predations of the Christian majority that Worcester claimed would happen if the United States were to withdraw from the islands. The three articles were "Field Sports Among the Wild Men of Northern Luzon"

(March 1911), "Head-Hunters of Northern Luzon" (September 1912), and "The Non-Christian Peoples of the Philippine Islands" (November 1913). This last article was promoted as having thirty-two pages of full-color photographs, which was still a novelty in magazines in 1913 and may have drawn additional reader interest for that reason alone.

While it was unusual for *National Geographic* to give over an entire issue to a single article, Gilbert H. Grosvenor, the magazine's editor and a longtime supporter of U.S. control in the Philippines, allowed Worcester to do so twice, in 1912 and 1913. Like virtually all of Worcester's writings, these articles defended Republican policies in the Philippines. In addition, they reveal an undercurrent of apprehension about the future given the political changes that were occurring in Washington, D.C. This apprehension, however, did not intrude on the readability of the articles. As Vernadette Vicuña Gonzalez notes, Worcester's articles were written "in the fashion of expert travel guides."[6] They were not overly polemical, nor were they as strident and divisive as his 1910 annual report as secretary of the interior. Instead, Worcester wanted to let the images present the "truth" of the diversity of cultures in the Philippines, and to use the text to explain both the natural "savagery" of many non-Christian tribes and the great strides that those groups had made under U.S. guidance.

FOR A NUMBER OF OVERLAPPING REASONS, Worcester's *National Geographic* articles provide a particularly useful lens for understanding the growing prominence of photography in the magazine in the early twentieth century, and for understanding how Worcester was able to use his massive archive of photographs in an effort to influence the political debates about U.S. control of the Philippines. These reasons include the growing market for, and cultural significance of, monthly magazines in general at this time, the rapid growth of *National Geographic* specifically, the links between *National Geographic* and the U.S. government, and the role of photography in the magazine. Photography played a critical role in marking the degree of visual difference between the largely white readership of *National Geographic* and the darker-skinned Filipinos seen within the magazine's pages, a component of the racialized formations of national identity that were woven throughout U.S. imperialist ideologies and policies.[7]

National Geographic benefited from the fact that at the same moment that the United States asserted itself as a colonial power, a market of magazine readers was emerging that laid the groundwork for the dominance of monthly periodicals as the main source of information about the world. The historian Richard Ohmann notes that "there were no modern, mass circulation magazines in 1885." However, "by 1900 there were in the neighborhood of twenty—enough to make them a highly visible and much noted cultural phenomenon." Between 1890 and 1905, the circulation of monthly magazines increased from eighteen million to sixty-four million, surpassing the combined circulation of all daily and weekly periodicals within the United States.[8]

The rise of *National Geographic* to a position of influence needs to be understood both within this context of the overall rise in the popularity of magazines at that time and the role that such magazines played in helping to define an American national imaginary at a critical moment in American history. As the sociologist Matthew Schneirov notes, "By the turn of the twentieth century [magazines] were not only a regular form of entertainment, a source of pleasure for a national audience of readers, but a potent and powerful force in shaping the consciousness of millions of Americans."[9] Part of that shaping included the representations of other nations for American readers, representations that were never neutral. According to Schneirov, "an implicit cultural hierarchy . . . informed nearly all writing" on non-Western cultures in American popular magazines.[10] In this hierarchy, of course, the United States was always presumed to be at the top.

At the turn of the twentieth century, monthly magazines routinely presented the world outside of the United States "not just as a field for tourism and adventure, but as an imagined stage for American prowess."[11] This is a good description how *National Geographic* came to depict the world. First published in 1888 as a text-heavy journal, its initial subscribers ("members" in the magazine's parlance) were primarily tied to academic or scientific institutions. By the outbreak of World War I, *National Geographic* was a magazine that appealed to a wide swath of the American middle class, with its membership increasing from just over one thousand in 1898 to more than four hundred thousand in 1915. As historian Tamar Y. Rothenberg puts it, *National Geographic* portrayed the country's imperial agenda in the Philippines and elsewhere "as a positive and natural step in the spread of U.S. enlightened democracy and enterprise, a glorious expression of manifest destiny."[12]

Rothenberg discusses the role that the Philippines played in the development of *National Geographic*, pointing in particular to "three hallmark episodes" in the magazine's early history.[13] The first was the very fact of the takeover of the Philippines by the United States, an event that prompted the magazine to publish a flurry of fifteen articles on the islands between 1898 and 1900, over one-third of all the articles published about the Philippines prior to World War I. The second was the establishment in 1903 of the magazine's policy of publishing photographs of bare-breasted women. The third was the publication in 1905 of a number of photographs from the Philippine census of 1903. Although Rothenberg never mentions him, Worcester was instrumental in all three of these episodes.

Rothenberg refers to the June 1898 edition of *National Geographic* as the "Philippine Number" because all three of the articles published in that issue were about the Philippines. One of the articles, "Notes on Some Primitive Philippine Tribes," was the first Worcester article to appear in the magazine. Illustrated with photographs taken by Worcester and Frank Bourns during their 1890–93 Menage Expedition, "Notes on Some Primitive Philippines Tribes" is similar to Worcester's 1898 book, *The Philippine Islands and Their People,* in that both works were largely a recounting of the two men's experiences while searching for "rare or new birds and mammals."[14] In his *National Geographic* article, Worcester limited his discussion of his ethnographic observations to his encounters with Negritos, Mangyans, and Tagbanuas, whom he suggested to readers served as a representative cross-section of the population of the islands. Acknowledging the narrow scope of his article, he nevertheless asserted that his "brief notes concerning the more important of the tribes in question may not be entirely without interest at the present time" (284–85), an assertion that overstated the numerical significance of the cultural groups included in the article.

In this article, Worcester presented the Philippines as an exotic destination that would prove to be a challenge for whatever country would assume control over the islands after the Spanish. (Somewhat coyly, he did not state directly that the United States would be the controlling power, though there is little doubt that he believed and hoped that such would be the case.) Worcester said that the Negritos—whom he called "the most primitive of Philippine peoples"—were "well nigh extinct" and were destined to disappear from the islands (285). Of the Tagbanuas and Mangyans, he said that they would "afford an interesting problem in civilization to the nation whose flag is in future to float over their islands" (300). In a pattern that he maintained throughout his career, Worcester paid little attention to the fact that the overwhelming majority of the population in the Philippines was Christian and at least partly Hispanicized, despite the fact that Worcester used those identifiers as the criteria for what he believed it meant to be a civilized Filipino.

As noted in chapter 1, Bourns was the primary photographer during the Menage Expedition, and Worcester had not yet become an avid photographer when he wrote this article. In fact, Bourns took all eleven of the photographs included in the article. It was Worcester, however, who arranged them in a deliberate sequence. The first and the last photographs in the article are of Spanish military forts with their accompanying churches, the initial image taken in Dumaguete on the island of Negros, and the final image taken on the island of Culion. The photograph immediately after the first, and the one immediately preceding the last, both show Filipino houses. The earlier one is captioned "Tagalog House—Mindoro" and shows a small rural house constructed of bamboo and nipa. The other one is captioned "Bisayan Native and House" (45-F-001) and shows a man climbing a coconut tree, his bamboo-and-nipa house in the background framed by the tree he is on along with another tree.

Worcester's arrangement of photographs juxtaposed the large, solid, European structures with the smaller homes that Worcester suggested dominated the Philippine landscape. There is an implicit criticism of Spain's administration of the Philippines, as the photographs seem to suggest that the longtime colonial master devoted its time and resources to constructing monuments to the church and state instead of developing the resource potentials of its colony. The photographs also reveal Worcester's willingness to use the same image for different purposes in different contexts. For example, the photograph of the Visayan house had a very different caption in *The Philippine Islands and Their People:* "A Tuba-Gatherer—Sálag Dakó, Guimaras." In that book, Worcester wasn't interested in the house; he was interested in the activity of the man on the tree.

The four photographs of forts and homes frame seven other photographs in the *National Geographic* article. Five are photographs of people; one shows a boat; and one shows a granary. The photographs of people were captioned to mark the people as representatives of Mangyans on the island of Mindoro, and Tagbanuas on the island of Palawan. (There are no photographs of Negritos in the article, just as there are no photographs of Negritos in *The Philippine Islands and Their People.*) Shown individually and in groups, the photographs were mostly taken from a middle distance, showing people in environmental and social contexts instead of the more anthropometrically oriented photographs that Worcester favored in later years. One photograph (04-B-001) shows three Tagbanua men sitting in a row; the two seated on the outside wear traditional clothing while the one in the middle wears Western clothing, a visual juxtaposition that underscored both the potential to bring civilization to the Philippines and the failure of Spain fully to do so.

The entire article revealed Worcester's ambivalence about the presence of Western nations in the Philippines. He opened the article by criticizing Spain for "never seriously attempting to solve" the "problem" of bringing "good government" to the Philippines or of "developing their enormous latent resources" (284). He returned to that theme at the article's end, speculating about the "new order of things which is sure to follow when the blight of Spanish domination is finally removed from the islands" (301). However, in a prelude to the "imperialist nostalgia" that he would exhibit in his later articles in the magazine, Worcester encouraged anthropologists to come to the Philippines as soon as possible, "before the record of the daily life, the thoughts, and the ideals of these harmless and simple children of nature has been forever blotted out" (301).[15]

This article, then, established some of the themes that Worcester would keep coming back to for the next fifteen years. In addition to how he organized the images in the article, Worcester's belief in the ability of photographs to meaningfully reveal the Philippines to his readers is indicated by the simple fact that his article was relatively image-intensive at a time when *National Geographic* was still overwhelmingly a text-oriented magazine. One anecdote that he recounted further reveals Worcester's fascination with photography's ability to assign identities to individuals and to groups, and the technological gap between the Mangyans and Americans that photography could help delineate: "When shown their own photographs they failed to recognize themselves, although they at once pointed out the likenesses of their friends." He went on to make fun of the Mangyans's lack of understanding of optical devices that his readers were familiar with: "They [i.e., the Mangyans] made the most ludicrous attempts to catch or find the persons who stared back them from our pocket mirrors" (294). The use of the word "ludicrous" here served to separate the Mangyans from the supposedly more sophisticated readers of the magazine who would never fail to recognize themselves either in photographs or in mirrors.

Five years after the publication of this article, Worcester was once again a key figure in the second "hallmark episode" that Rothenberg points to in the early history of *National Geographic*—the editorial policy established in 1903 that made photographs of bare-breasted women a routine feature of the magazine. This policy needs to be understood as part of the larger shift toward photography in *National Geographic*'s early years. In 1902 Grosvenor attended a lecture about the recent eruption of Mount Pelée on the island of Martinique that killed around thirty thousand people, a lecture hosted by the National Geographic Society. While there, he overheard members of the audience complaining that the speaker was not showing any photographs of the eruption's aftermath. Grosvenor said that the moment provided him with a sudden awareness of "the character the Geographic should take . . . lucid, concise writing; material of general, not academic interest; an abundance of pictures."[16] Grosvenor wanted to shift the magazine's focus in order to tap into the rapidly expanding market of general-interest monthly magazines, and to take advantage of advances in photomechanical reproductions that simplified the inclusion of high-quality images in the print media.

Before he could convince his colleagues to move in that direction, Grosvenor had to fight against a perception that the halftone prints used by the magazine were "vulgar," and that the publishing of photographs of a general interest was beneath the magazine's loftier goals. This attitude may have been a reaction against the rapidly growing market of hobby photographers with their Brownie cameras, which made it increasingly difficult to separate professional photography from amateur photography. W. J. McGee, who at that time was the vice president of the National Geographic Society, believed that "the excessive use of picture and anecdote is discouraged . . . superficial description and pictorial illustration shall be subordinate to the exposition of relations and principles."[17] Unlike Grosvenor, McGee wanted to maintain the magazine's status as a serious, scientific journal, not a popular magazine for the general edification of an aspiring middle class.

Fortunately for Grosvenor, he had the full support of the president of the National Geographic Society, Alexander Graham Bell, who also happened to be his father-in-law. Perhaps more important, the overwhelmingly positive response by the magazine's readers to the inclusion of photographs was enough to convince Grosvenor "of the great value photography could have in increasing the circulation of the magazine."[18] Thus, by 1915, the magazine boasted about the primacy of photography in its pages: "The *National Geographic Magazine* has found a new universal language which requires no deep study . . . one that is understood as well by the jungaleer as by the courtier; by the Eskimo as by the wild man from Borneo; by the child in the playroom as by the professor in the college; and by the woman of the household as well as by the hurried business man—in short, the language of the photograph."[19] Worcester's belief in the teaching value of photographs, of the ability for images to tell the "truth" that he wanted to convey, merged seamlessly with the magazine's belief in photography as a universal language easily understood by everyone.

The photograph that is usually credited as establishing the magazine's policy for showing the bare breasts of women was a photograph of two Tagbanua women harvesting rice, published in the May 1903 issue of the magazine (fig. 13). Worcester took the photograph on the island of Culion in December 1902 when he was scouting the island for an appropriate site to establish a leper colony. The photograph shows the women (one of whom appears to be the same woman seen in figure 4 in chapter 1) standing stiffly in the middle of a rice field, the lower halves of their skirted bodies obscured by the ripe stalks of grain. Both women stare down toward the ground, avoiding eye contact with the camera. Save for its role in helping to establish the magazine's policy, it is an unremarkable photograph. In the Newberry *Index*, the photograph is described as showing "Tagbanuas harvesting rice. The heads are cut off one at a time with a knife, the blade of which is hardly larger than that of an ordinary jack knife."[20] In the magazine, the photograph's caption points to the "primitive agriculture" that the women are practicing, and notes that their "agricultural methods are exceedingly backwards."[21] The point of the photograph, then, was primarily to demonstrate how the Tagbanua people harvested their staple crop.

Although this photograph may have been the one to establish the magazine's editorial stance toward the subject, it was not the first time that bare breasts appeared in the magazine. In fact, Worcester's 1898 article included one such photograph. There are a couple of important distinctions, however, between the two photographs. The 1898 photograph in the article (03-B-003), captioned, "Married Mangyan Woman, Showing Typical Costume—Mt. Halcon, Mindoro," was accompanied by text reading: "Married women are distinguished by the fact that they expose the breasts, while unmarried girls cover them with a peel from one of the plantains, ornamented with finely braided rattan cord" (289). Another photograph (03-B-004) served to confirm that, in fact, unmarried Mangyan women kept their breasts covered. As a result, Worcester mitigated the potential eroticism of the 1898 photograph by establishing the woman as married and, as a result, sexually unavailable. In addition, the caption and the text worked to ground the fact of her bare breasts within a scientific discourse—we see her bare breasts because that is how married Mangyan women dressed.

Fig. 13. "Primitive Agriculture. Tagbanua Women Harvesting Rice, Calamianes Islands." *National Geographic Magazine*, May 1903. (UMMA 04-A-009.)

The photograph of the Tagbanua women was different, however, in that there was no accompanying text and no additional visual signifiers to ground the meaning of the breasts in the photograph. They were simple facts of the women's bodies, potentially erotic and not easily neutralized by the language of ethnology explaining the relationship between fashion and marital status. Consequently, this photograph was riskier than the one published in 1898. Moreover, by 1903 it had become clear that photography would be prominent in the magazine and that editorial policies had to be established for how to deal with such photographs in future issues of the magazine.

The Tagbanua photograph was included in an uncredited article titled "American Development of the Philippines," and although it has received the lion's share of attention by historians, as well as by Grosvenor, it was not the only photograph showing bare breasts in that particular issue of *National Geographic*. Less than ten pages later, in another uncredited article titled "Benguet—The Garden of the Philippines," another photograph showed another woman's bare breasts. This was the photograph of Worcester standing next a Negrito woman taken in Mariveles in 1901 that was mentioned in chapter 1. Much like the widely

reproduced photograph of Worcester standing next to Ibag seen in figure 5, Worcester and the woman were juxtaposed in order to show their
"relative size" as the caption informed readers. Worcester was presented
as a representative American, and readers were invited to carefully scrutinize the contrasts in size, dress, and skin tone.

This photograph may not have generated as much controversy or
attention as the Tagbanua photograph for the very fact that the woman
was Negrito. Worcester could have neutralized any potential eroticism
of the photograph by noting that, much like the Mangyans, only married Negrito women bared their breasts. He didn't, however. It may well
have been that neither Worcester nor Grosvenor could have imagined
readers having an erotic attraction to the woman in this photograph,
since Negritos were routinely referred to as "missing links" on their way
to extinction. The magazine invited readers to dismiss the significance,
and even the humanity, of the woman in the photograph, further miti-
gating any erotic reading of her breasts: "The Negritos are physical and
mental weaklings, and are rapidly disappearing."[22] This claim was similar
to the one Worcester made in his 1898 article for the magazine. In fact,
throughout his career he insisted that the Negritos were a disappearing
race existing at very bottom rungs of human evolution, an insistence
that had little basis in fact and that may have been more about Worcester's wishful thinking than anything else. Indeed, the 1903 census of the
Philippines revealed that the population of Negritos was higher than for
eleven other non-Christian tribes (including the Tagbanuas and Mangyans Worcester wrote about in his 1898 article), none of which Worcester described as "disappearing."

The decision to publish photographs of Filipinas with bare breasts
was not made lightly. As in his earlier battle to make photographs a more
prominent part of his magazine, Grosvenor relied on the support of Bell
to push for their inclusion: "I asked his opinion concerning some pictures of Filipino women working in the fields, naked from the waist up.
Should we publish them? The women dressed, or perhaps I should say
undressed, in this fashion; therefore the pictures were a true reflection
of the customs of those times in those islands." Grosvenor went on to
say that Bell told him to feel free to print the photographs, "agreeing
with me that prudery should not influence the decision."[23] That decision
would shape the magazine's reputation throughout the twentieth century. In the words of anthropologists Catherine Lutz and Jane Collins:
"Nothing defines *National Geographic* for most older American readers

than its 'naked' women. . . . [T]he magazine's nudity forms a central part of the image of the non-West that it purveys."[24]

The third "hallmark episode" that Rothenberg writes about, and that Worcester once again played a central role in, was the publication in 1905 of photographs from the 1903 Philippines census, the first comprehensive survey of the Philippines after the United States took over the islands. The inclusion of those photographs illustrates the close connection that the National Geographic Society had with the federal government in the early twentieth century as well as Worcester's centrality in that relationship. As Grosvenor himself put it, he discovered "gold in my own backyard" when he discovered that "Government agencies would lend me plates for illustrations in The Magazine."[25] In fact, the Society and government came together in the census, the director of which was Henry Gannett, a founding member and future president of the National Geographic Society.

The relationship between the federal government and the magazine worked out well for both parties. Grosvenor was able to secure photographs from government agencies, and those agencies gained an outlet for their work that went beyond the filing of official reports. Like Worcester and President Theodore Roosevelt, Grosvenor was part of the Progressive wing of the Republican Party that advocated a muscular foreign policy and, as Rothenberg writes, "Grosvenor's beliefs made themselves felt at National Geographic headquarters."[26] Grosvenor's ideas for the kinds of photographs he wanted in his magazine neatly dovetailed with Worcester's goal of using his photographs to influence public and political opinion about the role of the United States in the Philippines. This relationship proved beneficial to both Worcester and Grosvenor— Grosvenor got the images that would attract readers and Worcester got access to those readers.

The heavily illustrated article about the census, published in the April 1905 issue of the magazine, contributed to the rapid rise in the magazine's membership that year. In *The Blood of Government*, Paul Kramer says that the National Geographic Society "owed much of its success to the Philippine census photographs."[27] The article contained thirty-two uninterrupted pages of photographs—more than one hundred photographs in all—taken from the census report. The majority of those photographs were taken either by Worcester or by Charles Martin, with many credited as having come from "the collection of Dean C. Worcester." In addition to showing examples of different kinds of houses, boats, and churches

Fig. 14. Plate from 1903 Philippine Census. *National Geographic Magazine,*
April 1905. (Photos in top two rows and left-hand photo in bottom row,
UMMA 37-A-007, 37-A-001, 37-A-003, 05-F-030, 05-F-007. Bottom right
photo, Newberry 05-F-030.)

around the islands, the photographs show members of different cultural
groups of the Philippines. Many of the photographs were taken from
the Ethnological Survey—photographs showing men, women, or children against a simple white background. In such photographs, contex-
tual and environmental information was removed, with the photographs
insisting, instead, on the corporeality of their existence, what Vernadette
Gonzalez calls the "visual lexicon of native bodies" that Worcester "set
down and shored up."[28] The photographs were arranged on the page

in collage fashion, with as many as six photographs per page and simple captions identifying the people solely by what culture group they were said to represent (fig. 14).

In *Displaying Filipinos*, Benito Vergara critically examines the uses of photography in the 1903 census, which he calls "the American colonial state's first major attempt at ordering the colony and casting its net of surveillance over its colonized subjects."[29] Through the census, the United States was able to formally and officially fix boundaries separating "civilized" and "uncivilized" Filipinos. According to the census, there were eight "civilized tribes." Listed in descending order of population those were the Visayans, the Tagalogs, the Ilocanos, the Bicols, the Pangasinans, the Pampangans, the Cagayans, and the Zambalans. In addition, there were sixteen "uncivilized tribes": the Moros, the Igorots, the Bukidnons, the Subanos, the Mandayas, the Negritos, the Manobos, the Bagobos, the Mangyan, the Bilan, the Tagbanua, the Tiruray, the Ilongot, the Ata, the Tagabili, and the Batak.[30]

The census, notes Vergara, created a "sudden plurality of subjects" that "reinforced . . . a constant theme in American colonial discourse: the incapacity of the Filipinos to govern themselves."[31] He goes on to describe the uses of photography in the census: "The captions of the photographs accompanying the census . . . express representativity, enabling the suppression of context and individuality. . . . The white sheet (a familiar method used by anthropologists and police photographers) covers the background, depriving the photograph of its spatial context, and emphasizes the physical features of the photographed."[32] The photographs, and their arrangement on the page, were not taken with the intent of illustrating an article in *National Geographic*. They appeared in the magazine in the same fashion as they appeared in the official census report itself, a cobbling together of images from the Worcester archive.

In addition, at least some of the photographs were captioned haphazardly. For example, in figure 14, three of the individuals are identified as being "Gaddan" and three are identified as "Remontado," despite the fact that no such categories existed in the census. At both the Newberry and the UMMA archive, the "Gaddan" photographs are categorized as Kalingas. Moreover, one of the "Gaddan" individuals is called a "girl," but is actually a man (bottom left), and one of the "Remontado" individuals (middle left) is actually a Gaddan/Kalinga. The accuracy of what the photographs were said to show appeared to have been of less importance than their potential visual impact as indicators of the supposed diversity of the islands.

Seeing the census photographs in *National Geographic*, readers were invited to scrutinize the features of Filipinos, comparing their own sense of self—as individuals and as Americans—with the bodies of colonial subjects presented as representative types in a fashion similar to the comparative gaze that the photograph of the Negrito woman invited in the magazine in 1903. Such photographs were instrumental in shaping American perceptions of the Philippines. As one observer put it in 1907: "The average American knew almost nothing about [the Philippines] . . . until the newspapers and magazines began to educate him."[33] As they were being educated about the Philippines, readers also were being educated in how to think about themselves as representative members of a new colonial power, engaged in a process of bringing civilization to the Philippines. As Vergara writes, "The pictures of wild tribes not only showed the extent of civilizing needed but also fed the consistent doubt on the capacity of the Filipinos to govern themselves."[34]

In addition to the regular magazine articles, Grosvenor found other ways to capitalize on Worcester's photographs. For example, in 1907 several of the census photographs, along with other photographs of the Philippines published in various articles in *National Geographic,* were reprinted in a book put out by the National Geographic Society. That book, *Scenes from Every Land,* contained 250 images that had appeared in the magazine over the previous five years. Ten of the photographs were from the Philippines; the only country with more photographs was India, with eleven. Though clearly intended to spark increased interest in the magazine, Grosvenor adopted a humble tone in his explanation of the reason for the publication: "The reader must not infer . . . that this modest collection of illustrations has any great mission to perform." He went on to suggest that "those who desire further information can turn to the original number of the Magazine" if they found their interest piqued by any of the photographs they found in *Scenes from Every Land.*[35] If they decided to become members of the Society, Grosvenor certainly would have been delighted.

TUASON NOTES THAT the theme of "commercial expansion . . . tended to dominate *National Geographic* articles through the first half of the 1898–1908 period" that her study covered.[36] However, Worcester consistently utilized the rhetoric of "moral tutelage" in his writings about the relationship between the Philippines and the United States. This is not to say that he was uninterested in commercial development. As Rodney Sullivan and others have observed, Worcester's arguments in favor of

U.S. retention of the Philippines were at least partly self-interested in that his postgovernment activities included ranching and the processing of coconut oil in the Philippines, and it suited his financial interests to make sure that the United States maintained control of the islands.[37] Nevertheless, his writings tended to frame the discussion of the Philippines around the Kiplingesque idea of the "white man's burden" to bring civilization to the "savages." This was seen as early as 1898, and it was even more evident in three articles Worcester published in the magazine in 1911, 1912, and 1913. (He originally wrote four articles on the subject but, as will be detailed below, Grosvenor combined two of the articles into one, removing portions that he felt were unduly controversial.) Coming after more than a decade of living and working in the Philippines, these articles are a crystallization of Worcester's ideas about the Philippines, about Filipinos, and about the future of the colony. As always, he focused his articles on the non-Christian Filipinos.

In addition to summarizing his ideas about the non-Christian Filipinos, the articles also reveal Worcester's growing unease about the future, coming as they did in a period of Democratic ascendance in American politics. In 1910, Democrats gained fifty-eight seats in the House of Representatives, making them the majority party for the first time in fifteen years. In the committee reorganization that followed the election, William Jones of Virginia became the head of the House Committee on Insular Affairs. Jones, a staunch anti-imperialist, "had no patience with arguments that retention of the Philippines served either American or Filipino interests." Working with Manuel Quezon, one of two Philippine resident commissioners in Washington, D.C., "Jones introduced a measure calling for creation of an elected upper house of the Philippine legislature, to replace the Philippine commission, and for independence within a decade."[38]

The Jones bill was unable to advance at that time due to opposition in the Republican-controlled Senate, but the political terrain continued shifting in the next round of elections. In 1912, the Democrats picked up an additional sixty-one seats in the House and won control of the Senate. Even more importantly, Woodrow Wilson was elected president on a platform that called for Philippine independence. Filipinos followed the election closely, and when the results were cabled to Manila, "[a]n estimated 10,000 people paraded through Manila's streets." The nationalist newspaper, *La Vanguardia,* "called Wilson a modern Moses who would 'preside over our triumphal entrance into the Promised Land after redeeming us from the long captivity to which the imperial Pharoahs reduced us.'" By contrast, "Manila American opinion was . . . full of fear and foreboding: would the great 'experiment' with Filipinos endlessly enhancing their capacity for self-government under U.S. tutelage, be allowed to continue?"[39]

Worcester certainly hoped so, and he was determined to keep pushing the retentionist agenda in the face of strengthening headwinds. Even before the triumph of his Democratic enemies in Washington, D.C., Worcester was well aware of the shifting political tide, which may have prompted him to make arrangements with Grosvenor to publish a series of articles in *National Geographic*. Worcester hoped that these articles would help him gain the support of readers (and voters) for his argument that U.S. colonial policies in the Philippines were benevolent and were helping to civilize the islands. By this point he was fully convinced of the power of his photographs to sway public opinion, and he recognized that the most direct way of attracting the attention he desired was to make his articles overwhelmingly image-intensive, to use the "universal language" of photography in order to make his case. In a reflection of the changes taking place in the magazine in general, photographs dominated all three articles, with text taking on a decidedly secondary role.

Worcester put a great deal of care not only into selecting images for the articles that would help convey his argument but also in guaranteeing that the quality of the prints that were to be reproduced were of the highest possible quality. He relied on Martin to help him with this part of the image selection. On April 17, 1911, Martin sent a letter from Manila to the government retreat at Baguio, where Worcester was staying. The main purpose of the letter was to inform Worcester about an order that Martin had placed for a "cinematographic apparatus," film, and printing machine for the motion pictures that he and Worcester were planning to make. Martin also informed Worcester that his "order of types for your articles in the national geographic magazine [*sic*] is almost complete, with the exception of the negatives that can lend themselves to solio printing with better results; we have no solio now, but I shall have some to-morrow morning; it will take about 3 days to finish up the order and you might expect it complete by saturday [*sic*] or sunday [*sic*] at the latest; I am using the greatest care in the printing of these negatives for the purpose of half-toning."[40]

Negatives printed on Solio paper—a printing paper produced by the Eastman Kodak Company—were noted for their rich tonal gradations. Martin and Worcester were both concerned with getting the best quality images for the reproductions that would go into the magazine. In a follow-up letter dated April 24, Martin was pleased to report that "the prints you requested for your articles in the National Geographic magazine, were mailed to you on April 22nd." Providing additional details, he told Worcester that "in some instances solio paper produced the best print for half-toning and again with other negatives, velox gave better results. . . . I have found a method for developing Velox papers, that give wonderfully soft tones, softer even than solio."[41] Of course, some of these distinctions were lost when the photographs were mechanically reproduced for the magazine, but Martin and Worcester both took great pride in the quality of the images that were sent to Grosvenor.

Worcester opened the first of his articles, "Field Sports Among the Wild Men of Northern Luzon," by establishing his credentials as spokesman for the country's colonial policies: "My acquaintance with the wild men of northern Luzon began in July, 1900, shortly after the arrival of the second Philippine Commission at Manila."[42] Acknowledging the oft-revised categories of the various non-Christian Filipinos, Worcester told readers: "We now know that there are but seven non-Christian tribes in northern Luzon, namely the Negritos, the Benguet-Lepanto Igorots, the Ilongots or Ibilaos, the Ifugaos, the Bontoc Igorots, the Kalingas, and the Tingians" (215). He presented this number as definitive in contrast to estimates of thirty-six tribes given by Ferdinand Blumentritt or the twenty-six tribes that the Jesuits in Manila believed existed in northern Luzon, the two main sources of earlier estimates for the number of tribes.

Worcester seems not to have been persuaded by the official categories and counts of the 1903 census. Of the seven tribes in his 1911 article, only the Ilongots and the Negritos were identified as separate tribes in the census. There was only one general category for all Igorots, which included the Kalingas and the Tingians. Although it is tempting to think that Worcester's revised numbers came after eight additional years of thoughtful analysis and clarification, his 1905 *Index* also failed to match the categories of the census, with Worcester listing many more non-Christian tribes than the census acknowledged and the census claiming two categories (Batak and Tagabili) that Worcester didn't include. In the UMMA archive, too, Worcester included categories absent from the census. In other words, in 1911 there was still no consensus regarding the total number of "tribes" in the Philippines.

As he bolstered his claims of authoritative knowledge gained firsthand by multiple trips into the region, Worcester simultaneously bolstered the legitimacy of the U.S. enterprise in the Philippines. He pointed out to readers that the organization of a civilian colonial government in 1901 resulted in his being assigned "the control of all non-Christian tribes, except those of the Moro province. . . . It also fell to my lot to draft legislation as might be deemed necessary in the premises" (215). Thus, both the knowledge of the non-Christian tribes and their welfare depended on Worcester's efforts. He was proud of his results, claiming that because of his efforts "we have been able to cause 120,000 head-hunters to give up head-hunting" (266).

In the final passage of the article, Worcester summarized how he was able to bring the non-Christians closer to civilization: "We have been able to get results in dealing with the wild men by following the simple policy of always giving them a square deal; by not punishing them for a given course of action unless they had ample previous warning that such action would be followed by punishment; by never failing to punish when, *after due warning,* they have misbehaved; by making friends with them again whenever they were ready to be friendly, and by finding an outlet for their superabundant animal spirits in rough but innocent field sports" (266–67). If that course of action sounds much like how a parent would deal with a child, recall that in 1898 Worcester referred to Filipinos as "simple children of nature." Fifteen years later he evidently still felt much the same way.

The first photograph included in the article seemed to underscore both the childlike nature of the "wild men" and the tranquility that Worcester said he was able to bring to northern Luzon (fig. 15). The photograph certainly has little connection to the article's subject matter. It is, however, a well-composed photograph with a greater degree of aesthetic appeal than most of the photographs in the Worcester archive. A full-page image, it shows an Igorot man standing on a hillside holding a large bouquet of white lilies that he had gathered "near the trail to Cervantes" (217). Posed in such a way that he seems to have emerged organically from the surrounding landscape, the unnamed man smiles beatifically and gazes up past the camera toward something unseen in the sky.

The precise date of this photograph is unknown, since it is not included in the Worcester archive at UMMA. Worcester did sell the photograph to Ayer, including it in his 1909 supplement, where it is included in category 34, "Plants, their flowers and fruits." Of the five photographs of Benguet Igorots holding lilies in the UMMA archive, there are two that show a man posed in a similar fashion. Those photographs were made in July 1902 near Baguio. If this photograph was made at the same time as those, then the gentle look on the man's face had little to do

Fig. 15. "An Igorot Gathering Lilies Near the Trail to Cervantes." *National Geographic Magazine*, March 1911. (Newberry 34-A-197.)

with the efforts of Worcester and his colleagues to bring peace to the region, since they were taken only a year after the civil government was established at Manila, at a time when Worcester was still getting to know the region.

The lilies in this photograph are Philippine lilies (*Lilium philippinense*), and they closely resemble Easter lilies, long a symbol of hope and redemption in Christian iconography. It could be that Worcester was less interested in presenting an image of a pacified Igorot in this photograph than he was in metaphorically positioning himself (and, by extension his American readers) as the redeemers of the non-Christian Filipinos. He clearly suggested as much in the article's text. Worcester wrote that some people felt that the non-Christians in northern Luzon "believe the Secretary of the Interior, Lieutenant Governor [of Ifugao, Jeff] Gallman, and [Constabulary] Lieutenant Meimban to be genuine gods, recently reincarnated." Worcester demurred at that suggestion, saying: "In point of fact," they "believe nothing of the sort" (266).

It seems, though, that Worcester may actually have believed he was held in godlike esteem by the non-Christian Filipinos, a point noted by the historian Peter Stanley: "As he [i.e., Worcester] rashly wrote in a draft of his annual report for 1911—subsequently expurgated by more politic officials—*his* natives said, 'The Voice of Worcester is the Voice of God.'"[43] In the *National Geographic* article, too, Worcester boasted that he was treated with great respect when traveling through northern Luzon. On the page opposite the photograph seen in figure 15, he wrote: "The number of wild men who assembled to meet me at important points was at first small, and the meetings held them were very informal. The meetings are still informal, but the attendance now reaches 6,000 or 8,000." He portrayed himself as a peacemaker in the region, his annual inspections bringing enemies together: "When such people have once been brought into contact with each other it has often proved a comparatively simple matter to establish more or less permanent friendly relations between them" (216).

Worcester presented himself to readers as an intrepid explorer who had the temerity to travel into "previously unknown regions" that not even the Spaniards had explored in the nearly four hundred years that they ruled the Philippines. In his own decade of travel, Worcester "familiarized myself with conditions throughout practically all of northern Luzon" (215) and he included more than fifty photographs showing the Igorots, Ifugaos, and others dancing, engaging in foot races, and wrestling, suggesting that an almost festival-like atmosphere had taken hold in the region. According to Worcester, these organized sporting events succeeded in bringing peace to northern Luzon.

Worcester inserted himself into the article visually as well as textually. Although he didn't include any photographs in which he appeared himself, one photograph showed a group of Ifugao men gathered around Worcester's camera, several of them clustered under his focusing cloth in order to peer at the scene through the lens. The photograph is captioned "Making the Acquaintance of the Camera" (256). In another photograph, a man from Lubuagan crouches in front of the horn of a phonograph while an American officer crouches behind the phonograph in order to control the machine. It's captioned "Listening to the Talking Machine," and is one of several photographs (08-F-12 to 08-F-22) that Worcester made that show various men of Lubuagan posing singly or in groups next to the phonograph.[44] Such photographs illustrate Vergara's point about the impact of the introduction "of American technology, and its apparent capacity to entrance the inferior other."[45]

Gonzalez points out that through the travel-guide rhetoric that he employed in his *National Geographic* articles, "Worcester establishe[d] a practice of framing the Philippines as a colonial destination for the American public."[46] Worcester allowed readers to experience vicariously all that he had actually experienced in his years in the Philippines. After establishing himself as a reliable guide to the land of the "wild men," Worcester invited his readers to imagine themselves on a journey to northern Luzon: "We leave Manila on a coast-guard boat and 24 hours later land through the surf at Tagudin. . . . [W]e climb upward through wonderful tropical forests until at the crest of the Malaya range we reach the pines and lilies of the temperate zone; we then descend its eastern slopes, and as we approach our destination are met by a great gathering of Igorots on horseback and on foot, who escort us into town" (221–22).

Worcester structured the entire article as though he and his readers were traveling through northern Luzon, and he included a map marked with the different places they visited. In actuality, this "journey" collapsed multiple trips that Worcester had taken over the years in order to provide the illusion of a seamless tour through the region. Approaching the town of Bontoc, "we catch, now and then, wind-borne musical notes, which rise and die away again and again, but gradually grow clearer" (226). Later: "It is 5 a.m. and we are in the saddle and off for Lubuagan, distant 54 miles" (244–47), a distance that will require two days to cover. "As we continue our journey the Lubo men fall in behind us, and we keep a sharp eye on them. We reach Lubuagan after dark and are escorted into town by Igorots who have come out in the rain with torches to meet us" (247). As the trip comes to an end, Worcester and his readers descended "down from the mountains to the Christian town of Bagabag, in Nueva Vizcaya, escorted all the way by Silipan Ifugaos, who were the terror of the Spaniards." Their trip completed, at "Bagabag we receive an enthusiastic reception. The people of this town are more than grateful, because the government has made their lives and property safe" (266).

At each stop along this imagined journey, Worcester supplied vivid, sensuous imagery for his readers' benefit. As Gonzalez puts it, he was both the source, and the purveyor, of details satisfying his readers' "lasting fascination with the native body."[47] Worcester's own fascination extended equally to the bodies of men and women. About a group of dancing Bontoc men, he wrote: "The perfectly developed brown bodies of the dancers are naked save for handsome blue and scarlet clouts and an occasional boar's tusk arm ornament with its horse-hair plume. Not a man has an ounce of superfluous flesh. There is a beautiful rippling play of perfect muscle under clear skin. . . . Their steps are springing and panther-like" (226). The participants of an Igorot slapping game are "two lithe and muscular young men" (233). At the start of a tug-of-war game, the "teams have dropped exactly together and now how they pull and how their perfectly developed muscles stand out" (241).

One of the longer and more sensual depictions of women is this one, describing the "Champion Dancer" from the Igorot town of Bañgad:

> We go down and mingle with the crowd, and, noting unusual excite-ment among the women at the edge of a dance circle, force our way through to ascertain its cause. We are well repaid for our trouble. The men from Bañgad, in the far north, have the floor. They have brought only one woman with them to uphold the reputation of their town, but she is abundantly capable of doing this. . . . She wears only a bright-colored and handsomely embroidered skirt, reaching from the waist to the knee and open up the right side, so that her move-ments are absolutely unimpeded. Her arms are stretched upward and outward, palms up. Her chest is thrown out and her shoulders are held well back. Her arms and hands convey the impression of soaring wings, and she seems hardly to touch the ground. While the dance lasts she has no thought for anything else. When it ends and the crowd shrieks its approval, she becomes self-conscious, covers her face with her hands, and bounds away like a deer. (231–32)

To illustrate this scene, Worcester included two photographs that he said showed the champion dancer, but the images do little to capture the sen-suality of her dancing. In one photograph (08-A-155) she stands alone, posed stiffly facing the camera in an open field, a crowd of people in the distance behind her. In the second (08-A-156) she leans against a coco-nut tree, her ankles crossed, one hand on her head as she turns toward the camera.

Identifying her as the champion dancer served Worcester's pur-pose of providing visual evidence for what he had written. As Vergara writes: "The photograph does not merely illustrate, or represent, but also authenticates. . . . [T]he mere reading about a fact in print does not completely confirm reality, but seeing that fact captured in a photograph makes it seem even more 'real.'"[48] Worcester, of course, felt free to use photographs however he saw fit, even if the facts surrounding a photograph differed from the "truth" that Worcester ascribes to a photograph. In the case of the photographs of the "champion dancer," the text on the original negative sleeve at the UMMA says that they were taken on June 28, 1908, and that she was the winner of a women's foot race, not the champion dancer. The two photographs were part of a sequence of forty-five photographs taken that day showing not only the foot races but the slapping contest, a greased-pole contest, a wheelbarrow race, and a humiliating game where a small boy "is allowed to bury his face in a washbasin of flour and grope for coins, which, when found, must be seized with his mouth" (239) (fig. 16).

While much of this article was dedicated to showing Worcester's ability to find appropriate outlets for the "superabundant animal spirits" of the people of northern Luzon, the article's final sequence of five photographs took on a darker tone and showed a large group of Ifugaos swarming and attacking a carabao (a type of water buffalo) that had been let loose for that purpose. Readers could see the Ifugao men hacking at the animal with their bolo knives, and they could read about how even before the animal had died "his intestines have been torn out and the crowd has a tug-of-war with them, each individual retaining what he can get" (261). Moreover: "When such a mob of people hacks recklessly with war knives, it is inevitable that severe wounds should be accidentally inflicted" (261). In his 1913 article in the magazine, Worcester included a photograph that showed him treating an Ifugao man for an injury sustained during this same event, and in that article he referred readers back to the 1911 article, effectively linking the two articles into a larger narrative.

According to Worcester, the gruesome carabao-killing scene lasted fewer than ten minutes, and was about to be reenacted on another carabao until Worcester intervened: "We emphatically disapprove . . . and insist that he shall be killed with an axe" (261–66). In this passage, Worcester suggests to his readers that he was unaware that the first carabao was to be butchered in such a manner. However, the fact that he had his camera at the ready and was able to make several exposures in short order indicates that he knew precisely what was about to transpire. As a final scene to the imagined journey, however, it provided a powerful

Fig. 16. "A Bontoc Igorot Boy Who Has Been Burrowing for Coins in a Dish of Flour." *National Geographic Magazine*, March 1911. (Newberry 08-A-563.)

reminder to readers that despite the progress made toward containing their "animal spirits," the "wild men of northern Luzon" remain wild and that a strong American presence was required to continue the civilizing process.

Eighteen months after inviting readers to imagine themselves on a journey through northern Luzon, Worcester's next article about non-Christian Filipinos appeared in the pages of *National Geographic*. Titled, "Head-Hunters of Northern Luzon," it sprawled across nearly one hundred pages, and comprised the entire September 1912 issue of the magazine. Photographs dominate the article; page follows page with only captions for text. (By contrast, there are just three text-only pages.) The article served as a showcase for the accumulated images in Worcester's archive. There are traditional ethnographic photographs with the subjects posed against a white backdrop, photographs showing people engaged in their daily activities, photographs of the rice terraces built by the Ifugaos, and photographs emphasizing weaponry.

For this article, Worcester blended the voice of a tour guide with the authoritative and dispassionate tone of a scientist instructing his readers. He explained that he wrote the article in order to give "a brief account of each of the head-hunting tribes" that he had become acquainted with during eleven years of annual trips to northern Luzon. "The photographs," he told his readers, "were taken in part by me and in part under my direction by Mr. Charles Martin, the official photographer of the Philippine government. It should perhaps be said in passing that they are in every case strictly authentic and typical."[49]

Worcester reminded readers that "the number of non-Christian tribes in the northern part of the great island of Luzon had been grossly exaggerated, and that there were in reality but seven." Moreover, six of those "tribes have, until recently, engaged in head-hunting" (833). Although he didn't name the non-head-hunting tribe, he may have had the Lepanto-Benguet Igorots in mind, as they were the only group from the 1911 article that he did not include in the 1912 article. However, he did find a seventh group to include in this article, the people of "No Man's Land" where the Tingian, Kalinga, Ifugao, and Bontoc-Igorot regions met. According to Worcester, the people of this "No Man's Land" were "especially warlike, and among them are found some of the most famous head-hunting chiefs in northern Luzon" (930).

In his 1911 article, Worcester categorized the people of "No Man's Land" as Bontoc Igorots, but in 1912 he said that he was unable to categorize the people of this region because years of intermarriage had resulted "in a blending of physical characteristics and racial customs, and it is often difficult to state with any degree of certainty to what particular tribe, if any, the people of a given town belong" (930). To illustrate, he pointed to their houses, which "resemble the houses of the Kalingas more than those of the Bontoc Igorots," as well as the fact that "women have adopted some article of dress from the Kalingas and others from the Tingians" (930) and that the men have hats like the Bontoc Igorots. Despite the fact that the people of "No Man's Land" challenged his notions of fixed cultural boundaries, Worcester seems to have never seriously considered abandoning the tribal classifications that he used to organize both his photo archive and his conceptualization of the people of the Philippines. This article reaffirmed his faith in both, and it continued to utilize the hierarchical classifications that are a hallmark of his archive.

The first group Worcester wrote about in the 1912 article was the Negritos, whose intelligence he still believed was "of an exceptionally low order." Worcester continued to insist that there was little hope that the Negritos could be civilized, noting that efforts to "educate them or materially to better their condition . . . has resulted in complete failure" (847). Until a 1909 trip to the far north of Luzon, none of the Negritos he had encountered "were head-hunters; but there is no doubt the representatives of this tribe which now inhabit northeastern Luzon engage in this custom" (837–38). Having given them the status of "head-hunter," he had little choice but to discuss them alongside the Igorots, Kalingas, and others. However, while he found much to admire in the bodies of those groups, he was repelled by the Negritos, noting that they were "dwarfish," had skin that was "very dark brown, or black," had noses that were "broad and flat," and arms that were "disproportionately long" (838). He also reiterated his belief that "they must be regarded as a 'link' which is not now missing, but soon will be" (849).

Worcester included fourteen photographs of Negritos, including some that dated back to his February 1901 visit to Mariveles, including one of his favorite photographs, the one showing him standing next to Ibag, a "typical Negrito man," that he used to show the "relative size" of a Negrito in comparison to an American. In fact, there are more photographs of Negritos from 1901 than there are from 1909—when Worcester first encountered the "head-hunting" Negritos. Although he noted in their captions which photographs were made in northeast Luzon, he didn't specify that the other photographs weren't made there. In other words, he allowed readers to collapse any distinctions that might be made between different groups of Negritos. In this way, all Negritos could now be seen as headhunters.

He turned next to the Ilongots, whom he placed one step above the Negritos in his hierarchy. He didn't say that the Ilongots were destined to disappear despite the fact that they were "numerically even less important than the Negritos" (850). Worcester criticized Ilongot houses as "very filthy, and . . . scantily furnished with only the articles strictly necessary to make it possible for a rather primitive people to grow rice, yams, and corn, take fish and game, attack their enemies, and defend themselves" (862). About their head-hunting—which Worcester said was stopped only "very recently" (862)—the Ilongots "usually cut off the heads of their victims, sometimes tossing them about and playing with them, and again carrying them for some little distance only to throw them away" (862–63).

The Kalingas were the next group discussed in the article, and he told readers that the "dark-brown [Kalinga] bodies are, as a rule, kept quite clean, and are often beautifully developed" (863). The men "wear short, tight-fitting jackets made from cloth woven by their women, or from gaily colored cloth," and those "Kalinga men who can afford to do so purchase gaily colored blankets" that they would knot and wear draped diagonally across their bodies (872). The Kalinga women "usually wear a short *camisa,* or upper garment. It fits the body tightly and has sleeves" (873). About the head-hunting practices of the Kalinga, Worcester said that until U.S. intervention the Kalinga had been "constantly at war among themselves and with their non-Christian neighbors of other tribes. Furthermore, they frequently wiped out Filipino hunting parties and even attacked small Filipino villages" (875). In passages such as this, Worcester reiterated the distinction he made between "Filipino" and "non-Christian tribes," depicting the Philippines as a collection of diverse groups of people historically in conflict with one another, and not as a cohesive nation. Worcester then went on to provide vivid descriptions of "blood oozing from the severed head" of a Kalinga victim and a drink made from a mixture of fermented sugarcane (*basi*) and the brain matter of the victim (877). The "beautifully developed" Kalingas were thereby reinscribed as savages.

Worcester continued the same pattern of describing and revealing the other subjects of his article, alternating between the violence of the men and the erotic potential of the women, the inherent savagery of the "tribe" and the civilizing effects of the Americans. Thus, the Ifugaos, "like the Kalingas[,] have until very recently been inveterate head-hunters" (882). Their clothing "is as somber as that of the Kalingas is gaudy" (879), and Ifugao "women wear excessively short skirts wrapped about the body far below the waist and often not extending more than half way to the knee" (879) and rarely wear upper garments. The Bontoc Igorots are "physically a wonderful people" (895) who "until recently have been inveterate head-hunters" (895). Bontoc women wear "a narrow skirt reaching from the waist to the knee, and open up one side. Upper garments are practically unknown except in regions where the inhabitants have come much in contact with Filipinos" (896). The Tingians, "although . . . non-Christians . . . are in other respects quite as highly civilized as their Christian Filipinos" (911). Both men and women have "clean, well-developed bodies" (912).

In this article, Worcester included more photographs showing evidence of violence and death than he did in any other article for the magazine. There are photographs of human skulls, "trophies" adorning the outsides of houses, a photograph of a dead girl (called a Kalinga in the article, but cataloged as a Bontoc Igorot) propped up in a chair as part of ceremony prior to her burial (Newberry 08-I-010), and a horrific photograph of a headless Ifugao man whose hacked body was bound to a pole and was being carried to its grave (07-B-081). Worcester gave an account of the burial ceremony, portraying the Ifugaos as heartless in the face of such violence: "When the open grave was reached the body was deposited on the ground. The neighbors shouted to the spirit of the dead man, asking him why he had been careless enough to get himself killed, and why he had left his poor old mother and a house full of rice and tobacco. Even the gray-headed mother berated her careless son" (893).

The final photograph in the article (fig. 17) reinforced Worcester's argument that there was still work to be done to bring civilization to northern Luzon. The caption says that the two men in the photograph were from "No Man's Land," that they were "the last to come under government control," and that "isolated cases of head-taking still occur among them" (929). Readers may well have had their eyes drawn to the axe that one man holds in the photograph, seeing it as a weapon whose potential to inflict a lethal wound was still very real. They very likely would have had a very different reading of the photograph, a much more benign reading, had they read the caption that Worcester provided for Ayer: "Full length front view of two men in dancing costume."[50]

In fact, both men also appeared in a photograph in Worcester's 1911 article. In that photograph (Newberry 08-F-042), they posed with eight other men that Worcester identified as "picked men, who dance for their town on festal occasions" (250). In 1911, Worcester emphasized the celebratory aspects of the men; in 1912, he emphasized their potential for violence. Worcester's 1912 article, with its photographs and its graphic textual depictions of violence, likely struck many of his readers as both alluring and terrifying. Worcester wanted to show readers that the Philippines remained an uncivilized and potentially dangerous place, but a place of great exoticism and romantic allure. As Gonzalez writes, "As a readable, accessible visual marker of difference, the icon of the wild man reduced a vast and diverse territory with a long and complex history into an easily digestible and highly entertaining shorthand for the civilizing mission."[51] Worcester assured his readers of the authenticity and typicality of his photographs, and that "the conditions I have set forth are those which existed when Americans first came in contact with these people."

Fig. 17. "Two Men of 'No Man's Land,' Showing Typical Dress and Ornaments." *National Geographic Magazine,* September 1912. (Newberry 08-F-043.)

As a teaser for the next installment in his story, he gave this promise: "In a future article I shall tell of some of the changes which it has proved possible to bring about" (930).

Sensitive to the charge that he used the non-Christian Filipinos as representatives of the nation as a whole, Worcester finished his article with a caveat, telling any readers who had stuck with him all the way through that "the peculiar, and sometimes highly objectionable, customs which have prevailed, or still prevail, among the million of non-Christian inhabitants must not be credited to the Filipinos, the civilized and Christianized inhabitants in the Philippines, of whom there are some seven millions" (930). Even here, though, Worcester misled his readers, given that the 1903 census put the total population of non-Christians at under 650,000, and that the non-head-hunting Moros accounted for more than 40 percent of the non-Christian population. Even more important is the likelihood that Worcester's caveat had very little impact on readers, given the sheer volume of images that Worcester devoted to revealing the bodies and the customs of the non-Christian tribes of northern Luzon, and given that Worcester provided no images, and almost no textual information, about those seven million "civilized and Christianized" Filipinos.

AMONG THE PEOPLE whose attention was grabbed by Worcester's depictions of the "Head-Hunters of Northern Luzon" was Edmund Felder, a New York-based film distributor who wrote Worcester a letter inquiring about movies that he had been told Worcester made while gathering material for his *National Geographic* articles. Felder wondered if, perhaps, he could enter into a business arrangement with Worcester, organizing screenings of any such movies for the rapidly emerging market of filmgoers. Worcester wrote back and explained to Felder that he did have such films and that he had been able to secure them based on the fact that Worcester had "executive control over the people of all the Philippine wild tribes outside of the Moro Province."[52] Although the two men were unable to reach a mutually agreeable business relationship, Felder's letter reveals that there was a wide audience in the United States that was receptive to the messages that Worcester was promoting through the pages of *National Geographic*. Felder believed that Worcester could have even more of a reach if he tapped into the film market, and that it would be profitable to do so.

Worcester wrote back to Felder saying that he had films of all the tribes represented in the 1912 article, and he pointed out to Felder that most of those tribes had also been written about in his 1911 article. Worcester also told Felder that he had two more articles forthcoming in *National Geographic*. He said that one of the articles, "What Has Been Done for the Non-Christian Tribes of the Philippines Under American Rule," was already in the hands of Grosvenor and that it would probably be appearing in print soon. The last article, which Worcester said he was "just ready to transmit . . . contains descriptions of all the wild tribes of the Philippines, and will be copiously illustrated with color plates."[53]

As it turned out, Grosvenor decided to combine those two articles into a single article, "The Non-Christian Peoples of the Philippine Islands, with an Account of What Has Been Done for Them under American

Rule." It comprised the entire November 1913 issue of the magazine, and the magazine's cover promised readers that inside they would find "32 Pages of Illustrations in Eight Colors." In some ways, the article was an extension of Worcester's 1912 article. It even picked up where the previous year's article left off, beginning with this sentence: "The non-Christian peoples of the Philippine Islands constitute approximately an eighth of the entire population of the islands." If that sounded like a small number, Worcester assured readers of their geographic significance: "It is not too much to say that at the present time approximately half of the territory of the Philippine Islands is inhabited by them, so far as it is inhabited at all." Then, in a footnote, he added: "There are probably no regions in the world where within similar areas there dwell so large a number of distinct peoples as are to be found in northern Luzon and in the interior of Mindanao."[54]

The majority of his article was organized in an encyclopedic fashion, with his coverage of the non-Christian peoples beginning with the "Atás" and ending with the "Tirurayes." After giving accounts of each tribe, he shifted to his discussion of American successes in the Philippines. As with his 1912 article, Worcester told his readers that the photographs he included were necessary for conveying his message: "Typical individuals, houses, settlements, and scenes are shown, so that the reader obtains at a glance facts which it would be impossible to state in words within the limits of any publication smaller than a bulky monograph" (1157). He accompanied his photographs with an abundance of enthusiastic praise for the clothing and the bodies of the people he wrote about, calling the Kalingas "the Peacocks of the Philippines" for their bright clothing (1192), and saying of the Bontoc Igorots: "Both men and women are splendidly developed" (1202).

Aware of the fact that he was revisiting some of the same ground he had already covered in the previous two articles, Worcester insisted that the 1913 article remained relevant, in part because he had expanded his coverage to include all the non-Christian tribes, including those in the southern Philippines: "[A]s the convenience of having even brief descriptions of all Philippine non-Christian tribes included in one article seems obvious, I venture here to record some additional facts concerning these peoples, and to restate some few of the facts already set forth" (1158). Here, Worcester came full circle back to his 1898 article in which he wrote that "brief notes concerning the more important of the tribes in question may not be entirely without interest at the present time" (284–85). By 1913, he was able to provide notes and give facts about a great many more peoples than he had done fifteen years earlier.

Worcester's 1913 article was even more heavily illustrated than his 1912 article, with some pages having as many as six photographs showing "typical" members of the different cultures represented. Once again viewers were able to read about and gaze at the bodies that Worcester admired, as well as the bodies that Worcester disliked. The use of hand-colored photographs made the clothing and ornamentation of the non-Christian Filipinos all the more striking. Here, again, were Igorot women wearing almost no clothing, and the shapely bodies of Kalinga men that Worcester was so clearly drawn to. Here, again, were the assertions that the Negritos might be a missing link and are certainly destined to die out. New were the bodies and costumes of people like the "strong, robust" Bagobos (1158) and the "exceedingly timid" Bilans, both of Mindanao (1166). The Mangyans, the "wild people of the mountains of Mindoro" (1178), appeared for the first time since his 1898 article.

One striking feature of the article was the revelation that Worcester felt some ambivalence toward the changes he was helping to facilitate in the Philippines. Take, for example, this passage about the Bukidnon people of Mindanao: "The people are converting their beautiful and naturally rich country into a checkerboard, with roads and trails for dividing lines. They are giving up their picturesque native costume so rapidly that typical garments are even now hard to obtain—a fact which is to be regretted, as the garb of the Filipinos which they are adopting is not more modest or more serviceable and is far less picturesque" (1193). Like his analysis of the clothing of a Kalinga woman in his 1906 article in the *Philippine Journal of Science,* Worcester admits to a preference for clothing that, to him, signaled "display rather than modesty."[55] Mere modesty seemed to be a disappointment to him.

The effects of the American occupation could be felt in the north, as well. About the Benguet Igorots, he wrote: "The daily wage has risen steadily since the American occupation and opportunity to work can practically always be had by those who wish for it. The people of this tribe have prospered under American rule and today live in better houses, are better fed, wear better clothes, and enjoy better health than ever before" (1202). There was a downside, however, in that some of the more picturesque elements of native life were disappearing. Of the Bontoc Igorots, he wrote: "Upper garments were in the past almost never worn, but are now gradually coming into use as a result of contact with whites and Filipinos, who are teaching these light-hearted and innocent-minded daughters of nature to be ashamed of the beautiful bodies with which the Creator has endowed them" (1204).

Worcester's ambivalence is an example of "imperialist nostalgia" prompted by the changes that he both facilitated and witnessed from year to year on his annual inspection tours. The wistfulness of his article may also have been prompted in part by the fact that he knew his time as secretary of the interior was coming to an end and, with it, his ability to travel with authority and photograph with impunity whoever he wanted, wherever he wanted, and however he wanted. Despite his mixed emotions, he clearly was proud of all that the Americans had been able to accomplish during his time in office.

In the second part of this article he summarized some of the changes in the Philippines since the imposition of American rule there, and discussed (in less poetic language) the building of roads and trails over mountains and through the forests, the construction of schools, and the establishment of an American-style judicial system. Sounding at once optimistic and melancholy, he predicted that "it will be but a few years until the Bontoc Igorot is hammering out head-axes for the tourist" (1243). He finished by giving credit to "the provincial and subprovincial officials, who, in the face of innumerable and insuperable obstacles, have carried on their country's work with dogged persistence and unfaltering courage, content to do the right thing *because it ought to be done*" (1256).

Worcester was on his way back to the United States by the time the article was published, having resigned his position as secretary of the interior. In a November 26, 1913, letter to Gilbert Grosvenor mailed from San Francisco, Worcester wrote:

> I was glad to learn on arrival, of the publication of the matter on "The Wild Tribes" in the November number of the magazine. I had not previously had any acknowledgement of the receipt by you of the manuscript or the colored transparencies and was beginning to feel some concern regarding the matter. . . . The illustrations are fine as usual, and I think that the article in the form in which you have issued it, gives a very fair presentation of the subject. In combining the two articles you were of course, quite within your right, as I had no agreement with you relative to the publication of the articles, but only one relative to my furnishing them.[56]

Worcester went on to note peevishly that Grosvenor neglected to pay Worcester upon the receipt of the article, and pointed out that this was not the first time the magazine had failed in this regard.

Worcester's annoyance with Grosvenor may have gone beyond the question of payment or the combining of two articles into one. In the articles that he submitted to Grosvenor, he apparently included material of a highly controversial nature that was edited out of the final published article. In a letter dated November 19, 1913, Grosvenor wrote to Edward Fallows, the president of the American Philippine Company (where Worcester had assumed a position as vice-president), about Worcester's upcoming lecture before the National Geographic Society. After assuring Fallows that he has been following Worcester's work for twelve years "with much interest and appreciation," and that he believed that Worcester was "a man of whom all Americans ought to be proud," Grosvenor went on to say that Worcester was "very fond of controversy, which sometimes is unfortunate." He alluded to "a long discussion of a controversial nature" that Worcester included in the original manuscript that he submitted to Grosvenor and that Grosvenor felt he couldn't publish without damaging his relationship with the Wilson administration.[57]

Given the cozy relations between the National Geographic Society and the federal government, it makes sense that Grosvenor wanted to avoid controversy. With his history of making inflammatory remarks and his clear opposition to Democratic policies toward the Philippines, there is little reason to doubt that whatever the controversy was that Worcester wrote about in his article, it was directed at least in part at the Wilson administration. It would have done Grosvenor little good to allow Worcester to use *National Geographic* to directly attack either the president or the new colonial administrators working in the Philippines.

THE OVERARCHING THEME of all three of the articles about non-Christian Filipinos that Worcester published in *National Geographic* between 1911 and 1913 was Worcester's oft-stated argument that there was no singular national identity in the Philippines and, as a result, that any calls for Philippine independence were incoherent. This was the rationale he consistently presented for why the United States must keep control over the Philippines. Not only was the notion of Filipino national identity an illusion, or so his argument went, but the non-Christian minority groups would also be put at risk if the Christian majority were allowed to assume control over the islands. Thus, it was incumbent on the United States to maintain its position of authority in the islands in order to guide the Philippines toward U.S.-style civilization that might result in the country's independence at some future, though far distant, point.

It is, of course, impossible to state precisely how much direct influence Worcester's articles had on the readers of *National Geographic*, but there are clues that his influence was considerable. As noted above, his 1912 article caught the attention of the film distributor Edmund Felder, who recognized an audience for films on the same topics as his magazine articles. There were also loud denunciations of Worcester's writings and photographs from many quarters, as will be discussed in chapter 5. In addition, in 1913 and 1914, Worcester embarked on a lecture tour where he brought his photographs and films to large and enthusiastic audiences, with some of his lectures essentially reworked versions of his *National Geographic* articles. Significantly, one such audience was a committee of the U.S. Senate, before whom Worcester testified against the Jones bill, a bill that would have granted independence to the Philippines. Despite having come to the end of his career as a colonial administrator, Worcester still had very much to say.

CHAPTER 4

Lecturing against Philippine Independence: Photography, Film, and the Lyceum Circuit

———

THE MORE THOROUGH READERS of Dean Worcester's 1913 article in *National Geographic*—particularly those who liked to browse through the magazine's back matter—would have come across a full-page advertisement promoting a series of lectures that Worcester was prepared to give during the 1914 lyceum season (fig. 18). Noting Worcester's thirteen years of service in the U.S. colonial administration in the Philippines, the advertisement highlighted Worcester's use of motion pictures in his lectures. If the use of color plates in the article was one step toward greater realism in visual culture, the use of movies in his lectures was another step. The boldface font used for the words "Vivid Motion Pictures" was intended to grab the readers' notice and get them excited about the possibility of seeing in action some of the same exotic sites and people that they had only been able to see in Worcester's still photographs. The advertisement noted that Worcester would give lectures under the management of the Philippine Lyceum Bureau, a newly created company that Paul Kramer points out was "conveniently located in the New York offices of the American-Philippine Company,"[1] of which Worcester was a vice-president, a position he accepted on March 15, 1913, six months before he officially resigned as secretary of the interior.[2]

Through the autumn of 1913 there was a great deal of buzz about

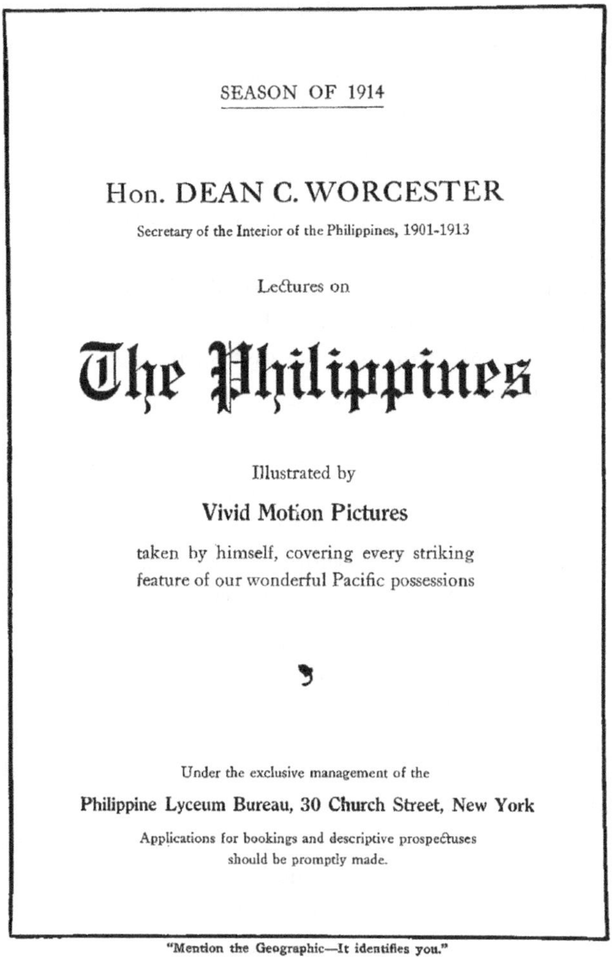

SEASON OF 1914

Hon. DEAN C. WORCESTER

Secretary of the Interior of the Philippines, 1901-1913

Lectures on

𝔗𝔥𝔢 𝔓𝔥𝔦𝔩𝔦𝔭𝔭𝔦𝔫𝔢𝔰

Illustrated by

Vivid Motion Pictures

taken by himself, covering every striking
feature of our wonderful Pacific possessions

Under the exclusive management of the

Philippine Lyceum Bureau, 30 Church Street, New York

Applications for bookings and descriptive prospectuses
should be promptly made.

"Mention the Geographic—It identifies you."

Fig. 18. Advertisement for Dean C. Worcester's lecture series. *National Geographic Magazine*, November 1913.

Worcester's lectures and the films he had made in his final two years in the Philippines. A September 7, 1913, article in the *New York Times* announcing Worcester's resignation said that his lectures

> will begin early in November. He plans to cover the entire country. Mr. Worcester possesses the most complete series of photographs of the Philippines in existence, and he has made many moving pictures of the wild tribes and the bird life in the island jungle. He will deliver

nine different lectures on the islands, three of which will deal with the wild tribes and the head-hunters of the Philippines and what the United States has done for them. Two other lectures will be devoted to the forest resources and commercial possibilities of the Philippines. A sixth will describe the health and sanitary campaign in the islands, and in another lecture Mr. Worcester will describe the methods of educating the Filipinos and tell what has been accomplished in this direction.

One address will deal with the modern Manila, built by the Americans. In the last lectures of his series, which is bound to attract a great deal of attention, Mr. Worcester will discuss the question of Philippine independence.[3]

The income that Worcester expected to draw from these lectures and from his new position with the American-Philippine Company was enough to assure him that he would "be sure of being able to look after my wife and children" after his resignation, an important concern of his after more than a decade of government service.[4]

WORCESTER BEGAN LAYING the groundwork for this next stage of his career more than a year before his resignation, corresponding with a variety of people in New York City about the possibility of securing a contract with a commercial distributor for the films that he and Charles Martin had been making. As noted in the previous chapter, one correspondent was Edmund Felder of the Paragon Feature Films Company, who contacted Worcester after reading his 1912 article in *National Geographic*. Felder offered to help Worcester market the films he and Martin had made. Worcester was interested in profiting off of the films and he planned to incorporate them into lectures that he intended to give once he returned to the United States. Those lectures, in turn, were designed to push for U.S. retention of the Philippines, which would benefit Worcester's own business plans. Indeed, the *New York Times* article announcing his resignation noted that Worcester "expects to devote his time to making the Bukidnos [*sic*] region [of Mindanao] the source of supply in the Philippines for meats and cattle."[5]

Worcester apparently was sensitive to perceptions that he may have shirked his official duties or else abused his position of power in order to make the films. Worcester told Felder that the films "were secured during a period extending over several months." However, "I naturally did not devote myself exclusively to this matter during such period."

He went on to explain how the films were made. Martin "was employed by me during vacation leave which he took in the Philippines, in order to accompany me on official trips and take such motion pictures as I requested, I having previously purchased the best camera and other accessories obtainable. Mr. Martin is a very skillful operator—the best, by far, in the Philippine Islands."[6]

Although he was interested in bringing his films to as wide an audience as possible, Worcester declined Felder's offer of going into business together, explaining: "An official holding the position which I now occupy can hardly afford to be 'exploited' in cheap motion picture theatres, and I personally object very decidedly to that sort of thing," especially as he appeared in a number of the films himself. Lest Felder assume that Worcester was grandstanding by appearing in the films, Worcester went on: "There is no impropriety in this, as the film is intended to show, and does show, the manner in which I deal with these people, but so far as concerns making a show of myself at home, I do not care to do it."[7] Worcester was concerned that his reputation might suffer if he was not present to control the terms of the representations of himself on screen.

Worcester expressed two other concerns about entering into an arrangement with Felder. First, if he parted with the film negatives, Worcester would "have no check upon the number of copies" made and distributed. Second, he did not like the offer of receiving a percentage of the profits, preferring, instead, the idea of receiving a percentage of the gross receipts that film screenings might bring in. Part of his concern in this regard was that "profits are obviously dependent upon good management, among other things, and as I have no voice in the management, that would make my returns subject to something which I could not myself in any way control."[8] Worcester demonstrated his understanding of the business side of the still nascent film industry, pointing out to Felder that two other film companies had approached him based on what they had seen in *National Geographic*.

By late 1912, Worcester knew his time as secretary of the interior was nearing its end, and he strongly felt the need to retain control of the films for use in what he no doubt imagined would be a profitable series of lectures he would give upon his return to the United States. To Felder he wrote:

I am especially desirous of bringing home to the American people the importance of continuing the policy thus far pursued in dealing with the wild tribes of the Philippines, and have had a good deal of experience in illustrated lecture work. I, of course, own large series of very fine lantern slides, which can be used to supplement films for certain purposes, and it is my desire to devote a considerable amount of time to this work during my next visit to the United States.

If Felder had any suggestions for how to manage such a lecture tour, Worcester was eager to hear them.[9]

On February 11, 1913, Felder responded to Worcester. He advised Worcester to retain control of the films himself, saying, "If the pictures were mine, and I had your gifts as a lecturer, I would never part with them." Felder may have been sincere in giving Worcester this advice, or he may have wanted to discourage Worcester from entering into any agreements with Paragon's competitors. Felder suggested that Worcester make sure that any screenings and lectures accompanying the films be held in "theatres of the highest class," since the rapidly proliferating "moving picture houses" drew audiences whose "general intelligence . . . is not above that of children." Felder predicted great success for Worcester, especially with appropriate publicity ahead of time. After all, one of the more popular film/lecture combinations of the 1912–13 season, Paul Rainey's *African Hunt,* was expected to "clear as much as $200,000 in this country alone"[10] (more than $4 million in 2012 dollars). Felder noted that Rainey's receipts were much stronger in "first-class theatres" than they were in "picture houses."

Felder acknowledged the value of Worcester's films and believed that the films would have a real impact in the political arena: "They will play for several years in this country, and judiciously managed, at the end of that time the United States would have a far better idea of the problem confronting Government in the Islands, and such resolutions as have been introduced in Congress looking to the turning over of the Philippines to the Filipinos would stand small chance of adoption for several generations." If Worcester was looking for investors to help this endeavor along, Felder knew several who might be interested.[11]

Felder wasn't the only potential collaborator wooing Worcester. The day before he wrote to Felder, Worcester had written a similar letter to M. Douglass Flattery of Marcus Loew's Boston Theatres (proudly billing itself as "world's best vaudeville"). Worcester's letter was in response to one he had received from Flattery. Worcester told Flattery that "photography has been my recreation during the past fourteen years, and that I know a lot about moving picture cameras." Letting Flattery know that he had already received an offer for distributing his films (from Felder),

Worcester added that "I like the way you are handling what you have, as shown by the circular which you inclose [*sic*], and if, after reading this letter, you care to make a definite offer, do so, and it will be considered if it reaches me in time." He added a sense of urgency, telling Flattery that he may leave the Philippines "at almost any time."[12]

If Flattery was prepared to make him a business offer, Worcester had two stipulations. First, he believed "that there should at all events be a minimum compensation payable in cash at the time the negative film is turned over." Second, "I should prefer to reserve for myself the right to use these films in illustrating *lectures* in the United States. I have had considerable experience in this line of work and expect to do a good bit of it while at home. . . . I am particularly desirous of interesting sober-minded people in the United States in the importance of continuing the policy thus far followed so successfully in dealing with the wild people of the Philippines."[13]

Flattery responded to Worcester on March 8, 1913. Like Felder, he provided advice to Worcester for how best to go about his plans for his film-based lectures. Also like Felder, Flattery predicted that "the publication of these films will cause a large amount of discussion amongst the people interested in the vital questions of Philippine Government." Unaware that Worcester was already preparing to sign on as a vice president of the American-Philippine Company, Flattery suggested that Worcester "form a corporation" to take care of the business end of his plan. He cautioned, however, that because of Worcester's position as a colonial administrator "it might not be proper for you to hold office in a private corporation." Flattery offered himself as one of the officers of the proposed corporation, and he suggested that Worcester allow other people to deliver the lectures given Worcester's continued commitments in the Philippines. He recognized that there were risks in such a plan, but that the most profitable way to get the films before large audiences would be to sell "state rights" to the films to promoters in different states, and to "prepare a descriptive lecture for the use of the manager of such state rights." Of course, "such lecture would use your name as far as proper dignity and respect would allow."[14]

Flattery acknowledged Worcester's interest in being the one to give the lectures, and he was willing to talk that over with him when Worcester was next in the United States. "In the meantime, I hope you will have sent on, [*sic*] the negatives by express as it takes such a long time to get communications from Manila, and of course, it will take some time to prepare this field to properly sell state rights." In an effort to demonstrate to Worcester the urgency of moving forward with this plan, he added: "A man has recently arrived in the United States with 9,000 feet of films which he has taken in the Philippine Islands including records of the Moros. Of course, there is no comparison between your films and his but it makes me impatient to get the work started."[15] The rapidly expanding film industry tapped into the nation's already established interest in the Philippines, and Worcester risked facing stiff competition getting his films before audiences.

Worcester took his time responding to Flattery's letter, not writing back until September 21, six days after his resignation as secretary of the interior became official. Worcester provided a number of different excuses for the tardiness of his reply, including the change of plans regarding his resignation, his annual inspection trips to northern Luzon, Mindoro, Mindanao, and Palawan, and his desire to finish writing the manuscript of his book *The Philippines Past and Present*. It is clear, however, that Worcester was not happy with Flattery's proposal for how to move forward with the films and lecture series, writing that "there was one very definite and important reason" why Worcester did not provide Flattery with copies of his films: "I had endeavored to make it clear that I considered it imperative that I should be free myself to lecture and this obviously did not meet with your approval."[16]

Exhibiting his usual self-confidence, Worcester continued: "I consider these lectures of fundamental importance and could not think of confining them to clubs and learned societies. I want to get to the people who really count and try to influence public sentiment that it will not be possible for the succeeding administration to drop the work for the non-Christian tribes which has already attained so large a degree of success." Worcester let on that he "had been offered and had accepted a position as one of the vice-presidents of the American-Philippine Company." In order to make it quite clear that they would not be working together, Worcester told Flattery that the president of the American-Philippine Company, Edward H. Fallows, "has expressed his approval of my taking the lecture platform for the entire lecture season." Worcester then presented himself as being bound to the terms set forth by Fallows: "Under the circumstances I feel that he has the right to a vote in the way in which I shall spend my time and accordingly cabled to him a short time ago to make such arrangements relative to my lectures as he might deem best."[17]

While still serving as secretary of the interior in the Philippines, Worcester had practiced his lectures combining films and lantern slides, developing combinations of movies, lantern slides, and his own oratory so that his message would have maximum impact. In his November 14, 1912, letter to Felder, Worcester wrote: "I have thus far made no effort to place this film. Really my only motive in showing it here was to try it out on the screen, and the proceeds have been devoted to charity. The bird film and the Negrito film were run one evening in Manila at the Grand Opera House, and the net receipts were $2425, which would seem to indicate that the Manila public was interested. Of course, such things as these films show are much less of a novelty here than they would be in the United States."[18] In addition, Worcester's January 20, 1913, lecture, also at the Grand Opera House (the one with the memorandum reading "Camera can be made to tell the truth"), included Worcester's films of the Tingians, Ifugaos, Bontoc Igorots, and birds.[19]

The Grand Opera House was the site for other Worcester lectures as well, dating back to before his use of films. As mentioned in chapter 1, the Grand Opera House was one of the most important cultural institutions in Manila. In 1907, it served as the site for the swearing-in ceremony of the Philippine Assembly, a newly created lower house of government that was comprised entirely of Filipinos. Worcester's antagonistic relationship with the Assembly is revealed in his 1913 report, *Slavery and Peonage in the Philippine Islands,* with its allegations that members of the Assembly held people in peonage. Through such allegations, "Worcester sought to discredit the Philippine national elite's ability to speak for and about the people of the Philippines, reserving that authority to himself and American colonialism."[20]

In 1910, Worcester gave an illustrated lecture at the Grand Opera House titled "The Non Christian Tribes of the Philippine Islands and What the United States Has Done For Them." In a signed, handwritten note on the top of the transcript for that lecture, Worcester wrote: "These are the notes of a lecture delivered by me at the Grand Opera House, Manila before the largest audience I ever had there. They caused no comment so far as I know. *Many* Filipinos were present."[21] Worcester's notes were an attempt to put into context the uproar caused by the serious outcry he provoked with two illustrated lectures he had given at the YMCA auditorium in Manila, "The Non-Christian Tribes of the Philippines" and "What has been done for the Non-Christian Tribes under American Rule."[22] In a memorandum he prepared for Governor-General Cameron Forbes dated October 31, 1910, Worcester wrote: "The fuss that has been raised in the present instance is the more interesting from the fact that on a former occasion when speaking at the Grand Opera

House to an audience in which there were a large number of Filipinos, I
stated the case, so far as concerns the attitude of the Filipinos toward the
non-Christians, far more fully and bluntly than I did the other evening,
but at this time no one thought it worth while to misquote my remarks,
and they caused no subsequent public comment."[23]

Among the charges he leveled in his lecture at the Grand Opera
House was an accusation that until quite recently "[a] large proportion of
the Tagalog inhabitants of Mindoro lived off the poor Mangyans whom
they kept in a state of peonage closely approaching slavery."[24] He also said
that male Benguet Igorots, Bontoc Igorots, and Ifugaos "are physically
very superior to the lowlanders,"[25] and that "[i]t would be impossible to
find in the Philippines a Christian municipality more cleanly, more orderly, more prosperous or better governed than is the Igorot settlement of
Kabayan in Benguet."[26] What he didn't say, however, but what newspapers
reported him to have said at the YMCA, was that it was his belief that "six
Moros with barongs could stampede any civilized town in the Philippine
Islands where there was no Constabulary guard" and "If original ownership is to be the determining factor in the sovereignty of these islands,
then they should unquestionably be turned over to the Negritos, who are
universally admitted to be the aboriginal inhabitants. . . . If they are to be
controlled by those who are best able to deal out even-handed justice . . .
then I believe that we shall have to remain here for some time yet."[27]
While criticizing Worcester for his argument, newspapers also noted, and
complimented him on, his use of lantern slides.

Worcester's 1913 lecture at the Grand Opera House seems to have
been less inflammatory than some of his earlier lectures. He began with
an explanation for why he used lantern slides in his lectures, and he
noted his "previous use of film" before other audiences. He then showed
slides of the Tingians, whom he called "highly civilized" and "[e]xtraor-
dinarily cleanly." After describing how he was able to obtain a film of
the Tingians, he proceeded to show that film. He then showed slides of
the Ifugaos, including members of the Constabulary. He also showed a
re-enactment of an Ifugao headhunting scene after explaining why he
wanted to do so. (The explanation itself, unfortunately, was not recorded.) After an intermission he showed more film on the Ifugao, then
slides of the Bontocs and a film of them dancing. He finished by showing
slides and a film of birds, a film that he seemed particularly proud of.[28]

WHILE WORCESTER WAS laying the groundwork for his lecture series,
he also had to guarantee that he had ownership over the films that he

planned to use and distribute. Apparently, there was some uncertainty on that front, or, at the very least, there were competing claims over who had the rights to those films. An article in the *Chicago Evening Post* in July 1913 said Worcester "has taken miles and miles of moving pictures of these various tribes in their war dances and native festivals. Manila doesn't know whether these films belong to the American government or to the professor himself."[29] The government wasn't the only potential claimant to the films, either. In his letters to Felder and to Flattery, Worcester omitted the fact that the equipment used to make the films was purchased, in part, with other people's money, and that at least two additional people had an interest in the films.

The decision to make the films appears to date to late 1910 or early 1911. They seem to have begun as a collaborative effort between Worcester, Martin, and William Dinwiddie, a man with whom Worcester had long-standing friendly relations. Dinwiddie had originally traveled to the Philippines as a war correspondent during the Spanish-American War. In 1899 he was appointed the first military governor of the Province of Ilocos, and he later served as the governor of Lepanto-Bontoc. He and Worcester maintained ties after Dinwiddie returned to the United States. In a June 21, 1911, letter to Worcester, Dinwiddie, who by then was living in New York City, wrote: "It has taken me a long time to get the moving picture game worked out in this City as to its commercial possibilities."[30]

Dinwiddie encouraged Worcester to make films that had some kind of narrative element to them, not films that just showed a number of scenes depicting various aspects of the different cultures, as "an audience will not stand any protracted exhibition for an example of the dance alone, that while every movement may appeal to a scientist, it does not entertain the public." (Somewhat tellingly, Dinwiddie said that one thing that would entertain the public would be a scene showing a "nursing woman" going "into the rice fields to cultivate rice.") Dinwiddie also told Worcester that he was willing to join "you and Martin in this project and [was] willing to pay one-half for the equipment and the three of us to pay each one-third of any expenses that may accrue for materials, etc." In return, none of the men would "draw salary for services," but would "secure our remuneration from a division of profits."[31]

Dinwiddie's desire to work with Worcester and Martin was in response to an invitation to do so by Worcester in a letter dated April 22, 1911, that, in turn, appears to have been prompted by an even earlier letter from Dinwiddie inquiring into the possibility of securing films from the Philippines. Dinwiddie was aware of the general interest in the Philippines in the United States, and he wanted to profit off of that interest through the growing demand for motion pictures. Worcester wanted to nurture a business relationship with Dinwiddie, telling him: "There is a man in the Islands trying to get moving pictures now and I understand contemplates remaining some time, but his results are practically certain to be faked up, and you can lay emphasis on the fact that we will get the *real thing*."[32] Whether this is the same man that Flattery mentioned in his letter the following year is unknown.

While assuring Dinwiddie that any films by competitors would be inferior to his own films, Worcester also sought to prevent competitors from even having the opportunity to make their films. In 1912, a proposed law originating in the Philippine Commission would have prohibited "the introduction into the Philippine Islands and the manufacture, sale, or public exhibition therein of moving-picture films or of pictures of immoral, indecent, obscene, vicious, or a disorderly character or tendency."[33] There is little reason to doubt that Worcester was the originator of that proposal, which was broadly enough written that it could have prevented the filming of bare-breasted Filipinas or head-hunting scenes by any filmmaker who wasn't acting under the authority of the colonial regime. Although the proposal failed to pass through the Philippine Legislature, it was enough to scare off some potential competitors. As the article in the *Chicago Evening Post* put it: "[T]he representatives of the moving-picture companies, whom Worcester has forbidden to photograph the native tribes, are full of resentment at him. They claim that he has attempted an unfair monopoly. He retorts that they can't be trusted to manage a ticklish 'war dance' without stirring up far-off dreams of revolt."[34]

Worcester told Dinwiddie that Martin was skilled both as a photographer and as a filmmaker: "Mr. Martin has spent a lot of time with the Pathe Bros. in Paris and with the best German people, is thoroughly posted as to apparatus, has taken numerous lessons from the best possible instructor, and has actually turned out very excellent results, doing all the work of exposure, developing, making of positives, etc., himself. There is no reason why he should not spend holidays and vacation periods in this work." To Worcester's mind, Martin's technical skills, Worcester's own "ability to secure the opportunity to do the work desired," and Dinwiddie's "knowledge of conditions in the United States" made for a powerful combination that could potentially be lucrative for all concerned. While claiming a spirit of collaboration, however, Worcester desired to keep the negatives himself in "view of the danger of loss or injury" that shipping the negatives would entail.[35]

Worcester was stretching the truth in his letter to Dinwiddie. At that point, no films had been made, and Martin had yet to successfully demonstrate his skills as a filmmaker. In fact, they had not even acquired the filmmaking equipment that they would need for this endeavor. In the April 17, 1911, letter that he sent to Worcester in Baguio (mentioned in chapter 3), Martin broke down the costs of purchasing cinematographic materials, as well as the potential profits, and he requested that Worcester pass the information to Dinwiddie: "If Mr. Dinwiddie can dispose of 20 to 25 films 1000 ft. long from each negative, a handsome profit can be expected."[36]

In the same letter, Martin let Worcester know that competition for such films was emerging in the Philippines: "There is now a man in Manila whose sole business is to take cinematographic views; he intends to travel all over the Philippines, north and south, presumably for the same purpose as we do." Although Martin was confident that he could secure superior quality films, the viewing public "is fairly ignorant of first class results." Moreover, if the unnamed man (possibly Albert Yearsley, an American who lived in Manila and is sometimes credited with being the first filmmaker in the Philippines) was able to bring his films to market before Martin and Worcester, it "might possibly influence the sale of ours." Consequently, Martin suggested that Worcester ask Mr. Dinwiddie "to clinch a market in advance if such a thing is possible."[37]

Martin's April 24 follow-up letter included a revised estimate of the profits from the films. In a conversation that he had with Manila-based theater owner Frank Goulette, Martin learned that they could expect to sell a thousand feet of film for only $80, not the $125 that Martin had expressed in the previous letter. He added: "The cost of producing such a positive will be at least $45.00; a profit of only $35 on one positive is not enough to cover the original expense of the taking of the negatives, unless we can sell 25 to 30 positives from each negative." In a more detailed breakdown of expenses and revenues, Martin estimated that his traveling expenses would be $500 for five weeks in northern Luzon, where he would secure films of Bontoc Igorots, Ifugaos, Ilongots, and Tingians. The cost of making the films themselves would be around $3,900. He then added in an incidentals expense of $600. Returning to the earlier assumption of a sale price of $125 per 1,000 feet of film, if they sold eighty films, they would have revenues of $10,000, which would result in a profit of $5,000 (the equivalent of roughly $115,000 in 2012 dollars).[38]

On November 27, 1911, Worcester shipped to Dinwiddie a print of the first film that he and Martin had made, one that showed "the wonderful bird life on the corral [*sic*] reefs of the Sulu Sea." Worcester appeared to have reservations about the film, or, at least, he anticipated that Dinwiddie might have some, writing: "You, of course, understand that this is Mr. Martin's first film,"[39] an oblique admission that his earlier letter praising Martin's skills as a filmmaker may have been more anticipatory than experiential. Worcester also admitted that the printing machine that Dinwiddie helped purchase was delayed, setting back the date that the films could be shipped to the United States.

Worcester informed Dinwiddie that Martin had been improving his filmmaking skills by making both negatives and positives for Yearsley of subjects "which could be of no possible interest to people at home . . . in other words we have made Yearsley pay for Mr. Martin's experience." In addition to the film about birds, Worcester and Martin were preparing a second one about growing rice "which, of course, cannot be complete until harvest time." Worcester said that they also had "a good start on the coconut growing industry." Their first film about people would begin soon, Worcester having "arranged to get a whack at a group of 100 particularly interesting Negritos in the Province of Bataan."[40] In a sense, Worcester was coming full circle here, returning to the same place where he had made his first large series of ethnological photographs, the site where he had made the oft-used photograph of himself standing next to Ibag.

As for the films that Martin had suggested making in northern Luzon, those would have to wait until the following February, when Worcester's annual inspection trip would commence. Worcester explained that he had "not sent the outlines for the future films" because he had been "caught up to my ears with a big hospital investigation" that involved some very powerful people. Now that he had that investigation out of the way, he assured Dinwiddie, the film plans would move forward: "Mr. Martin will take his month's vacation leave and go into the North country a month ahead of me to get the individual scenes requiring special selection, training and grouping of actors, while those incident to the subsequent great crowds that always assemble when I go through, will be obtained in connection with my trip. You can, therefore, look for results to come fast when they begin to come."[41]

Worcester's statement that Martin would select, train, and group "actors" reveals the blurred lines separating science and entertainment in Worcester's films. Worcester wasn't interested in simply filming the people as they went about their regular lives, as such scenes would have only limited dramatic appeal. Instead, he had particular aspects of their

Fig. 19. Charles Martin (attributed), "Philippine Islands—N. Luzon.
Ifugao. Scene from head-hunting episode. Staged for Dean C. Worcester.
The head is papier mache. The jawbone was formerly used for this
purpose" (ca. 1912). (Courtesy of the Penn Museum, image #218994.)

lives that he wanted to show audiences, and so he and Martin worked
together to get the kinds of scenes that Worcester felt best represented
the culture being filmed. Such reenactments were common in ethnographic filmmaking at that time.[42] For example, Worcester was interested in showing the Ifugaos engaged in head-hunting. However, for a
variety of reasons, it was unrealistic to film an actual incident of head-

hunting. Consequently, Worcester had Martin stage such a scene. Evidence for that staging can be seen in figure 19, which shows an Ifugao man holding a papier mâché head that was constructed specifically for the filming.

While assuring Dinwiddie that filming would commence shortly, Worcester also provided an itemized list of expenses to date. According to Worcester's calculations, Dinwiddie's portion of what was still owed for the making of the films was just over three hundred Philippine pesos. He proposed that Dinwiddie deduct what Worcester owed him for "work you did for me after I left the United States, together with any necessary expenses of your own and remit" the balance to Worcester. Adding a note of urgency, he suggested that Dinwiddie "send the cash by cable as my pocketbook will be pretty flat by the time you get this letter and we shall presently have considerable expense for negative films."[43]

In the same letter, Worcester also updated Dinwiddie on his photographic activities as they related to the articles that Worcester was writing for *National Geographic*. He told Dinwiddie that he had already sent three articles to the magazine, and he was completing a fourth article about the recent eruption of the Taal Volcano. Worcester had collected "a series of photographs on this volcano for a long time" and so was able to create a number of "before and after" sequences showing the effects of the eruption. He had considered sending the Taal article to Dinwiddie to allow him to attempt to sell it to other magazines, an idea that Dinwiddie apparently had proposed. However, Worcester decided that "the National Geographic Magazine will probably publish more photographs than would any other magazine." In a conciliatory gesture, Worcester instead sent Dinwiddie a copy of an article on birds that he published in the *Philippine Journal of Science*, "thinking you would at least be interested in the illustrations."[44]

It's difficult to know exactly how Dinwiddie responded to Worcester's letter and his news of the films. However, a few months before receiving this letter from Worcester, Dinwiddie had received another from George Magie, one of three partners in the Solax Company, a film production company based in Flushing, New York. Magie stressed to Dinwiddie that successful motion pictures required "a capable director in charge, a man who has staged and produced picture plays and who will get the most out of any situation that may present itself." Conversely, "All hit or miss pictures are classed as *scenic* and are of little value as compared with the staged picture with a positive theme." In addition, successful films required action, a "leading character" that can be identified throughout the film, and a clear storyline.[45]

With these tips in mind, Dinwiddie may have cringed when he read Worcester's description of films about birds, rice growing, and the coconut industry. Unfortunately, whatever Dinwiddie's immediate response was to Worcester's November 28 letter, it is now lost. What is clear, though, is that their relationship turned acrimonious. On April 15, 1913, two years after they began planning the films together, Dinwiddie wrote a letter to John Blair, a Manhattan-based attorney who represented Worcester, in which Dinwiddie defended his own activities and charged Worcester with failing "to live up to his side of the contract with me." Dinwiddie singled out two of the films that Worcester sent him for special criticism, saying that the one about Negritos "was technically bad and dramatically without any point," and that "Bird Island" was especially bad, since it had "nothing in it except endless flocks of birds, and of the thousand feet of film on this subject not over two or three hundred feet would ever be used by any film company."[46]

Dinwiddie told Blair that Worcester had promised him that the film about Igorots would come closer to the kind of films that Dinwiddie felt would be profitable: "complete picture plays, with good plots in them." Dinwiddie also reminded Blair that Worcester had assured him that because of the access that his position as secretary of the interior provided him, Worcester and Martin's films would be superior to any others coming out of the Philippines. To date, Dinwiddie had not received any such superior films.

Judging from what Dinwiddie wrote to Blair, Worcester was trying to get more money out of Dinwiddie. In response to Blair's accusations that he had "not paid [his] share of the costs in this venture," Dinwiddie quoted from two letters he had received from Worcester, including the one from November 28, 1911, in order to demonstrate that, if anything, Worcester owed him money. He concluded: "If Worcester believes we cannot carry out this contract to the mutual advantage of both of us; I would suggest that he make me a cash offer for my interest in the contract. If he will not do this then it is clearly up to him to live up to his part of the contract with me, and send me promptly films of marketable value."[47]

Blair seemed not to be too eager to pursue this matter for Worcester. On April 16, 1913, he wrote a brief letter to Worcester enclosing copies of the letter from Dinwiddie and Blair's response to that letter. In the letter to Dinwiddie, Blair made a halfhearted attempt to cast Dinwiddie in an irresponsible light, writing: "I am disappointed that I have not received . . . the promised list of magazines to which the article on salt water fishing was submitted. May I request that you will take the trouble to have this list prepared and send to me as soon as convenient."[48] To

Worcester, he suggested, "the best thing to do will be for you to take this matter up upon your arrival in New York in the autumn."[49]

If Dinwiddie felt that Worcester was in breach of contract, there are hints that Charles Martin also believed that he had been taken advantage of by his former boss. On April 2, 1914, a little more than six months after Worcester's departure from the Philippines, Martin wrote a letter to Worcester in care of the American-Philippine Company in which Martin struck a defensive posture about some filming that he did in preparation for the Philippine exhibit at the 1915 Panama-Pacific Exposition. Now that the Philippine government had "secured a complete cinematographic equipment," he explained to Worcester, "I am subject to orders of my superiors which may cause me to take films of any nature for any purpose in my capacity as official photographer."[50]

Martin was concerned that he might be contravening his agreement with Worcester regarding the making of films in the Philippines, and he asked Worcester for his thoughts on the matter. Martin pointed out that in their original contract "it was quite well understood between us" that Martin would remain the government photographer and that he would "undertake to do whatever work our contract called for during hours of leisure and vacation." Given that his portion of the profits from the filmmaking was not enough for him to quit his job, he had no choice except to make whatever films the current Philippine government asked him to make. He offered to resign his position if Worcester "wish[ed] to retain [his] services," but Worcester would have to enter into a contract with Martin "for not less than two years at [his] present salary" in addition to compensating him for "accrued leave and allowances" that Martin would lose were he to resign.[51]

Although no response from Worcester has been found to answer the question about whether or not he thought Martin would be in breach of contract if he was to make similar films for the Philippine government, a correspondence that Martin entered into a few months later with George Byron Gordon, the director of the Penn Museum at the University of Pennsylvania, may shed some light on the matter. In preparation for resigning from his position as government photographer, Martin was looking to secure work back in the United States. Although Gordon could not see any "immediate use for the services which you mention" (presumably, services as a photographer), he invited Martin to check in with him if Martin happened to be in Philadelphia.[52]

Gordon was more interested in the films that Martin had made in the Philippines, asking: "Do I understand that you have and are prepared to sell forty thousand feet of cinema film printed from the films which you took in the field? If so, we would be interested in this and especially in that part which illustrates the native life." Gordon was also interested in Martin's "collection of coloured lantern slides which illustrates the natives and the native life."[53]

In his response, dated November 7, 1914, Martin explained that he had "taken 40,000 feet of cinema film in the P.I., 25,000 feet illustrate nine different wild tribes, the remainder are of industries." Unfortunately, he couldn't offer the films to Gordon, explaining that "though half owner of these films, I have lost control of the same, through my lack of business sense and over-confidence." Although he doesn't mention Worcester by name, the implication is that Worcester somehow wrested control of the films from Martin. In an echo of the contractual struggle between Worcester and Dinwiddie, it seems that Worcester turned the tables on Martin to make it appear as though Worcester was the aggrieved partner. Martin continued, "today, I am in debts to my partner according to his figuring; but, from information received by the Pinkerton agency, I was simply juggled and swindled."[54]

In an effort to secure films for Gordon, an offer that can be viewed either as game or as desperate, Martin proposed that he travel up to northern Luzon prior to his return to the United States in order to secure the kinds of films that Gordon was interested in. Martin was willing to front all of the expenses for materials, provided that Gordon was willing to take a look at the resulting films and pay him twenty-five cents a foot for ten thousand feet of film, or twenty cents a foot for fifteen thousand feet of film. At the same time, Martin would gather ethnological artifacts for Gordon.

Gordon apparently didn't take Martin up on his offer, as the next letter in their correspondence was written the following September, when Martin had returned to the United States, bringing with him his lantern slides and photographic negatives. An album containing sample prints of his negatives was due to arrive shortly, as were a few ethnological artifacts, and he wanted to know if Gordon remained interested in the materials.[55] Gordon expressed an interest in both the artifacts and the photographs, and he inquired once again about the films that Martin had written about the previous year. Martin reminded Gordon that he "did own a half-share in 40,000 ft. of films of Philippines views, but was 'outgeneraled' by my partner; however, it is barely possible that I may yet manage to secure my share of the same."[56] Martin and Gordon came to terms on the sale of photographs and lantern slides, and Martin delivered those by the end of the year, just before he moved to Washington, D.C., to begin what would turn out to be a long career as the director of the photography lab at the National Geographic Society.

DESCRIBING IN DETAIL the films that Martin and Worcester made is difficult, as there are only remnants known to exist, and these are in the possession of the Penn Museum in Philadelphia.[57] Beyond an analysis of that footage, any understanding of the making of the films and what the films show has to be done by reading about them, a more elliptical approach. For example, in his 1912 official report as secretary of the interior, Worcester briefly alluded to the making of the films, which he said began "immediately after the adjournment of the Legislature" when he departed for his regular trip to northern Luzon:

> The need of entertaining the great crowds of wild men who meet the secretary of the interior on these trips is imperative, and at times embarrassing. The gatherings often include large numbers of men who have until recently been bitter enemies, and who are liable to indulge in untimely reminiscences, with unfortunate results, if not kept actively occupied. This problem was solved in part in a somewhat novel way by taking with us a portable moving-picture outfit and showing our wild friends something of life in a world heretofore beyond their ken. At the same time we ourselves took cinematograph films designed to afford an accurate and permanent record of characteristic scenes and events in the now rapidly changing methods of life of these comparatively primitive tribes.[58]

In this report, Worcester suggested that the filming was done primarily in the name of dispassionate science; he did not reveal that he had plans in the works to profit from activities undertaken while doing his government work. At the same time, he echoed the call he made in his 1898 article in *National Geographic* to have anthropologists study the people of the Philippines before their ways of life had irrevocably changed.

Worcester didn't say how the "wild men" responded to the movie camera or movie projector, but a tantalizing hint can be found in Cornélis DeWitt Wilcox's 1912 book, *The Headhunters of Northern Luzon*, a book liberally illustrated with photographs from Worcester's collection. Commenting on the "spread of friendly relations" in northern Luzon due to Worcester's frequent visits to the region, Wilcox wrote: "this year (1912) more people 'came in' to meet Mr. Worcester than ever before. . . . A moving picture machine was taken along in a four-wheeled wagon . . . and created both enthusiasm and alarm: enthusiasm when some familiar scene with known living persons was thrown upon the screen, and alarm when a railway train, for example, was shown advancing upon the spectators, causing many of them to flee to safety to the neighboring hills and woods,"[59] an anecdote that recalls the perhaps-apocryphal reaction of audiences to the Lumière Brothers' 1895 film of a train arriving at a station.

Although Worcester's letters clearly indicate that his interest was in *making* films of the non-Christian Filipinos, his *showing* of films to them has been the subject of more attention by anthropologists and historians. In her 2002 book, *Wondrous Difference: Cinema, Anthropology, and Turn-of-the-Century Visual Culture*, Alison Griffiths writes:

> Worcester devised a program to use cinema as part of a propaganda effort to educate members of the Bontoc Igorot, Ifuago [*sic*], and Kalinga tribes in the U.S.-occupied Philippines. The main aim of these government-produced educational films was to inculcate Western standards of hygiene among the indigenous subjects, although as a way of sustaining audience interest colonial administrators decided to exhibit nonpropaganda subjects (featuring both Western and native cultures, according to anthropologist Emilie de Brigard) between the propaganda films. But the decision to show films representing white Americans was probably motivated by another subtext, the idea that exposure to "civilized" culture would reinforce the object-lesson by representing white metropolitan culture as the idea to which colonial subjects should aspire.[60]

Worcester's own explanation for showing the film is a bit different than what Griffiths argues. According to Worcester, his actual subtext was primarily to keep people entertained. It is possible, too, that showing motion pictures made it simpler to explain his motives and to minimize the resistance of the Kalingas, Ifugaos, and others to his filming of them.

The Emilie de Brigard article that Griffiths references places Worcester as among the first to use film in "applied anthropology" and one of the originators of "colonial cinema." De Brigard goes on: "Worcester . . . devised a program of sanitary education for the provinces. To hold the interest of the Bontoc Igorot, Ifugao, and Kalinga between health films, Worcester's subordinates projected scenes of native and foreign life. The program achieved the desired results; when shown moving pictures of better conditions, the people showed a disposition to change."[61] De Brigard based her analysis of Worcester's use of films on Leonard Donaldson's 1912 book, *The Cinematograph and Natural Sciences,* one of the first references to Worcester's use of films.

In that book, Donaldson wrote: "Wonderful results have been achieved among a number of wild Philippine tribes by the use of motion pictures. . . . The natives of the non-Christian tribes have lived in appalling squalor, but, when shown pictures of better conditions, contrasted with the old, have manifested a most encouraging disposition to profit by the lesson." Donaldson then quoted at length from Worcester about the changes taking place in the non-Christian areas of the Philippines: "A good state of public order has been established. . . . Life and property have been rendered comparatively safe, and in much of the territory entirely so. In many instances the wild men are being successfully used to police their own country." Donaldson concluded with a hearty "Such is the power of the motion picture!"[62]

The only problem with Donaldson's discussion is that the Worcester quote he used had nothing to do with motion pictures. It came from Worcester's highly emotional and divisive 1910 annual report, and was written before Worcester had introduced motion pictures into the non-Christian territories of the Philippines. Worcester wrote the passage that Donaldson quoted in order to highlight the accomplishments of the U.S. colonial regime in those areas where Worcester had executive control. Worcester's point in the passage was to contrast his successes in helping to "civilize" the non-Christian Filipinos with what he called the "lamentable lack of initiative" on the part of the governors of the provinces that were outside of Worcester's direct control.[63]

Nowhere in that discussion does Worcester mention motion pictures. He does, however, mention the use of films several pages later, but this reference was not to the use of films in anthropology, and had nothing to do with the non-Christian Filipinos. Worcester described how motion pictures were being used as part of a public health campaign:

> The moving-picture craze, long since developed in Manila, is now invading the provinces to some extent. As a result of the cooperation of Mr. A.W. Yearsley, many of the cinematographs of Manila are now showing nightly films of great educational value in connection with the recently inaugurated antituberculosis campaign, and it is purposed to extend and develop this plan of reaching the common people through the eye, both in Manila and in provinces. . . . Lec-

tures illustrated by the stereopticon or reflectoscope will be given by officers of the bureau of health in the provinces and will cover such subjects as tuberculosis, intestinal parasites, hygiene, diet, etc.[64]

Given Worcester's usual way of writing about non-Christian Filipinos, his use of the term "common people" here instead of "wild men" strongly suggests that the educational films were being directed toward Christian Filipinos and not, as Donaldson indicated, toward the non-Christians. The use of films in that territory wouldn't begin for at least another year.

Word began to spread in the United States that Worcester was making use of films in the Philippines. As filmmaker and historian Nick Deocampo notes in his book, *Film: American Influences on Philippine Cinema,* in April 1911 Worcester "urged the use of motion pictures to bring about education and peace among native, non-Christian tribes" in the motion picture trade publication, *Film Index.*[65] That same year, another trade publication, *Motography,* published an article titled "Pictures in the Philippines" that praised the ability of motion pictures to aid in the civilizing process: "After centuries of fruitless effort on the part of the Spaniards to wean the wild men from their unholy pastimes, it has remained for Uncle Sam to adopt the only means to reach their hearts, all with the assistance of the ever-fascinating picture show." (The same article also made reference to Worcester's 1910 annual report and Worcester's use of before-and-after photographs, including the series of photographs of Don Francisco Muro discussed in chapter 2.)[66]

Although neither of those articles claimed that Worcester was making motion pictures of the non-Christian Filipinos, both conveyed a sense of anticipation that such films would be much desired. When he did begin making films in the non-Christian territories, Worcester appears to have had his lectures in mind more than he had in mind the "moral tutelage" of the non-Christians. His prepared memorandum of the films he made includes both descriptions of what the films showed and what the "announcements" (i.e., intertitles) said. The memorandum thus gives some indication about what he wanted to get across through each film. For example, the "Negrito Film" began by describing the Negritos as "the aborigines of the Philippines" and "nomadic forest dwellers." Film segments show scenes such as "a Negrito family camped under the trees, building a fire, cooking, overhauling belongings, etc.," Worcester interacting with the Negritos "so that there is an opportunity to see relative size," and activities such as a wedding ceremony, shooting bows and arrows, and dancing.[67]

The memorandum goes on to talk about the films that Worcester and Martin made of the Ilongots, the Ifugaos, the Bontoc Igorots, the Kalingas, the Lepanto Igorots, the Tingians, bats, and birds. All of the films of people except for the Lepanto Igorots show scenes of people dancing. One intertitle for the Ilongots reads: "Ilongot dancing. The dances of this tribe differ radically from those of any other tribe in the Philippines." The accompanying description of the scene reads: "Film shows a series of dances. The extraordinary contortions of the performers are brought out with great clearness." For the Bontoc Igorots, the intertitle reads: "The historic dance on the Bontoc Plaza, in which every town in the subprovince joined. Only friendly Igorots dance together."[68] The description says that there were "thousands of dancers" in the scene. According to Griffiths, "native dance" was one of the "enduring tropes" of ethnographic films from that time period.[69]

The existing footage from Worcester's films shows several dance scenes, including scenes at an Ifugao wedding, a scene of two Kalinga men in what the intertitle listed on the memorandum says is a "war dance. Two men engage in mimic combat, keeping step with the music meanwhile,"[70] and a scene of Ilongot musicians with two dancers behind them. The intertitle reads "'Oh, Listen to the Band!'"[71] Perhaps unsurprisingly, given Dinwiddie's prediction that a scene showing a "nursing woman" working in a rice field would entertain the public Worcester and Martin also captured quite a bit of footage showing the bare breasts of women, including a scene of Tingian women hulling and winnowing rice, a scene of Kalinga women carrying jars of water on their heads, a scene of women harvesting and carrying baskets of root crops, and a scene of several young women grooming each others' hair. In many of the other dance scenes described in his memorandum, the women undoubtedly were seen dancing bare breasted.

In addition to the dance scenes and the repeated scenes showing bare-breasted women, Worcester and Martin also filmed people engaged in activities that they had previously photographed, reenacting scenes previously captured only on still film. Thus, the Ifugao head-hunting reenactment mentioned above allowed Worcester to give a filmic representation to the photograph of a beheaded Ifugao man published in his 1912 article in *National Geographic.* He also filmed a series of "field sports," much like those seen in his 1911 article in that magazine, and the carabao slaughter, also written about and shown in the 1911 article.

WITH THE FILMS MADE, and with control of the films firmly in his hands, Worcester was ready to move ahead more forcefully to lay the groundwork for his proposed lecture series. He didn't want to waste any time capitalizing on his films, photographs, and his name as soon as he returned to the United States. On July 18, 1913, Worcester sent a cablegram from Manila to the Philippine Lyceum Bureau listing nine lectures that he was prepared to give, lectures that would be "illustrated with slides and motion pictures." Worcester authorized the Bureau to "make the best arrangements possible" to secure speaking engagements.[72]

In an interview with a reporter from the *New York Times*, given shortly after he disembarked in San Francisco from the Pacific liner *SS Manchuria*, Worcester is quoted as saying: "There is cause for grave alarm that the placing of the balance of power of the Commission in the hands of the Filipinos will work irreparable damage" to the various accomplishments of Worcester and his colleagues. The lectures that Worcester proposed to give were designed, in part, to convince his audiences that the United States ought to maintain tight control over its colony. The *Times* article concludes by noting that Worcester "seems profoundly in earnest in his desire to tell the American truth about conditions in the Philippines. He brings with him 1,500 stereopticon slides and 20,000 feet of film of moving pictures of the various tribes, and he purposes to deliver lectures throughout the country."[73]

Paul Kramer says that Worcester's lectures combined "the traditional lyceum lecture and the novel motion-picture feature, allowing him to narrate and interpret the film to his audience. Worcester's descriptions of the film's goal would combine hopes for non-Christian uplift, retentionist argument, and commercial boosterism."[74] Kramer also points out that the American-Philippine Company, the umbrella organization through which Worcester operated, was "a major sponsor of publicity against present or future Philippine independence" and that its members, according to company president Edward Fallows, included "a large number of people of power and prominence, having a personal interest in the Philippines" who would "prevent the Government from doing something which might be prejudicial to their interests in the country."[75]

The New York Times noted the renewed popularity of public lectures in a December 29, 1913, article announcing a lecture by Worcester at New York's Carnegie Hall: "We have spoken lately of the revival of the lecture as a means of information and culture. We demand of the modern lecturer that he shall not only have the vocal training and vocabulary of the orator, but also an accurate and exceptional knowledge of his subject. To these qualifications Mr. Worcester adds the zeal of a teacher. He has a lesson to impart."[76] That lesson, of course, was that the United States should not relinquish control of the Philippines, both for the good of U.S. interests in the region and for the good of the people of the Philippines.

The use of motion pictures in public lectures was still a relatively new phenomenon when Worcester embarked on his speaking tour, and lecturers and the institutions that hosted them did not always have the same goals in mind when films were used. For many lecturers, the primary goal was often the simplest goal—to reach as wide of an audience as possible in order to maximize profits. Some venues shared that goal. Other venues, particularly cultural institutions such as "learned societies," libraries, and museums, needed to balance the novelty and entertainment value of the films with their educational mission.

What this meant was that lecturers and their host institutions sometimes had to negotiate the format of the lecture. At the American Museum of Natural History, for example, museum president Henry Fairfield Osborn insisted "that either physical artifacts be displayed or slides be shown *before* motion pictures in public lectures." According to Griffiths, this insistence suggested that Osborn perceived "an opposition between the presumed nonscientific nature of mimetic movement [i.e., films] and the reflective qualities of stasis, even in the form of a magic lantern slide. Osborn's concern that scientific principles would be undermined or trivialized in the case of unaccompanied moving pictures invokes a hierarchy of visual representation in which stasis is afforded greater scientific exactitude than movement and spoken or written texts imbued with more authority than visual images."[77] (Worcester gave a lecture at the American Museum of Natural History on February 5, 1914, and likely would have had to conform to Osborn's demands.)

IN THE AUTUMN OF 1913, a press release announcing Worcester's return to the United States, his opposition to Wilson's policies in the Philippines, and Worcester's upcoming lecture series was sent out to newspapers around the country. Accompanying the release was the 1901 photograph of Worcester standing next to Ibag, a photograph that many newspapers dutifully published. Despite the fact that Worcester routinely depicted the Negritos as a disappearing race far different from the majority of Filipinos, he recognized the power that the photograph had to represent the stark differences between Americans and Filipinos. Worcester may have hoped that the photograph would prompt viewers to wonder about the wisdom of the president's plan to turn over control of the colonial bureaucracy to Filipinos, if men like this—short, dark-skinned, slouched, weary looking, and wearing only a loincloth—would be left in charge of the Philippines. If Worcester had chosen a different photograph, such as one showing the success already achieved by the United States in "civilizing" the non-Christian Filipinos, readers might interpret it to mean that the United States had achieved its goals in the Philippines and that, perhaps, Philippine independence was a good idea. Worcester didn't want to risk such a response.

The same photograph was used on the front of the official brochure that the Philippine Lyceum Bureau distributed to promote Worcester's lectures (fig. 20). Prominently placed alongside the list of nine lecture titles that Worcester was prepared to give, the photograph was captioned "Mr. Worcester and a Full-Grown Negrito." Two other photographs are found on the back of the flyer, a photograph of "A Head-Hunter With His Trophy," and a photograph of "The Busy Wharves of Manila." The first one shows a man grasping the hair of a disembodied head lying on the ground in strong sunlight.[78] The man wears only a loincloth and his hair appears to be up in a topknot. He grasps the hair of his "trophy" with his left hand, while his right hand reaches behind him and seems to be grasping the handle of a knife. The other photograph, taken from middle distance, shows a bustling scene of men loading and unloading goods from the boats moored in Manila Bay, evidence that modern commerce had come to the Philippines as a result of U.S. efforts.

The three photographs worked together to show what the Philippines had been (i.e., savage and head-hunting), what the Philippines had become, and the role that Worcester played in moving the country toward civilization and prosperity. The text of the flyer reinforced this message: "As the 'White Father' of the wild peoples in the Philippines, his experience has been a novel one, and his work, first in winning their confidence and friendship, and then in turning them from intertribal warfare, head-hunting and other barbarous pursuits to the simpler works of husbandry, handicraft, education and friendly rivalries, is probably without parallel anywhere in the world."[79] To hear about Worcester's activities in greater detail, all you had to do was book him for one of his nine lecture titles.

Fittingly, the first two lectures Worcester was scheduled to give upon his return to the United States were set for the afternoon and evening of December 5, 1913, at the National Geographic Society. These lectures were intended for members of the Society; technically, then, they were not part of his public lecture series. Desirous of taking advantage of Worcester's time in Washington, D.C., Fallows wrote to Gilbert Grosvenor to solicit his advice about scheduling other lectures in the city shortly

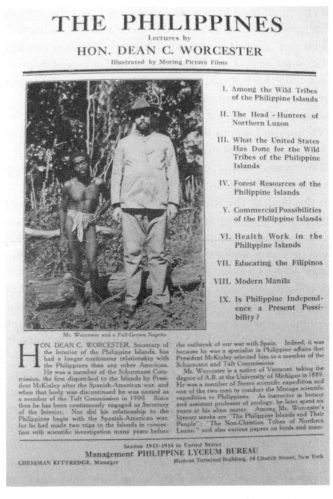

THE PHILIPPINES
Lectures by
HON. DEAN C. WORCESTER
Illustrated by Moving Picture Films

I. Among the Wild Tribes of the Philippine Islands

II. The Head - Hunters of Northern Luzon

III. What the United States Has Done for the Wild Tribes of the Philippine Islands

IV. Forest Resources of the Philippine Islands

V. Commercial Possibilities of the Philippine Islands

VI. Health Work in the Philippine Islands

VII. Educating the Filipinos

VIII. Modern Manila

IX. Is Philippine Independence a Present Possibility?

Mr. Worcester and a Full-Grown Negrito

HON. DEAN C. WORCESTER, Secretary of the Interior of the Philippine Islands, has had a longer continuous relationship with the Philippines than any other American. He was a member of the Schurmann Commission, the first dispatched to the Islands by President McKinley after the Spanish-American war, and when that body was discontinued he was named as a member of the Taft Commission in 1900. Since then he has been continuously engaged as Secretary of the Interior. Nor did his relationship to the Philippines begin with the Spanish-American war, for he had made two trips to the Islands in connection with scientific investigation many years before

the outbreak of our war with Spain. Indeed, it was because he was a specialist in Philippine affairs that President McKinley selected him as a member of the Schurmann and Taft Commissions.

Mr. Worcester is a native of Vermont, taking the degree of A.B. at the University of Michigan in 1889. He was a member of the Steere scientific expedition and one of the two men to conduct the Menage scientific expedition to Philippines. As instructor in botany and assistant professor of zoology, he later spent six years at his alma mater. Among Mr. Worcester's literary works are "The Philippine Islands and Their People", "The Non-Christian Tribes of Northern Luzon," and also various papers on birds and mam-

Season 1913-1914 in United States
Management PHILIPPINE LYCEUM BUREAU
CHESSMAN KITTREDGE, Manager   Hudson Terminal Building, 50 Church Street, New York

Fig. 20. Dean C. Worcester lecture brochure (1913). (Courtesy of the Bentley Historical Library, University of Michigan Historical Collections, Dean C. Worcester Papers, Box 2.)

after the December 5 lectures. Grosvenor advised Fallows to wait at least two weeks after that lecture to schedule a second, "public pay lecture" in Washington, noting that "we have invariably found that if there is an intermission of 2 weeks, the second lecture is very much better attended" than if it came quickly after the National Geographic Society lecture.[80]

In addition, Grosvenor warned Fallows that Worcester should avoid causing any controversies during his lecture: "Of course, in all lectures before the National Geographic Society all politics and references to the new administration in the Philippines must be omitted." Grosvenor told Fallows that he was a bit concerned that Worcester would raise controversial topics, given that Worcester had done so in one of the articles that he had submitted to Grosvenor. (It is possible, perhaps likely, that the controversy surrounded accusations of slavery and peonage in the Philippines, a topic that Worcester included in other lectures, and that he issued a report on in 1913.) Grosvenor wrote:

> Mr. Worcester probably was right in his controversy, but I made the point that the main argument and purpose of this article [i.e., the November 1913 article in *National Geographic*] was to draw attention to the splendid work that he and his associates had done for the non-civilized tribes of the Philippine Islands. Anything of a sharp controversial nature in the article would draw attention from the real purpose of the article . . . and I therefore omitted the entire controversy. The result is that everyone is talking about the splendid achievements of the Americans in the Philippines.[81]

The cozy relationship with government bureaucracies that Grosvenor had nurtured through the years made him pragmatic in his politics. After all, this relationship allowed him access to photographs from those bureaucracies.[82] Indeed, the relationship between Worcester and Grosvenor originally grew out of Grosvenor's relationship with William Howard Taft when Taft served as secretary of war. Although Grosvenor was a registered Republican "for most of his life," the election of Woodrow Wilson in 1912 did not worry him as much as it did Worcester, as he had less personally at stake if the country's colonial policies changed. Indeed, by 1914 Grosvenor switched political parties, writing to his mother, "I believe everyone should uphold President Wilson."[83]

Grosvenor made it clear that he intended to distance himself as far as possible from any controversial position that Worcester planned to stake out: "If Mr. Worcester desires to assail the new administration in the public lecture which is to follow his National Geographic Society lecture, it is very important that there be an interval of at least two weeks between the National Geographic Society lecture and the public lecture, or otherwise the Society will become involved in a controversy on subjects which are not within its province." In case that reason wasn't enough for Fallows, Grosvenor added his opinion that Worcester would "seriously injure the popularity and attendance at his lectures throughout the country" if he was too controversial in his talks.[84] Fallows and Worcester appeared to have taken Grosvenor's words to heart, as they scheduled no immediate public lectures in Washington.

Worcester steered away from controversy when he spoke before the Society. In the lecture, "The Great Adventure and the Great Experiment," the closest Worcester came to condemning the policy plans of the Wilson administration was at the end, when, in language he lifted from the ending of his forthcoming book, *The Philippines Past and Present,* he said: "The work undertaken for the physical, mental, and moral advancement of Non-Christians in the Philippine Islands has succeeded far beyond the hopes of those who initiated it and of those who have carried it out. Let us hope that the men who have done these things may not be forced to watch them broken and then derived [*sic*] the poor privilege of building them up again." He then asked, rhetorically: "The splendid results obtained at the cost of so much efficient, faithful, self-sacrificing and successful effort have not been paid for too dearly if they are to be permanent but if the[y] were to be lost, would not the dead who gave their lives for them, turn in their graves?" He closed by saying: "The greatest of the Non-Christian tribe problem [*sic*] in the Philippine Islands, at present, is: SHALL THE WORK GO ON!"[85]

The bulk of the lecture covered less controversial territory, and had a somewhat reflective tone. Worcester opened with an overview of the country under the heading "What Did Magellan Find?" This section included details of the geography, forest resources, minerals, and agricultural prospects, accompanied with a series of slides and his beloved bird film. He then moved into a discussion about the peoples of the Philippines, under the heading "What Peoples Did Magellan Discover?" According to his notes there were "[o]utright savages" and "[s]lightly civilized barbarians," and there were "[t]wo distinct races represented." He then showed his Negrito film. A handwritten note in the margins of his lecture notes reads "A link that is not missing," suggesting that Worcester may have expanded on his belief in racial hierarchies for his audience.[86]

Having dispensed with the Negritos, Worcester went on to discuss the eight civilized groups of Filipinos identified in the 1903 census that he said were not tribes and that had in common "their physical appearance; their religion; their manners and customs, and their dress." Despite their similarities, "They differ in industry, in self-assertiveness and in other ways. They are kept apart by dislikes and prejudices—handed down . . . from the days when their ancestors were members of mutually hostile tribes. The differences between are not so great and are constantly becoming less. The important thing is that they themselves consider these differences very great." Continuing to ignore the protestations of many Filipinos that they did, in fact, have a national identity, and conveniently overlooking the fact that the Philippine-American War demonstrated the lengths to which Filipinos were willing to fight and die for their independence as a sovereign nation, Worcester told his audience that "the great experiment" that the United States had undertaken was "welding into one people the extraordinarily diversified aggregation of human beings which today comprises the population of the Philippine Islands."[87]

Somewhat unusually, Worcester did not dwell in great length on the non-Christian Filipinos in his talk. He apparently did not show any other films other than the Negrito and bird films, and only made brief references to the "27 distinct Non-Christian tribes." He was more interested in talking about advances in education and health, and the potential for increased trade with the Philippines. He spent even more time talking about some of the Americans he had worked with during his time in the Philippines and their commitment to the cause of U.S. colonialism there. He quoted at length from the Rudyard Kipling poem, "If," copies of which he said that he had sent "to each governor and lieutenant governor employed in the special provincial government service of the Philippine Islands. Kipling wrote for these men of mine up in the hills, without knowing it. They understood him, and he would understand them."[88]

WORCESTER'S PUBLIC LECTURE SERIES started three weeks after his talk at the National Geographic Society, with a two-night engagement at New York's Carnegie Hall. The first, which the *New York Times* described as "Wild Tribes of the Philippines," was given on December 30, 1913, and the second, "The Picturesque Philippines," was delivered on January 6, 1914. The *Times* was excited about the lectures, explaining to readers that the "future of the Philippines concerns us all, and the knowledge the citizen may obtain from books and newspaper articles could not be better supplemented than by these lectures, illustrated with lantern pictures from photographs taken by the lecturer in his extended official tours and founded on the closest observation of the people of varied races and ethical ideals whose relations with us are now so generally discussed."[89]

Worcester was introduced to the audience by the Reverend Samuel Fallows (Edward Fallows's father), who praised Worcester for "his unwearying labors among the wild tribes of the Philippines that has gradually brought those people of the darkness into the light of civilization." The *Times* quoted Worcester as saying during his lecture that "[w]e have set the feet of these backward wards of the United States firmly on the road that leads onward and upward, and they are traveling it much faster than are their Filipino neighbors." Here, Worcester seems to have rhetorically inverted his typical depiction of the Philippines as having a civilized, Christian majority theoretically suitable for self-government at some unspecified point in the future but with a non-Christian population needing a much longer tutelage. Indeed, he went on to say that their "Filipino neighbors" were the greatest threat to the non-Christians: "The results thus far achieved would go down like a house of cards if American control were permanently withdrawn. If they were lost, would not the dead who gave their lives for them turn in their graves?" Then, echoing the end of his lecture at the National Geographic Society, Worcester closed by asking: "The greatest of the non-Christian tribe problems in the Philippines at present is 'Shall the work go on?'"[90]

A partial description of Worcester's remarks at Carnegie Hall reveals the message that Worcester wanted to drive home in his lecture: "There is no such thing as a Filipino people, the inhabitants of the Islands being divided between eight civilized peoples . . . and some 27 non-Christian tribes."[91] Worcester relied on his slides and his films to drive home the argument that there was no coherent Philippine nation, that the work of building a nation remained incomplete. His slides showed "Speaker Osmena of the Philippine Assembly, General [Emilio] Aguinaldo and a highly educated Filipina on one hand and a Negrito warrior, a headhunter, and women of the hills clad in banana leaves on the other." What Kramer says about the bifurcated model of colonialism in the Philippines, and what Vergara writes about the 1903 census photographs, was at work here, too: "The pictures of the wild tribes not only showed the extent of civilizing needed but also fed the consistent doubt on the capacity of the Filipinos to govern themselves. The civilized pictures, on the other hand, showed that there were well-groomed and 'educated-looking' Filipinos . . . potentially willing to be taught democracy. But it is the contrast between the two kinds that was meant to stress the heterogeneity even more."[92]

During the course of his lecture Worcester referred to the Negritos as "curly headed black dwarfs . . . incapable of civilization" whose "peculiarities and customs were shown by lantern slides and by the first motion pictures ever taken" of them. Worcester contrasted the Negritos with the

Bukidnons who "have progressed more rapidly under American rule than have the people of any other non-Christian tribe." There were also slides showing many of the same things that Worcester depicted in still photographs in his *National Geographic* articles, such as Igorots playing baseball and the construction of roads, and films of "a great gathering awaiting the arrival of the Secretary of the Interior and the welcome extended to him and his party" and "a tug of war between representatives of two hostile [Igorot] towns."[93] Through the films and the slides, Worcester was able to extend his arguments from the *National Geographic*, interpreting and explaining for the audience what is they were witnessing on the screen.

In its review of the lecture, the *New York Sun* quoted Worcester as saying: "We have checked head hunting, murder, slave taking, selling and keeping, robbery and theft, and have made life and property safe throughout vast regions where a few years ago the former was cheap indeed and the latter was apt to find its way into the hands of the man strong and brave enough to seize it and hold it." The audience was "a large one" and was "keenly appreciative," and the *Sun* listed the names of several prominent clergymen, military officers, professors, and physicians who were in attendance—precisely the kind of people Worcester wanted to reach.[94]

The review in the *New York Times* enthused about the evening's entertainment: "A brilliant audience listened to the lecture, which was illustrated by some of the most wonderful moving pictures ever seen in New York. Each picture told a story of the marvelous progress made by Americans in teaching civilization to the savage tribes of the Philippines. . . . The savage, naked, dirty, and unkempt, was shown in still photographs, while that same one-time savage, clothed, intelligent in appearance, and clean, later was shown in moving pictures."[95] A similarly glowing review in the *New York World*, titled "Shows Regeneration of the Filipinos in Movies," read: "Motion pictures showed the head hunters during the earlier days of American occupation and as they are now. The one portrayed life in its most savage form . . . the other showed a transformation almost unbelievable, uniformed soldiery maneuvering with precision."[96] In addition to hand-colored slides showing "types of men and women, their peculiar dress, or, rather, undress," the *Sun* took note of "the evolution of well disciplined constabulary soldiers from naked head-hunters," which may well have included the Igorot sequence.

After completing his two lectures at Carnegie Hall, Worcester's lecture tour began in earnest. The first two engagements after Carnegie

Hall were in Boston on January 8, 1914, and Chicago on January 10. In Boston he spoke on "Health, Schools, and Commerce," which means either that he gave three separate lectures, or else that he blended three of the lectures from his promotional brochure. In Chicago he spoke before the Association of Commerce, giving his speech on "Commercial Possibilities of the Philippine Islands." Following those early dates, it appears that he was asked fairly consistently to give (or else he suggested that he be allowed to give) his lecture "Among the Wild Tribes of the Philippine Islands." Of the eleven speaking engagements he had booked in February, nine were the "Wild Tribes" lecture; the other two bookings had yet to choose which lecture they wanted to hear. Similarly, seven of the eleven dates he had booked for March also requested that he give his "Wild Tribes" lecture. The only other specified lectures on his agenda were on January 17, in New Haven, where he gave his lecture on "Commercial Possibilities," and on January 24, in Brooklyn, and March 3, in New Bedford, where he lectured on "What Has the United States Done for the Wild Tribes of the Philippine Islands."[97]

The brochure from the Philippine Lyceum Bureau listed nine different lectures for audiences to choose from, but Worcester was willing to make adjustments when necessary. With movies still a new technology, not every venue was set up for him to show films. For example, in a letter dated January 7, 1914, Worcester discussed options for a lecture that he was scheduled to give at Rutgers University on January 11, presenting two options for Rutgers' president, the Reverend William Henry Demarest, to consider. Of the first possibility, "The Wild Tribes of the Philippines and What Has Been Done for them Under American Rule," Worcester said that he was "accustomed to depend to a considerable extent on motion picture films which show them in action." As an alternative, he said that he could give a lecture called "What Has Been Done for the *Filipinos*," in which he discussed "particularly, educational work, health work, the opening up of means of communication, etcetera." Worcester apparently was concerned that he would be limited to the use of slides for his lecture, and he had "a very large series of fine slides" for the latter title.[98]

Worcester's ability to adapt his lectures to different audience needs stemmed in part from the overlaps that existed between them. That is, he used the same slides and the same films in different lectures, giving them slightly different meanings depending on what the scheduled lecture was about. For example, a typed synopsis of his January 24 lecture at the Brooklyn Academy of Music says that the subject would be "Fifteen Years in the Philippines," not the lecture on the "Wild Men." In his Brooklyn lecture, Worcester was still able to use many of his films, including the "scenes on the bird islands in the Sulu Sea," the same scenes that Dinwiddie had predicted would be of little interest to anybody. Worcester took his audience on a tour of the islands, noting "their picturesque features" and the effects of the recent eruption of the Taal Volcano, illustrated by his slides. Other films included one "showing Bontoc Igorot women in strange banana leaf costume clearing trail in anticipation of the arrival of the Secretary of the Interior," and a "strange dance to the music of head-axes beaten by sticks." He also showed slides of the Igorots being "civilized." Seemingly less heavy-handed and didactic than the "Wild Man" lecture, it nonetheless was able to get many of the same ideas across.[99]

Worcester's lectures regularly drew large crowds, and local newspapers frequently printed lengthy reviews that included excerpts from the lectures. This gave Worcester an even longer reach, as his words could be read by thousands of people who were unable to attend any of his talks. On January 22, he delivered his "Wild Tribes" lectures in Wilmington, Delaware. The next day the *Wilmington Journal* carried a headline reading "Wild Tribes Drop the Bolo for Baseball." The review itself opened: "The Philippine Islands, their inhabitants and all that seems strange about them, were transported to Wilmington for two hours and a quarter last night in moving pictures and a highly entertaining and educational lecture by the Hon. Dean C. Worcester perhaps the greatest living authority on the people and conditions of the islands. . . . His lecture was a departure far out of the ordinary, and almost every minute contained a laugh or an incident gripping the interest of those present."[100]

In a confirmation of Worcester's optimism that his lectures would reach "the people who really count," his audience that night contained "many of . . . the foremost residents of Wilmington and vicinity." Worcester repeated his main theme, telling the audience that "[t]here is no such thing as a Filipino people," and using photographs and films to visually convey his argument about the diversity of the islands. Like the review of his Carnegie Hall lecture, the review in the *Wilmington Journal* also singled out the series of photographs showing Speaker Osmeña and General Aguinaldo as representatives of "civilized" Filipinos, and Negritos and Igorots as representatives of the "wild tribes." Quoting extensively from Worcester's descriptions of the advances being made among the "wild tribes," the review finished with the same words that Worcester kept coming back to time and again: "Shall the work go on?"[101]

A slightly more measured review appeared the following day in the

Baltimore Sun, after Worcester's January 23 lecture in that city. The review opened with Worcester's sober assessment: "The only kind of government that the Filipinos could set up at the present time would promptly develop into a military oligarchy, under which would occur things that would not only justify but demand intervention." This reviewer was less enthralled than others about the films and slides, noting only that Worcester used them in order to show "the progress made by some of the hitherto savage tribes in the attainment of civilization." Worcester also accused Filipino political leaders of graft: "There is a crowd of politicians there, half-bloods, most of them, who would love to see us leave these people to themselves. These plunderers would then have a chance to feed and fatten themselves on spoils. The best thing we can do for these people is to ease this cry of self-government until they are ready for it—and that day is distant."[102]

Worcester's pattern of public engagement was established fairly quickly. He was able to give lectures before the kinds of audiences he wanted, the people he felt could make a difference in the political arena. He gave lectures at New York's American Museum of Natural History; at the Economic Club of Portland, Maine; at the Detroit Club; at the Chicago Geographic Society; at the Englewood (New Jersey) Armory; at Vassar College, in Poughkeepsie; at the Columbia University Institute of Arts and Sciences; and at the 20th Century Club, in Hartford, Connecticut. His printed schedule shows that he gave more than two dozen lectures between late December 1913 and late April 1914, and an advertisement for his films in the motion picture trade journal *Moving Picture World* said that he had given lectures with his films before more than fifty audiences. Not every venue was able to accommodate his desire to show films but when they could, he did. When they couldn't, he made do with his lantern slides.

ALTHOUGH HE HAD EXPRESSED an interest in giving lectures before respectable and influential audiences, Worcester also decided to broaden his reach through commercial distribution of his films. It is clear that Worcester saw deep interconnections among his articles and lectures, and that the films he had made in the Philippines were an extension of the work he previously had to rely solely on photography to accomplish. In a letter that he wrote to Grosvenor on February 14, 1914, Worcester requested permission to use a number of photographs that he had published in the magazine "in advertising some of my motion pictures."[103] Grosvenor granted Worcester the request, but noted that it would "be advisable in your circular to print a footnote to the effect that they are copyrighted by the National Geographic Society."[104] Although Grosvenor may have wanted to distance himself from some of Worcester's more controversial proclamations, the fact remained that his magazine had been one of Worcester's most prominent supporters during Worcester's career in the Philippines. Perhaps anticipating the popularity of Worcester's films, Grosvenor was interested in reaffirming the link between his magazine and Worcester.

Two weeks after Worcester's letter to Grosvenor, a full-page advertisement appeared in the trade journal *The Moving Picture World* (fig. 21).[105] Deciding to reach out to commercial movie theaters in addition to the learned societies he favored for his lecture series, Worcester granted Pan-American Film Manufacturing the right to distribute two different films under the umbrella title of *Native Life in the Philippines*. One film focused on "The Headhunters," and the other focused on "From Savages to Civilization." The advertisement included ten photographs of non-Christian Filipinos, one man and one woman at each of the top corners, and eight photographs of "Our Little Brown Brothers of the Philippines" printed along the bottom.

The advertisement's copy makes reference to Worcester's belief in the ability of the camera to tell the truth, extending it to motion pictures, too. It asked: "Shall the hundreds of millions of dollars spent in the Philippines and the result of years of development be turned over to our 'Little Brown Brothers' or retained by the United States?" The implication here is that the people seen in the advertisement were typical representatives of the Philippines, signaling a complete collapse of any distinctions between Christian and non-Christian Filipinos. The advertisement then challenged viewers to think about the consequences of their vote in that year's congressional elections, and posed two questions: "What do you know? How shall you decide?" The answer to both questions was "It is up to the picture to tell you."

A review of Worcester's films was published in the April 18, 1914, issue of *The Moving Picture World*. Written by the journal's full-time film reviewer, W. Stephen Bush, the review said that although the "production has considerable educational value," Worcester's "zeal for a complete portrayal of Philippine life" resulted in the inclusion of footage "that might well have been omitted and that, as I understand it, will be eliminated in all the films intended for public use."[106] Nick Deocampo points out that Bush "lauded the use of film to show American voters what their country had done in the Philippine Islands."[107] In a hint that

Fig. 21. Advertisement for *Native Life in the Philippines. The Moving Picture World*, February 28, 1914.

Bush may have held political views similar to Worcester, he applauded how "manfully" the United States "has shouldered the white man's burden and how, with infinite patience and toleration, it has conquered the superstitions, the evils, and the crimes of savagery."[108]

Much like with his articles in *National Geographic Magazine,* the precise amount and kind of impact that Worcester's lectures and the public screenings of *Native Life in the Philippines* had on civic and political leaders is impossible to measure. It is clear that both the lectures and the publication in 1914 of his heavily illustrated two-volume book, *The Philippines Past and Present,* allowed Worcester to give prominent voice to the argument for long-term U.S. retention of the Philippines. As Congress debated the Jones bill and the question of whether the Philippines ought to be granted independence at some fixed date in the future, Worcester's influence was felt. In fact, in December 1914, a year after he began his lecture series, Worcester was invited to testify about the Jones bill before a committee of the U.S. Senate. Tellingly, his testimony included his lecture, including his lantern slides (though not his films). There, before a captive audience, he was able to bring his argument to the highest levels of power.

CHAPTER 5

Final Acts and Reactions

WORCESTER'S CAMPAIGN AGAINST Philippine independence was not limited to his lectures and the commercial distribution of *Native Life in the Philippines*. Indeed, despite the number of lectures he gave, the large audiences he attracted, and the positive newspaper reviews and recounts he routinely received, lectures have a limited reach. In addition, although motion pictures at that time were rapidly increasing in popularity, many sober-minded Americans found them to be a bit uncouth. Books, on the other hand, had a wider reach than lectures and had higher prestige than films.

Worcester knew the power of books firsthand. After all, his first book, *The Philippine Islands and Their People*, helped earn him a spot on the Schurman Commission back in 1899. In February 1914, he published his second book, the two-volume *The Philippines Past and Present*. Like his lectures and *National Geographic* articles, *The Philippines Past and Present* made heavy use of the photographs that he had amassed over the previous fifteen years. In fact, the book's title page highlighted its photos, telling readers that the two volumes contained 128 plates (some of which contained two photographs on the same plate).

According to Rodney Sullivan, *The Philippines Past and Present* was written partly as a response to James Blount's book, *The American Occupation of the Philippines, 1898–1912*. Blount's book was published in the midst of the 1912 presidential campaign that landed Woodrow Wilson in the White House. Blount "aggressively challenged the legitimacy of American acquisition of the Philippines and alleged that the insular administration was despotic, exploitative, and unacceptable to the great majority of Filipinos." Sullivan continues: "Both President Taft and Governor General Forbes were anxious that Blount's charges should be countered in print." Because of his demonstrated proficiency at attacking his opponents in writing, Worcester "was the obvious choice" to lead the counterattack. Sullivan goes on: "The prospect of writing a book . . . as a lucrative rejoinder to Blount's volume was one of the reasons Worcester tendered to his family . . . for his decision to resign as Philippine commissioner and secretary of the interior."[1]

Blount was an active member in the anti-imperialist movement in the United States. He had fought in the Philippine-American War and had served as a judge in the Philippines from 1901 to 1905, giving him firsthand experience with the U.S. colonial regime there. In his book's preface, Blount said that he wrote the book in order "to make audible to a great free nation the voice of a weaker subject people who passionately and rightly long to be free, but whose longings have been systematically denied for the last fourteen years, sometimes ignorantly, sometimes viciously, and always cruelly, on the wholly erroneous idea that where the *end* is benevolent, it justifies the *means,* regardless of the means necessary to the end."[2]

Blount's anti-imperialist message resonated with many Americans in 1912, and his book went into multiple printings. Sullivan writes that the "book dramatically brought together much material that challenged the dominant rhetoric of benevolent assimilation with allegations that treachery, misrepresentation, self-delusion, brutality, and incompetence were the hallmarks of America's colonial enterprise."[3] However, a review in the *New York Times* argued that the Blount's tone, characterized as "undignified, unjust, intemperate, and abusive," undermined the book's potential impact. The reviewer doubted "whether public opinion in this country will be affected much" by it. To demonstrate Blount's intemperate tone, the review quoted from the book's caustic depictions of Elihu Root, William McKinley, Theodore Roosevelt, and President Taft, and of Worcester, whom Blount called "the direst calamity that has befallen the Filipinos since the American occupation, neither war, pestilence, famine, reconcentration, nor tariff-wrought poverty excepted."[4]

In a published response to the *Times* review, Blount complained that the *Times* had taken out of context his criticisms of Root, McKinley, Roosevelt, and Taft. About Worcester, however, Blount conceded: "It is true I criticise Prof. Worcester severely, and I believe he deserves it."[5] Indeed,

Blount's book reserved special scorn for Worcester, who was the only person who was neither a military commander nor a governor-general to whom Blount devoted an entire chapter. Linking Worcester's training as a zoologist with his work as colonial official, Blount referred to him as "the grand official digger-up of non-Christian tribes. He takes as much delight at the discovery of a new non-Christian tribe in some remote, newly penetrated mountain fastness, as the butterfly catcher with the proverbial blue goggles does in the capture of a new kind of butterfly."[6] Blount's one personal encounter with Worcester was in 1901, and Blount wrote that this encounter left him with the impression that Worcester was "an overbearing bully of the beggar-on-horseback type."[7]

Blount wrote that Worcester's most significant accomplishment in the Philippines was the "discovering, getting acquainted with, classifying, tabulating, enumerating, and otherwise preparing for salvation, the various non-Christian tribes." However, this accomplishment was the very "thing out of which has grown, most unfortunately, what seems to be a very cordial mutual hatred between him and the Filipinos."[8] Blount was not particularly sympathetic to non-Christian Filipinos and had no problem referring to them both as "savages" and as largely irrelevant to the social, economic, and political conditions in the Philippines. However, he correctly identified Worcester's desire to keep the non-Christians a central issue in the debates about Philippine independence. To Blount, as well as to many other people both in the United States and in the Philippines, the repeated and prolonged attention to non-Christian Filipinos by Americans served as a gross misrepresentation of the Philippines as a whole, a misrepresentation that Worcester was instrumental both in creating and perpetuating.

Much of Blount's criticism revolved around Worcester's use of photographs, which he sarcastically depicted as an unintended consequence of Worcester's scientific background:

> Of course, it was not a desire to misrepresent the situation [i.e., life in the Philippines], but only the enthusiasm of a zoölogist, anthropologically inclined, and accustomed to carrying a kodak, which started the Professor to photographing the dog-eating Igorrotes and specimens of other non-Christian tribes soon after the Taft Commission reached the Philippines. But you cannot get far in the earlier reports of the Taft Commission, which was supposed to have been sent out to report back on the capacity of the Filipinos for self-government, without crossing the trail of the Professor's kodak—pictures of naked Igorrotes and the like.[9]

More than most contemporary observers, Blount recognized the convergence of science and politics in Worcester's photographs. He also understood the very real consequences of Worcester's ethnographic archive, saying that Worcester's photographs had "distinct political value in 1900 and 1904" and they "must have greatly awakened the philanthropic interest of exporters of cotton goods to learn of those poor 'savage millions' wearing only a loin cloth, when they could be wearing yards of cotton cloth."[10]

In perhaps his most scathing criticism, Blount called Worcester "the P.T. Barnum of the 'non-Christian tribe' industry," and said that Filipinos understood "the malign and far-reaching influence of the work of Professor Worcester, and his services to the present Philippine policy of indefinite retention with undeclared intention, through humbugging the American people into the belief that the islands must be retained until the three hundred thousand or so Negritos, Igorrotes, and other primitive wild peoples sprinkled throughout the archipelago are 'reconstructed.'" Worcester's main tool for this "humbugging" was photography, "the Worcester kodak" that Blount said led the influential magazine publisher S. S. McClure to oppose Philippine independence. McClure, whom Blount believed "is trying to make his life one of large and genuine usefulness for the good . . . must have seen some of Professor Worcester's pictures of Igorrotes and Negritos scattered through public documents related to the question of Filipino capacity for self-government. Mr. McClure has never, I believe, been in the Islands; and the cruelly unjust impression he had innocently received was precisely the impression systematically developed all these years through the Worcester kodak."[11]

For more direct evidence of the influence of Worcester's photography, Blount pointed to a February 1911 article in *Sunset* magazine written by the former governor-general, James F. Smith, titled "The Philippines As I Saw Them." Smith actually published four articles with that title in *Sunset* in 1910 and 1911, articles that were intended to "present a careful study of the Islands by a man who knows and loves them and who is largely responsible for what they are to-day."[12] Directly under the article's title in the August 1910 issue of *Sunset,* readers were told that the article was "Illustrated by Photographs through the Courtesy of the Bureau of Insular Affairs," about which Blount wrote: "If you read this legend understandingly, you can, in so doing, hear the click of the Worcester kodak."[13]

Blount provided a lengthy (and critical) description of the article's use of photographs, saying that the article is "smeared all over" with Worcester's photographs, which included "Eighteen Igorrot Fledgings

Hatched by the American Bird of Freedom" and a photograph of "some other specimen with a curious name, in which there is a woman naked from the waist up and a man in a loincloth." Recognizing Worcester's pervasive influence on how Americans perceived the Philippines, Blount wrote: "I do not so much blame General Smith for this libelous panorama of pictures. . . . He probably illustrated his article with what the Bureau of Insular Affairs sent him, without giving much thought to the matter. But the Bureau of Insular Affairs appears to neglect no occasion to parade the Philippine archipelago's sprinkling of non-Christian tribes before the American public, fully knowing that the hopes of the Filipinos for independence must depend upon impressions received by the American people concerning the degree of civilization they have reached."[14]

Blount's criticisms of Worcester's photographs couldn't compete with the spectacle of the images and the films that Worcester deployed time and again. Indeed, just two months after the publication of *The American Occupation of the Philippines,* the first of Worcester's two full-length articles in *National Geographic* was published. Worcester continued to hammer home his arguments using photographs in his 1913 *National Geographic* article, in his lectures, and, ultimately, in *The Philippines Past and Present.* Sullivan notes that despite its "initial popularity, Blount's book has had little impact on American writing on the Philippines, its message largely overwhelmed in 1914 by the splash and continuing ripples of Worcester's *Philippines Past and Present.*"[15]

Worcester responded directly to some of Blount's criticisms in the first volume of his book, characterized by Paul Kramer as "a massive, two-volume broadside against his and the regime's critics."[16] Early in the book, Worcester sought to dismiss Blount outright: "Judge Blount has indulged so freely in obvious hyperbole, and has made so very evident the bitter personal animosities which inspire many of his statements, that it has been a genuine surprise to his former associates and acquaintances that his book has been taken seriously."[17] One contemporary reviewer of *The Philippines Past and Present* thought it "perhaps unfortunate that Mr. Worcester should give so much specific attention" to Blount's book. However, "Mr. Worcester has seemed to think that upon the whole the best way to meet many of the attacks that have been made upon our Philippine record is to regard Mr. Blount as the latest and most aggressive of all the critics, and to answer all opponents by the process of taking up Mr. Blount's charges and meeting them seriatim." The reviewer concluded, admiringly: "It can hardly be denied that Mr. Worcester does this with conspicuous success."[18]

One thing Worcester didn't rebut, however, was "Blount's fundamental allegation that Worcester was using his position to lobby against Philippine independence." Indeed, as Sullivan writes, "If anything, Worcester's response corroborated Blount's charge: it was a reiteration of the divisive propositions that so enraged Filipinos in 1910," namely, that the departure of the United States from the Philippines would result in widespread violence and chaos throughout the Philippines.[19] Nor did Worcester rebut Blount's comments regarding Worcester's use of photography. In fact, in what may have been partly a deliberate provocation aimed at Blount, Worcester loaded both volumes with scores of images all intended to drive home the point that the Philippines was too diverse to constitute a nation, that "savagery" was still a very real presence in the islands, and that the United States was a benevolent force in the Philippines.

The photographs that Worcester chose as frontispieces for each volume set the tone for the photographs that followed them. They were carefully selected to show how the United States was able to contribute to the advancement of both the Christian Filipinos and the non-Christian Filipinos. They signaled the transformations that had occurred in the Philippines since 1898 and pointed to the role of American-style education in that process of transformation. According to the eminent historian Alfred W. McCoy, photographs that emphasized education in the Philippines became, over the first half of the twentieth century, "a visual cliché in colonial photography. . . . Across the archipelago, US colonial schools, the photos tell us, are imposing the social order, personal discipline and productive skills necessary for nationhood—whether upon Tagalog girls in Manila, tribal girls in the northern Mountain province, or Cebuano boys in the central Visayan."[20]

For the first volume of his book, Worcester chose a photograph of Emilio Aguinaldo standing in a cornfield taken in late 1913 or early 1914. The photograph was captioned, "Peace and Prosperity. This chance photograph showing General Emilio Aguinaldo as he is to-day, standing with Director of Education Frank L. Crone, beside a field of corn raised by Emilio Aguinaldo, Jr., in a school contest, typifies the peace, prosperity, and enlightenment which have been brought about in the Philippine Islands under American rule."[21] The photograph powerfully depicted the supposed transformation in the Philippines from 1898 to 1914. In Benito Vergara's words, the photograph shows a "confluence of time" linking the struggles of the past with the "peace" and "prosperity" of the present.[22] The image presents Aguinaldo as a pacified former enemy now living life as a farmer and a "good citizen," hearkening back to the Jeffersonian image of a yeoman farmer. The fact that the corn was raised by Aguinaldo's son points toward a prosperous future free of the struggles of the recent past, but only, however, if the United States maintained control of the islands. After all, Crone is seen standing next to Aguinaldo, representing the colonial state and the American-style schooling that the photograph suggests is the reason for the fertile field of corn.

A similar depiction of transformation, of the "Philippines past and present," is found in the frontispiece to the second volume (fig. 22). Here, two photographs of the same person were placed next to each other. The caption reads: "The Metamorphosis of a Bontoc Igorot. Two photographs of a [sic] Pit-a-pit, a Bontoc Igorot boy. The second was taken nine years after the first."[23] According to Vergara, the first photograph was taken by Charles Martin, probably in January 1903.[24] In the Newberry *Index*, the photograph (number 8-A-070 in that archive) is captioned: "A young boy called Pit-a-pit. This is the brightest boy in Bontoc. He has been in school for some time and speaks excellent English."[25] In this photograph, Pit-a-pit faces the camera directly, smiling, arms relaxed at his side, standing in the bright sun in front of what appears to be a small river. He is the only figure in focus and he is dressed in traditional Igorot clothing, with a loincloth and long-cut hair with bangs. Blurred figures can be seen on the opposite shore. The focus of the photograph is exclusively on the young boy.

In the second photograph, Pit-a-pit has grown into a young man. He stands on a brick-lined path in a tended garden space. He again faces the camera directly, but this time with a serious look on his face. Now his hands are crossed in front of him, the right holding the wrist of the left, the left holding a hat. He wears a white suit and his hair is cut fashionably short, parted on the left and combed back. For American readers, he would visually be identified as "civilized," and his more recent photograph stood in stark contrast to the evidence of "savagery" seen in the younger Pit-a-pit. As Vergara writes, "The photographs graphically illustrate, authenticate, and ultimately legitimate the process of colonialism for the readers. They display quite succinctly and effectively the transformation of the colonial subject."[26]

In addition to the deliberate selection of photographs to serve as frontispiece images, Worcester also made conscious decisions about which photographs to include inside the book, and how to organize them. The arrangement and sequencing of the sixty-five plates in the first volume of *The Philippines Past and Present* can be divided into six general catego-

Fig. 22. "The Metamorphosis of a Bontoc Igorot: Two photographs of a Pit-a-pit, a Bontoc Igorot boy. The second was taken nine years after the first." Frontispiece to volume 2 of Dean C. Worcester, *The Philippines Past and Present* (1914).

ries. Worcester opened with eight photographs illustrating the Spanish-American War and the subsequent Philippine-American War, including the photograph of Filipino prisoners that Worcester was especially proud of and that is reprinted in chapter 1 above. (In the book, Worcester cropped the photograph to remove his shadow.) After the war photographs, Worcester included six photographs representing the establishment of the American colonial regime in the Philippines, including formal portraits of both the Schurman and the Taft Commissions, and photographs of Governor-General Smith and Governor-General Forbes. Significantly, both of these photographs showed the men surrounded by non-Christian Filipinos, emphasizing (perhaps misleadingly so) both their role in bringing civilization to the Philippines and the centrality of the non-Christian Filipinos to the work of the colonial regime.

The next three sets of photographs all deal with different aspects of the "improvements" that the United States made in the Philippines. For example, there are before-and-after photographs of streets, wells, and jails, and photographs showing improvements in medical care—the first six graduates of a new nursing school, a leper colony, and a before-and-after sequence showing a young boy treated for yaws. After these photographs are eleven photographs showing the construction of the road to Benguet and the government retreat and summer capital established in Baguio, including the Baguio Country Club, which Worcester felt the need to defend "[b]ecause of the extraordinary false statements made concerning it by certain unscrupulous politicians." Worcester explained that the purpose of the Baguio Country Club "was to afford a meeting place for the people of the town and to give them an opportunity for outdoor sports."[27] Moreover, "It knows no race or creed, and Filipinos take advantage of its privileges quite as freely as do Americans. . . . No more democratic institution ever existed."[28]

Worcester then shifted back to scenes of modernization, particularly in and around Manila. He included photographs of the Bureau of Science building and the General Hospital. He also showed more before-and-after photographs, including two sequences of schools, both of which contrast an "old-style" school with a "modern" school. The photographs of schools revealed two different aspects of what Vergara says were common elements of colonial photography, both of which were "based on the passage of time." The before-and-after photographs stem from the common colonial narrative of "inferiority and improvement,"[29] and they suggest that an end to the colonial endeavor puts the colony at risk of reverting back to the "old-style." Including multiple images of schools heightened this message: "Images of the present colonial improvements implied that this represented the future too. This is perhaps why pictures of children, in and out of school, were so common. More effective and more poignant than pictures of newly-constructed bridges, images of children being educated almost naturally connoted, by the virtue of their sheer potentiality, a forward movement into the future."[30]

Worcester was generally unconcerned about whether the placement of the photographs matched the accompanying text. In this way, the photographs operate less as illustrations than as a separate strand of argument, a visual rhetoric for readers (perhaps most readers) who weren't committed to reading the entirety of the more than one thousand pages that comprised the two volumes. For example, the photograph of the Baguio Country Club was located in a chapter of the book that talked about the Philippine-American War, while Worcester's written defense of the country club came almost two hundred pages later. In a similar vein, Worcester's turn to photographs of non-Christians (the sixth category found in the first volume) did not come while he was writing about the subject. In fact, the first image focusing on that subject appeared in a section of the book where Worcester discussed some of the health and sanitation problems that he witnessed during his first two visits to the Philippines. Despite the inclusion of photographs of non-Christians in the first volume of the book, Worcester's detailed discussion of non-Christians didn't appear at all in that volume, though it did comprise a significant portion of the second volume.

Worcester included thirteen photographs in the first volume of his book showing different aspects of non-Christian Filipinos and his experiences with them. Vergara writes about one such photograph, captioned "Entertaining the Kalingas. They are listening with great interest to the reproduction of a speech which one of their chiefs has just made into the receiving horn of a dictaphone."[31] Worcester is the central focus of the photograph, the largest figure and the individual working with the equipment. Vergara notes that the photograph "illustrates effectively . . . the entrance of American technology, and its apparent capacity to entrance the inferior other."[32] Like the photographs showing the modernization of the educational and health systems in the Philippines, this photograph informed readers that Worcester—and, by extension, the whole colonial enterprise—was working hard to modernize the Philippines.

Worcester appeared in another photograph of Kalingas, too, taken in 1905 while on one of his "inspection tours." Samuel E. Kane, a soldier-turned-prospector who later served in the colonial regime and who accompanied Worcester on a trip into the Kalinga region, wrote in his 1934 book, *Thirty Years With the Philippine Head-Hunters,* that Worcester had brought with him "two cameras, several hundred plates, and a complete developing outfit." He also brought trading supplies that required forty carriers to transport through the mountains of northern Luzon.[33] Worcester also wrote about the journey and about how he supposedly had interrupted a head-hunting celebration and had almost lost his own life: "Six of them [i.e., the Kalinga chiefs they encountered] were in favor of killing us immediately, arguing that we were the first white men to penetrate their country; that they might have to carry our baggage, which would be a lot of trouble; and that if they allowed us to pass through others might follow us, whereas if they killed us they would have no further trouble with strangers."[34]

Worcester went on to describe rising tension between his party and the Kalingas that seems to have been based on misunderstandings of the conventions of hospitality based on gifts of food. While Worcester's book suggests that he alone was able to find the way to reach a diplomatic resolution to the tension (having introduced himself to the Kalingas as "the ruler of all non-Christians"[35]), Kane's book suggests that

Kane was instrumental in the affair, as well.[36] After an understanding was reached between Worcester's party and the Kalingas, led by their head-man, Saking, Worcester spent the night among the Kalingas. Worcester wrote: "The following day was spent in distributing presents to the Kalinga head-men, in taking photographs, and in getting a little much needed rest."[37]

One of the photos taken is the one seen in figure 23. The photograph suggests some of the tense atmosphere in the setting, with the caption filling in the details: "In Hostile Country. Colonel Villamor and the author at Bakídan's place in the Kalinga country. The four chiefs were not as yet ready to lay down their shields or head-axes."[38] Worcester and Villamor stand flanked by four Kalinga men, all six of them standing in front of a house in which two Kalinga women can be seen. Worcester's right hand grips a walking staff, but the angle of the shot makes it appear as though he is gripping one of the shields. It is a classic kind of photograph meant to show the moment of contact between an intrepid white explorer and a heretofore-remote tribe.

Worcester stayed with Bakidan and Saking long enough to make more than a dozen photographs in their town of Bunuan, including multiple portraits of both men in front of a white sheet (axes in hand) and photographs of the houses. Kane wrote that he helped Worcester with the photography and that he "was busy most of the day" doing so.[39] Worcester recalled that the evening after distributing gifts and making photographs, "Bakidan suggested that it was time we formally made friends with each other."[40] Here, Worcester suggests a direct connection between his photographic activities, gift giving, and the formation of important alliances in his efforts to establish U.S. control of the region.

The photographs included in the second volume of Worcester's book were not organized into thematic clusters as apparent as those in the first volume. What stands out, instead, is the repeated use of the adjective "typical" to describe the photographs. In the first volume, the word "typical" was used only five times in the captions to the plates, scattered throughout the volume; the second volume used the word seventeen times, frequently in clusters of plates. For example, four photographs listed sequentially in the book's table of contents showed a "Typical Street in a Filipino Town," "A Typical Bukidnon Village Street," "A Typical Improved Bukidnon House," and "A Typical Neglected Filipino House." The photographs were printed in pairs on the same plate, separated by only eight pages of text. In each pairing, the Bukidnon photograph shows a more orderly and, consequently, a more desirable

Fig. 23. Dean C. Worcester, "Blas Villamor, Bakidan, Saking, and two other brothers of Bakidan, and myself. There are six brothers in this family and they rule the upper Nabuagan River valley. Bakidan is the most powerful" (1905). Description of photograph as found in UMMA archive. (Courtesy of the University of Michigan Museum of Anthropology, UMMA 05-A-010.)

scene. The pairings were chosen to show the contrast between Christian Filipinos and non-Christian Bukidnons. Worcester clearly favored the latter, revealing his bias both in the book's text and in its photographs. For example, the caption accompanying the photographs contrasting "typical" Bukidnon and Filipino houses reads, "In the Bukidnon villages all the people now take pride in keeping their houses in good repair. Houses like the one here shown are frequently seen in neighboring Filipino towns."[41] There is, of course, no way to verify the typicality of the photographs as asserted by their captions. Instead, Worcester relies on viewers to trust his apparent objectivity to show things as they really are.

One thing these photographs suggested was that the positive transformations seen in Worcester's before-and-after sequences might not last without continuing governance by Americans. Worcester told readers that the orderly towns that could be found in Bukidnon were the result of the diligent efforts of the government officials there. Worcester reported a "marvellous change" that had taken place in Bukidnon in just one year: "Model villages had taken the place of the ramshackle affairs which I had found on my first visit. The houses were grouped around spacious plazas on which the grass had been so carefully cut that they had already begun to look like lawns. Streets were kept so clean that one could literally pick up a dropped pin without the slightest difficulty."[42] Worcester also told readers that there had been ongoing attempts "to destroy the government which we had established in Bukidnon, and to reestablish the system of peonage under which its peaceful, industrious inhabitants had so long groaned."[43] The clear message sent both by text and by photographs is that if independence is granted to the Philippines, the hard work of bringing civilization to the Bukidnons and the other non-Christians would be undone.

The flipside to all of this, however, can be seen in the very last photograph of the book, a widely reproduced image of a non-Christian man standing next to a head set on a post that stares lifelessly at the camera (fig. 24). The man is dressed in a loincloth and he holds a spear, his eyes seeming to glance at the disembodied head. The photograph's caption reads: "A Possible Office-Holder. The man with the lance could be elected senator for the Mountain Province were the Jones Bill to be enacted. He has the qualifications therein prescribed as necessary to eligibility for this high office." This image was intended to horrify Americans with the thought that someone so obviously "savage" might be entrusted with helping to run a nation. As Kramer writes, Worcester's "imperial indigenism conveyed the image of non-Christians as both fierce and barbaric (as here) or as vulnerable and in need of protection," as in the case of the Bukidnon. From either perspective, Worcester presented the non-Christians as "permanently incapable of self-government and in need of indefinite tutelage."[44]

What Worcester doesn't say, and what his readers had no way to know, is that the photograph was almost certainly faked. It's not only that the photograph is not included in any of the known archives of Worcester photographs; it also bears little resemblance to any of those photographs. The only photographs taken by Worcester showing the aftermath of head-hunting were those surrounding the funeral of an Ifugao man (discussed in chapter 3). The composition of those photographs reveals the dynamic and fluid nature of the situation, unlike the carefully posed and framed composition in the photograph above. In addition, figure 19 in chapter 4 shows a man holding a papier mâché head prepared specifically for Worcester's filming, and the head on the post

Fig. 24. "A Possible Office-Holder. The man with the lance could be elected
senator for the Mountain Province were the Jones Bill to be enacted. He
has the qualifications therein prescribed as necessary to eligibility for this
high office." Facing page 972 of Dean C. Worcester, *The Philippines Past and
Present* (1914).

has the frozen look of a mask with no details indicating the brutality of being beheaded by an axe.

The photograph also matches some of the details Worcester provided in his notes for the film, *Native Life in the Philippines,* where he described some of the scenes surrounding the reenacted Ifugao head-hunting episode in the film: "The people of the towns to which the successful head-hunters belong have heard that they are returning with the head of a new victim, have prepared a post on which to place it, and a chief receives them with a speech. The head-hunters wear ornaments of scarlet leaves as a sign of success." In the next scene: "Immediately after the head is placed on the post, one of the warriors smears it with ashes, while another makes a speech."[45]

This description more closely matches what is seen in the photograph than does the description provided by Worcester in the September 1912 issue of *National Geographic.* In that article, Worcester wrote that it was difficult to describe in print "the weird effect" of an Ifugao head-hunting celebration, "but I hope yet to be able to use a moving-picture camera on a file of men engaging in this strange ceremonial, which they will doubtless soon forget, as head-hunting has now practically ceased among them." He also wrote that, rather than placing the head on a tall post, "the head is impaled on a short stake and the warriors circle around it in the characteristic war dance of this tribe. Some of them take off their ornaments and hang them on the head, at the same time jeering at it as if it were capable of hearing and understanding them. Dancing and feasting may last for days."[46]

BY THE AUTUMN OF 1914, Worcester was all but finished giving lectures about the Philippines. *The Philippines Past and Present* was selling well, and *Native Life in the Philippines* was being shown in public theaters. He had few new writing commitments, and his thoughts were starting to turn to his planned return to the Philippines, where he had a variety of business interests in the works. In mid-November, Worcester received a letter from a man named Elmer Silver, inquiring whether Worcester would be willing to deliver a lecture before the Vermont Association of Boston. Worcester, himself a native of Vermont, responded that he would get "very real pleasure to have an opportunity to meet the members of the Association and to tell them something of the Philippine Islands, their peoples and their possibilities, and the work which Americans have already accomplished there." After providing Silver with a quick run-down of his visual aids, Worcester gave Silver the option of five thousand feet of films and one hundred slides, or else 150 slides if no films were to be used.[47]

With the income earned from the "fairly stiff fee" he charged for his lectures the previous winter and spring, royalties from his book, profits from his film, and salary from his position in the American-Philippine Company, Worcester was financially secure. He didn't need to make any money from his lecture before the Vermont Association, and he told Silver that he was "proud of my Vermont origin and in talking to a Vermont audience should be glad to do this so that the only expense to which you would be put would be my bare expenses from New York to Boston and return."[48] If he wanted Worcester to show films, Silver could also expect to pay more than twenty dollars for the equipment and someone to run it, and only half that amount if they were content with Worcester just showing some of his lantern slides.

The lecture before the Vermont Association was of little consequence to Worcester; he agreed more as a favor to a fellow Vermonter than anything else. However, the end of 1914 saw him give a lecture to the most important audience he ever had—the United States Senate Committee on the Philippines. Of all the "people who really count" that Worcester wanted to reach, this committee counted more than any other. This lecture almost didn't happen, though, and it seems that the chair of the committee, Gilbert Hitchcock, a Democrat from Nebraska, wasn't especially eager to hear from Worcester. The invitation that Hitchcock sent may have been designed to be one that Worcester could easily refuse. On December 11, 1914, Hitchcock wrote Worcester a letter in care of the American-Philippine Company, inviting Worcester to give testimony at a committee hearing regarding the Jones bill, which, as Paul Kramer puts it, would have "provided for the election of a Philippine Senate as the upper house of the legislature and 'independence' eight years afterward, with U.S. troops remaining in the islands to 'protect' against outside intervention for twenty years."[49] This was a bill that Worcester vehemently opposed, and Hitchcock knew it.

Hitchcock, on the other hand, was a supporter of the bill. Hitchcock had already arranged to have testimony provided by Lindley Miller Garrison, the secretary of war; General Frank McIntyre, the chief of the Bureau of Insular Affairs; former president (and former governor-general of the Philippines) William Howard Taft; and other officials of the Philippine government. The tone of the letter to Worcester suggests that he was something of an afterthought to the committee. Or, at least, Hitchcock was lukewarm to the idea of hearing from Worcester, whom Hitchcock likely predicted would have little new to add beyond what was readily available in *The Philippines Past and Present*. However, as Hitchcock wrote to Worcester, "[m]embers of the Committee expressed a desire to hear from you on the subject" of the Jones bill, and Hitchcock asked Worcester to "indicate to me whether you would be willing to appear before the Committee and whether you can conveniently do so in December or early January." Given the timing of the request, just before the Christmas and New Year holidays, Hitchcock may well have hoped that Worcester had already committed to his holiday plans.[50]

However, Worcester was not one to shy away from an opportunity to air his views, especially before such an important audience, and he let Hitchcock know that he was more than willing to make himself available to the committee. In his response, dated December 12, Worcester noted that he had "important engagements" the following week on Tuesday, Wednesday, and Saturday, but that he had "no further engagements of importance until the eighth, twelfth and thirteenth of January." Moreover, he was willing to keep his schedule "as free as possible until advised of the date on which the Committee" wanted him to testify, and would be ready to travel to Washington "on short telegraphic notice." In an acknowledgement of the inconvenience of traveling on short notice during the holidays, Worcester wrote: "It would be a great convenience if the giving of my testimony might be delayed until after the holidays, but I shall, of course, hold myself at the disposal of the Committee."[51]

Worcester also requested that he be allowed to present one of his slide lectures to the committee. He didn't, however, raise the prospect of showing any of his films to the committee. The particular lecture he had in mind sounds very much like the one that he suggested he give at Rutgers almost a year earlier. As he wrote to Hitchcock:

> I have in my possession rather an unusual series of lantern slides showing some of the practical results of the American occupation in the Philippines in safeguarding the public health, in generalizing education, in providing better means of communication by land and sea, and in otherwise improving conditions. If the Committee is interested in these matters and should care to devote an hour or two to their consideration preferably in the evening, although daytime would answer, I could use slides in such a way as to communicate information more quickly and accurately than would otherwise be possible.[52]

Two days later, Hitchcock reported to the committee: "I have a letter from Dean C. Worcester stating that he would like to appear before the committee, and that he can illustrate his remarks with lantern slides to show the conditions of the islands before and after the American occupation." The response of Iowa Republican senator William Kenyon was that Worcester's lecture "will be very interesting."[53]

Worcester's request to deliver a lecture before the committee delighted those of his supporters in Congress who—like Worcester—believed in the power of images to make compelling arguments. Clarence Miller, a Republican representative from Minnesota, wrote Worcester a letter on December 26 in which he said: "I am delighted to know that the Senate Committee will give you an opportunity to present your slides showing the American work in the Philippines and the progress of the people there. This will be infinitely more effective than all the talking you or anybody else could do." Miller clearly saw this as a political victory for the retentionist argument. He asked Worcester to send him an outline of the lecture so that Miller could bring it to Massachusetts senator John Weeks—a fellow Republican—and together they could determine if there were certain topics that Worcester should either expand on or omit.[54]

Many of the people called to testify prior to Worcester had been asked about the status of the non-Christians in the Philippines. The Jones bill contained a provision that would "divide the islands into 12 districts—1 district to be the non-Christian territory and 11 districts to be in the Christian provinces."[55] Two senators from each of the Christian districts would be elected to the legislature, and two would be appointed by the governor-general to represent the non-Christians. Among the questions before the committee was one that asked whether or not the non-Christian Filipinos ought to be considered as truly Filipino, and, if so, whether or not the non-Christian Filipinos, particularly the "savage" Igorots and Ifugaos, were ready to take a role in governing the nation.

Manuel Quezon, who had been serving as resident commissioner for the Philippines (a nonvoting delegate to the U.S. Congress) since 1909, certainly felt that there would be little problem in moving toward full Philippine independence, telling the committee that the non-Christians would have a place in the nation: "Racially all the Filipinos, whether Christian or non-Christian, with the exception of the negritos, are the same—Malays." When asked if there was not "a great difference . . . in the physical type of characteristics of the people of Mindanao and the Filipinos of Luzon," Quezon replied: "No sir; I do not believe there is;

I do not think you could distinguish between a Moro and a Christian Filipino, if they were dressed alike." While admitting his belief that the "non-Christians are backward people," Quezon argued that the question of the non-Christians was a red herring used to distract people from recognizing that the seven-eighths of the population that was Christian was "a homogenous people in their religion, civilization, costumes, ideals, and do constitute a people in the strict sense of the word."[56]

Upon the conclusion of Quezon's testimony on December 19, the committee adjourned until December 30, when Worcester brought his lecture to Capitol Hill. Introducing Worcester, Senator Hitchcock stated: "Dr. Worcester offered to bring his lantern slides and illustrate his lecture. His offer was accepted; and he will now proceed to make his statement in a continuous form, probably without interruptions of any sort—unless members of the committee desire to interrupt him— and he will illustrate what he has to say by views taken in the Philippine Islands."[57] Worcester's introduction was met with applause, and then he commenced to speak. He began his lecture at 3:30 p.m. and spoke continuously until 5:00 p.m. The official transcript of his lecture reveals that his statement was punctuated with applause and laughter from members of the committee.

It seems that Worcester made few adjustments to his speech to take into account the specific audience he was addressing. Although the committee consisted solely of men, he began his lecture with the words, "Ladies and gentlemen," a habit he no doubt had gotten into during his lecture tour. He opened by invoking the kind of mental voyage that structured his 1911 article in *National Geographic:* "It is a great pleasure to me this afternoon to have an opportunity of taking you on a flying trip to the islands, and I can promise you that both seasickness and politics will be left out; so that you will have nothing to trouble you. My only object is to give you some idea of what the islands are like, and what the people are like; some notion of the conditions which we found there and of the conditions which exist there to-day."[58] Like his book, *The Philippines Past and Present,* Worcester's lecture was intended to demonstrate to the senators that the United States has been a beneficial presence in the Philippines and that the United States ought to maintain control there indefinitely.

Working without his films, Worcester relied solely on his lantern slides to help him make his points. He began by showing the islands on a map, followed by slides showing various geographical features of the country, including the Mayon Volcano and pine trees in Baguio. Then,

Fig. 25. Dean C. Worcester, "Skull house ornaments with the gentleman who
took the heads from which the skulls were obtained. Note particularly the
shouldered piles of the house" (ca. 1903). (Photo courtesy of the Newberry
Library, Chicago, Ayer Photo, Philippine Collection, Box 29, 07-A-110.)

directly contradicting what Manuel Quezon had said eleven days earlier,
Worcester dove into one of his main arguments: "There is no such thing
as a Filipino people. There is in the Philippine Islands one of the most
complex aggregations of peoples to be found in the same land area anywhere in the world." To illustrate, he gestured to a slide of "a headhunter
standing before a house ornamented with human skulls" and asserted
that "the individual whom you now see on the screen . . . is not a Filipino."[59] The photograph was in all likelihood the one seen in figure 25,
one of Worcester's favorite images, one that found wide circulation and
that Worcester included in his 1912 *National Geographic* article.

In his lecture before the committee, Worcester used this photograph
to make explicit his belief that an Ifugao "headhunter" should not be

considered to be a Filipino, though he doesn't explain why. Apparently, the photograph, probably taken in 1903 during Worcester's first trip to the area around Banaue—site of the world-famous rice terraces—was supposed to speak for itself, to reveal an essential truth about the Ifugaos that is inscribed in the image itself. However, Worcester had the photograph speak in different ways at different times. In the Newberry *Index*, for example, Worcester wrote of the photograph: "Skull house ornaments with the gentleman who took the heads from which the skulls were obtained. Note particularly the shouldered piles of the house."[60] Here, the fact that the man was a headhunter was secondary to something else that Worcester found interesting about the photograph—details about the construction of the house. In *National Geographic*, the photograph was captioned, "An Ifugao Head-Hunter With Some of His Trophies: Evidently in the opinion of this warrior, 'Heads is heads,' whether human or animal."[61] In the text of the article itself, included in a section titled "Exhibiting Gory Trophies," Worcester again directed attention to the house, writing with mock admiration: "I have seen a house with a tasteful ornamental frieze of alternating carabao skulls and human skulls extending around it at the height of the floor!"[62]

The photograph was included elsewhere, suggesting Worcester's belief in the power of the image to convey his arguments about the Philippines. It was prominently featured in the January 10, 1914, issue of the *Bulletin of the Brooklyn Institute of Arts and Sciences* promoting a lecture Worcester was scheduled to give on January 24. There, the photograph was captioned: "An Ifugao Head Hunter and Some of His Trophies Before Being Civilized."[63] It had also been included in former Governor Smith's 1910 article, "The Philippines As I Saw Them," the article that Blount criticized in *The American Occupation of the Philippines.* In Smith's article, the caption read: "An Ifugao head-hunter at home, with several grinning trophies above his chamber door."[64]

In the published articles, and in Worcester's testimony before the committee, the photograph was intended to suggest that head-hunting remained a serious problem in the Philippines, and that it would be foolish to allow a man such as the one in the photograph to hold any kind of position of authority in the Philippines. However, such a use of the photograph stood in stark contrast to what Worcester wrote about the Ifugao practice of head-hunting in the 1905 *Index* that he prepared for Edward Ayer: "The Ifugaos have, until recently, been very warlike, and at the time the writer visited Banaue, in their country, in 1903, were actively engaged in head-hunting, which has, however, now been almost completely checked. They are very friendly toward the Americans, and at the present time one may safely ride anywhere through their country without a guard. An industrial school has been established for their children at Quiangan, and is well attended."[65]

In keeping with his established practice of juxtaposing images for maximum effect, after the photograph of the Ifugao headhunter, Worcester next showed the senators the photograph of Aguinaldo and Crone that served as the frontispiece to the first volume of *The Philippines Past and Present.* After that, Worcester showed a photograph of a Negrito man (most likely Ibag), followed by a portrait of Sergio Osmeña, the Speaker of the Philippine Assembly. Again he compared the two men, saying that the Negrito was "practically at the bottom of the human series," while Osmeña was "pretty close to the other extreme." Like the photograph of the Ifugao, the photograph of the Negrito was supposed to speak for itself: "A glance at the face of this Negrito [indicating] will give you some idea of the impossibility of developing him."[66] Here, Worcester revealed his belief that character and personality was inscribed in the face, an embrace of the physiognomic theories of people such as Francis Galton and Cesare Lombroso, theories that helped undergird the ethnological photography woven throughout the Worcester archive.

Worcester also contrasted women, drawing laughter with a photograph of Bontoc Igorot women wearing leaf skirts, saying that the women "have spring, summer, and fall styles, dependent not on the caprice of tailors, but upon the state of the neighboring vegetation."[67] The Igorot women were followed by "Miss Mendoza . . . a graduate of the University of the Philippines, the department of medicine and surgery, who is now employed in our general hospital. She is a young woman whose attainments would compare very favorably with those of graduates of our best women's colleges in this country." Worcester could have gone on making such comparisons, but time limits prevented him from doing so. The point of these, he said, was "to give you some idea of the extremes" that could be found in the Philippines.[68]

Worcester continued to use his slides to make comparisons, shifting from the supposedly inherent differences based on culture and civilization to before-and-after sequences showing improvements in housing, roads, health care, and agriculture based on U.S. occupation of the Philippines. Among the slides he showed were 1903 photographs of "warriors of the old school" and "warriors of the new school": "There [indicating a row of armed savages] is the old fighting line, which was always out on mischief except when it was necessary to work in the field.

And that [indicating a company of Bontoc soldiers] is the one which has replaced it. We have never had a case of disloyalty or disobedience to orders among those soldiers."[69] Worcester didn't mention that the photographs were made in the same spot at the same time, a fact revealed by other photographs in his archive, and by figures 10 and 11, seen in chapter 2. His argument of transformation relied on the illusion that the two photographs showed change over time, not simply the wearing of two different kinds of clothing.

Just prior to showing the two slides of the "old school" and "new school" warriors, Worcester showed the committee the sequence of photographs of Don Francisco Muro in order to demonstrate the success of the Constabulary for transforming Igorot warriors into efficient, loyal, Americanized soldiers:

I will show you the evolution of the first Bontoc soldier who ever enlisted. It was difficult to get them, at the beginning, to join the constabulary, because the old "guardia civil" had perpetrated many abuses. This man is a chief named "Francisco," dressed as he was when I first saw him [indicating]. This slide shows how he looked a year later, after he had been in contact with the Americans [indicating]. He was the first man who enlisted in the hills, and this is the way he looked after one more year. In other words, in the short space of two years, having been under discipline one year, he changed from a long-haired savage to the very efficient sergeant of infantry whom you see on the screen; and, believe me, he was efficient.[70]

In showing these slides, Worcester asked the committee to accept that the photographs actually showed what he said they showed, and that the changes in clothing and haircut could be read as a change in attitudes, beliefs, and civilization. Although some members of the committee likely were skeptical about what Worcester was showing them, no one directly challenged him on what the slides revealed.

There was no real narrative arc in Worcester's lecture, whose force of argument came less from logic than from the inundation of images he put on the screen. He continued to show slide after slide—more than two hundred of them over the course of ninety minutes—illustrating different aspects of life in the Philippines. It seems as though he believed that the sheer volume of images that he showed his audience was enough to convince them of what it was that he so fervently wanted them to believe. The last set of photographs showed the Bukidnon, whom Worcester called "[t]he people who have responded most readily to our efforts to improve them." Again he relied on juxtaposition to suggest that significant transformations had been made among the Bukidnon because of the Americans: "There [indicating] is a typical woman with the old dress, which was modest and rather striking; and that [indicating] is the way you will find those people looking to-day. We did not make the slightest effort to get them to change their costumes; they did it themselves; and I may inform you that they order some of their dry goods from Montgomery, Ward & Co., of Chicago, the parcel post bringing them what they want."[71]

What Worcester didn't say was that he had an interest in cattle ranching in the Bukidnon region of northern Mindanao, having "acquired large tracts of Bukidnon land for the American-Philippine Company in 1913," and that he was actively working to prevent the possibility that Bukidnon land would be opened to homesteading by Filipinos from other parts of the country.[72] In other words, his interest in the Jones bill may have had to do with his own financial interests as much, if not more, than the interests of the non-Christian Filipinos. He closed his lecture by saying, modestly: "Now, it has been alleged that when I begin talking about the hill people I lack 'terminal facilities,' and I fear some of you must feel by this term that such is the case, so I will not further impose on your time, although there are many more things I would like to tell you. I will simply thank you for your very kind attention and close."[73]

The next day, Worcester returned to the committee to resume his testimony. In his opening remarks, Senator Hitchcock brushed off Worcester's lecture: "Dr. Worcester, you gave us yesterday a very interesting review of what the islands had been and what they are now. Will you now please take up H.R. 18459 [i.e., the Jones bill], and give us your opinion upon it and any suggestion of a change that you may have?"[74] Not surprisingly, Worcester was opposed to the bill, both in terms of its preamble stating that the United States would guarantee independence to the Philippines in the future, and in terms of certain details about how the Philippine legislature would be constituted and financed.

Hitchcock asked, "Suppose independence should be given the Filipinos within a few years. What do you think would actually happen?" Worcester responded with a grim prediction:

I think that what would happen would be that there would be a quarrel for offices in the first instance; that elections would soon become farcical; that within a comparatively short time the different political

factions would become so at outs with each other that armed viola-
tions of public order would result; that we would soon have a state of
bloodshed and anarchy and that not very long after complete independence had been granted there would occur aggressions against
foreigners owing to the disturbance of the public order; that these
aggressions would be of such a nature as to justify foreign intervention and would be made the basis for such intervention; and that the
islands would be taken possession of by some foreign power or powers
beyond peradventure of doubt.[75]

By "foreigners," Worcester was implying the American population in
the Philippines, which was the largest population of foreigners. Consequently, the "foreign intervention" would likely be American in order
to protect the American population there. Best, then, to just keep the
Philippines in the possession of the United States in order to forestall
such a dire scenario.

During the course of his testimony, Worcester again resorted to racial-
ist arguments to explain why the Philippines would not be ready for independence for at least a generation, reiterating some of the inflammatory
remarks that he made during his 1910 speech at the Manila YMCA. Pos-
iting the Moros as separate from and antagonistic to the Philippine state,
he sounded a warning about violence erupting internally in the Philippines: "The Moros do not hesitate to say to people they know well, and
sometimes they do not hesitate to say in public, that they would resume
their attacks on the Filipinos if an attempt were made on the part of the
Filipinos to govern them. And my own belief is that it would be wholly
impossible for the Filipinos to govern them in their own country."[76]

Worcester's testimony made an impact on at least some of those present in the committee chambers. Douglas O. Morgan, a stenographer
retained by the committee, transcribed Worcester's lecture. In a letter
that he sent to Worcester in order to verify the accuracy of his notes,
Morgan observed that Worcester was "a very rapid speaker" but that he
took care to make sure that he accurately recorded Worcester's words.
That letter, dated January 13, 1915, was sent to Worcester in care of "The
Bukidnon Company," located at the same address in New York that earlier letters to the Philippine Lyceum Bureau and the American-Philippine
Company were sent.[77] In his response to Morgan, Worcester expressed
his appreciation for the accuracy of Morgan's transcription and further
explained his rationale for using his slides in his testimony: "I have always
considered it impossible to get anything approaching a connected and

intelligible statement from a lecture of this sort because I depend so much on slides to emphasize and illustrate, and even to make, my point." He concluded his letter with a prediction as to Morgan's (and his own) contributions to American understandings of the Philippines: "With a little trimming up, which I gave it, I think your report of this lecture will be really useful to those who read it, and I am both surprised and greatly pleased at the result."[78]

When details of Worcester's testimony reached the Philippines, his supporters there were thrilled at what he had said before the Senate Committee. John R. Wilson, the former assistant director of lands (Wilson resigned his position in 1913), wrote Worcester a letter praising Worcester's words. Wilson, at that point working as an official with the Visayan Refining Company, a subsidiary of the American-Philippine Company, fairly gushed with excitement and bravado in his February 15 letter: "It is only just now that we are getting any full reports on what you and Mr. Taft had to say. As far as your testimony was concerned it is true that nearly everyone says, 'Hell yes! We knew what he would say.'" Wilson went on: "There is no denying the truth of what you both said. We know what the result would be withing [sic] thirty days of the first elections. It seems, however, that most of our people in the States are from Missouria [sic] they insist on being shown." He shrugged off the condemnation of Worcester's testimony by Philippine newspapers, saying that "we could expect no more" than such hostility.[79]

Wilson also struck a pugilistic tone in defending Worcester from attacks by other Americans in Manila: "I heard a few days ago that a man named LaPoint had made the statement that he would do everything in his power to rid the islands of you or your influence. He is reported as having said that he would even go so far as to use personal violence to obtain the result." Wilson told Worcester that he had run into LaPoint and asked the man to either confirm or deny what he was reported to have said. LaPoint refused to do so, and Wilson let him know that he was willing to impart violence against LaPoint in Worcester's name: "That he made the statement, I have no doubt. That he will be a little more discreet in the future, I also have no doubt."[80]

ALTHOUGH IT IS IMPOSSIBLE to know precisely how much impact any given photograph has on a viewer, unless that viewer states directly that he or she was swayed by the image, it is undeniable that Worcester's deluge of images of non-Christian Filipinos into American society, particularly in the years between 1911 and 1914, helped shape many Americans' attitudes about the Philippines. Blount recognized this, as his criticism of "Worcester kodaks" reveals. However, assessing the precise influence of Worcester's photographs in the debates about Philippine independence has to be done cautiously, by looking at some of the reactions to him and his photographs. Rodney Sullivan credits Worcester's lectures with having "an undoubted impact on American public opinion." In addition: "To Worcester must go some of the credit for the failure in 1913 of the Democratic congressional majority to make good its platform pledge on Philippine independence."[81] Perhaps. His images certainly played a role in the debate; whether they directly influenced the outcome of the Jones bill is probably unknowable.

What is known, though, is that when the Jones bill was finally signed into law as the Philippine Autonomy Act of 1916 (Jones Act), there was no longer any promise of Philippine independence within a particular timeframe. Indeed, the Philippines did not gain its independence until 1946. The Jones Act provided for an elected Philippine Senate as a replacement to the Philippine Commission (though with appointed senators for the non-Christian Filipinos), with the U.S.-appointed governor-general maintaining veto power. In, addition, certain privileges were maintained for American business interests in the Philippines. Such privileges benefited Worcester's interests in coconut oil production and cattle ranching, interests that he maintained until his death in 1924.

Evidence that Worcester's photographs helped delineate the contours of the debate over independence can be seen in a variety of places, including the testimony of other individuals before the Senate Committee, and the efforts to suppress Worcester's images after he resigned from the Philippine Commission. For example, in an exchange between the committee members and General Frank McIntyre, the chief of the Bureau of Insular Affairs, the question of clothing came up. As discussed in chapter 2, Worcester's photographs routinely made the connection between clothing and civilization, and nakedness and savagery. While discussing population estimates in the Philippines based on Worcester's numbers, Rhode Island Republican senator Henry F. Lippitt suddenly asked McIntyre: "Now, how do the people dress in the Philippine Islands? Are there any considerable number that are practically without clothes?" There followed this exchange:

> GEN. MCINTYRE: Only among the wild people, and among those the dress varies somewhat with the section and the tribe. The people in the mountains of Luzon— the men wear very little clothing; the women are modest.

SENATOR LIPPITT: The same as the people in the tropical countries of India and Ceylon?

GEN. MCINTYRE: Yes; the women are modestly clothed.

SENATOR LIPPITT: What does that mean, "modestly clothed"?

GEN. MCINTYRE: I mean they cover those parts which we usually regard the exposure of as immodest.

The exchange continued on, pulling in the clothing of the Moros and the question of whether or not children in the Philippines routinely go without clothing.[82]

Sensing that Lippitt wanted to drive home the argument that states of undress in the Philippines reflected states of savagery, an argument Worcester made repeatedly, Colorado's Democratic senator, John Shafroth, jumped in: "In China, in Hongkong, in Shanghai, and even in Japan, is it not a fact that the people who work on the streets have no clothing on at all except a breech clout?" McIntyre responded that that was "quite true." Pressing the matter further, Shafroth asked: "And is it not a fact that the people of the Philippine Islands wear as much clothing, if not more, than the people of the same latitude over in Asia?" Lippitt, perhaps recognizing that he was losing his intended point of demonstrating the uncivilized nature of the Philippines through their lack of clothing, abandoned the subject and moved on to other topics.[83]

In his testimony before the committee, Philippine vice-governor Henderson Martin criticized efforts by Worcester and others to use non-Christian Filipinos in order to represent the nation as a whole:

The Igorots live in the mountains on the island of Luzon. The men wear what is known as a G string; that is, a thing like a towel that they wrap once around their waists, and then finally between their legs, and that is all they wear. They are frequently exhibited as specimens of the Filipinos. Then there is another tribe of little men, the Negritos, who evidently belong to some other wave, which live in some other mountains. They are shy men. If they hear you coming or see you coming they leave their villages and hide in the hills or woods. They are sometimes shown as representing the Filipinos. It would be just as fair to exhibit a Pueblo Indian as a representative of the people of the United States as to exhibit a Negrito or any of those other non-Christian tribes as samples of the Filipino people."[84]

Manuel Quezon, then serving as resident commissioner from the Philippines, also recognized the political influence of Worcester's photographs of non-Christian Filipinos. In a speech delivered in Cleveland on April 14, 1914, Quezon described the obstacles to independence that his nation faced, and he saw photography as one of those obstacles. As Rodney Sullivan points out, Quezon seemed to be referring to Worcester when he "denounced the political message" of photographs such as those in Worcester's *National Geographic* articles, as well as Worcester's film, *Native Life in the Philippines*.[85] Taking on the voice of a retentionist for rhetorical purposes, Quezon said:

> The masses of the people in the Philippines are in such a state of dense ignorance that they know nothing and care less about independence. Those people are semicivilized, if not entirely savages. Some of them eat dogs, and for proof we refer you to the St. Louis Exposition, where Igorots were exhibited engaged in that toothsome pastime. As further proof of the deplorable condition of those people behold the "moving" and "nonmoving" pictures of naked natives armed with bows and arrows and spears. It would be a pity to see this people adrift. The Government of the United States alone can civilize them, and it must for the sake of humanity, undertake and carry to its successful termination this altruistic work.[86]

In the Philippines, too, a Philippine legislature emboldened by the new colonial policies brought in by the Wilson administration sought to limit the impact of Worcester's photographs in the public sphere. In October 1913, the Philippine Assembly proposed an ordinance that would prevent anyone from appearing on the streets of Manila unless fully dressed. One newspaper article covering the proposal wrote: "[T]he passage of such an ordinance will mean the end to the sight of three-quarters naked men running on the streets of Manila with loads on their backs. The Chinese with the bared torso will be a thing of the past, and tourists will effect a savings in photographic film."[87]

Discussions of the impact of Worcester's photographs circulated through the Manila newspapers. For example, in December 1913, one newspaper discussed the editorial of a different newspaper, an editorial that demanded that the Philippine "Assembly should step to the front and take up the question of the establishment of a publicity bureau in the United States, for the purposes of offsetting and retarding the progress of the tactics followed by the enemies of the Filipino people." Quoting from the editorial, Worcester emerged as the central "enemy" in question: "Worcester himself, with the fierce look of a promoter or an explorer of virgin soils, appears with an aborigin [*sic*] by his side. At the foot of this photograph attention is called to the difference in stature between the two, which must indeed stir the vain heart of that great actor called Worcester. . . . In the face of such facts, do not the leaders of the people think that the time has come for action?"[88]

Two months later, in February 1914, the same month that Worcester published *The Philippines Past and Present,* began advertising his film, *Native Life in the Philippines,* and was in the thick of his lecture engagements, the Philippine Assembly passed a bill that prohibited the taking, exhibiting, possessing, or using of any photographs of nude or seminude Filipinos. In what appears to be a passage aimed squarely at Worcester, one newspaper article read: "Woe betide the amateur or professional photographer who dares to take a picture of Igorot, and Ilongot, Negrito, Tinguiane, or any member of the non or semi-civilized tribe of the Philippines, of a Christian Filipina woman bathing in the river semi or entirely nude, or of a rice-bellied Filipino youngster, or of any subject in the nude, semi-nude and not altogether clothed." The article went on to explain the rationale for the bill: "It was argued that such pictures tended to make it appear that the Philippines were inhabited by people in the nude. That people in Europe and in the United States where such pictures were circulated might go away with the opinion that the members of the August Assembly gather to legislate in the typical make up of the well known 'Senator from Bontoc,'" a reference to the photograph seen in figure 24 above.[89]

A different article was even more explicit in condemning Worcester's photographic legacy. Quoting an editorial in a rival newspaper that discussed an exhibit organized by Dr. Victor Heiser, the director of health in the Philippines, the article read, in part: "The impression we had of the recent health exhibit of the recent Philippine exposition is that Dr. Heiser is a worthy disciple of 'non-Christian' Worcester, in his abhorrent propaganda which tends to make the people of the United States believe that the Filipinos are still in a semi-civilized state, gee-stringed and without any idea of hygiene and the other benefits of civilized life. . . . An unpopular government official such as Doctor Heiser can never be as efficient, despite his good work, as an official who enjoys the esteem and cooperation of the people."[90]

In his Senate testimony, Worcester drew attention to these efforts to suppress his photographs: "[W]e have twice had bills passed by the lower house intended to make it a criminal offense for any person to take a photograph of those fellows up in the hills. The Filipinos want to conceal the very fact of the existence of such people. The Government photographer [i.e., Charles Martin] who took the pictures that I am now using to illustrate conditions in the Philippines has left his position, under pressure, since I retired; and there has been agitation in favor of the destruction of the whole series of Government negatives showing the customs of the non-Christian people, the conditions which we found among them and the conditions which prevail to-day."[91]

As Worcester prepared to continue with more general remarks regarding the political pressures that Governor-General Harrison faced in the Philippines, he was interrupted by Senator Lippitt: "You say they propose the destruction of the pictures showing the conditions that prevailed when you went there and those showing the conditions to-day?" Worcester: "Yes, sir; the whole series." Lippitt: "Do you mean that they do not want the proofs of the improvement to be in existence?" Worcester: "They just want the whole series of negatives blotted out, because it shows the fact of the existence of such people there." Senator Coe Crawford, Republican from South Dakota, then chimed in: "In other words, they would like to have us in the United States simply consider that class who make the best showing in intelligence and education and forget that there are any others over there except them?" Worcester: "Undoubtedly, sir, that is true. It is a natural attitude on their part; we can not wonder at it at all; but that is the case."[92]

The repercussions of the efforts to suppress Worcester's photographs resulted in Winfred Denison, Worcester's successor as secretary of the interior, making an attempt to clarify the situation in his first annual report, which covered July 1, 1913 to December 31, 1914: "Rumors which appear to have been current in America that the bureau's [i.e., Bureau of Science] collection of photographs has been impaired are entirely without basis." He insisted that "[n]ot a single photograph, negative, or film has been destroyed or disturbed," but he also conceded that "[c]ertain pictures have been withdrawn from general public sale for reasons which would be evident to anyone who inspected them, but even these are still available to applicants who have a legitimate claim." At the same time, however, Denison acknowledged that "ethnological research, with its attendant photography and publications" had been eliminated because "the ethnological research already made, and the publications and photographs connected with it are already sufficient for the necessities of practical administration over the non-Christians."[93] In an oblique reference to the magnitude of the changes taking place in the Department of the Interior, Denison noted the resignation of Martin, saying only that Martin left his position "to enter private business."[94]

Despite Denison's protestations that Worcester's photographic archive had been left undisturbed, he had already made known his plans to undo much of Worcester's work. As Paul Kramer writes: "On June 30, 1914, Denison laid out his plan to reverse Worcester's non-Christian policy in an address at the City Club of Manila. The crux of the speech was that Filipinos' taxes were being misspent on priorities that did not benefit them. To make his point about fiscal irresponsibility clear, Denison ridiculed two classic Worcesterian projects: the expense of 500 pesos 'for the photographing of molluscs' and of 14,000 pesos 'for printing the results of ethnological research into the habits of the Bukidnons and other non-Christian tribes.'"[95]

Other criticisms of Worcester's photographs continued to appear even after he withdrew from his active campaign against Philippine independence and returned to the Philippines in 1915 to attend to his business interests. In 1916, Maximo Kalaw's book *The Case for the Filipino* was published in the United States, the first book written in English by a Filipino. (Kalaw was Manuel Quezon's secretary.) In places the book reads like a direct response to Worcester's uses of photography to shape American ideas about the Philippines. For example, in a discussion about how retentionists portrayed the Philippines to the American public, Kalaw wrote:

> Many of these publicity agents have gone to the extreme of deliberately misrepresenting conditions in the Philippines, slandering the entire Filipino people, and picturing them as a mere conglomeration of contemptible savage tribes separated from one another by age-long jealousies and hatred. . . . There was hardly a magazine in the Union which did not embellish its pages with photographs of "head-hunters," directly or indirectly conveying to the lay mind that they were typical Filipinos. There was hardly a newspaper that did not open its columns to bizarre stories of the wonderful transformation of these savage Filipinos that was being wrought. American audiences have been regaled with the same stories, supplemented by pictures and told with more vividness, even with the glamour of romance, because the lecturer himself had been on the scene of action and had participated in the great enterprise![96]

Kalaw specifically mentioned Worcester's 1912 article in *National Geographic*, where Worcester placed at the very end of the article a disclaimer about the representativeness of the non-Christians for the country as a whole: "Worcester knows full well that 90 per cent. of the American readers would not stop to read those lines but would be content with reading the legends below the pictures, all of which are likenesses of savage men. It should be further noticed that these illustrations were published at a time when the American people were weighing the capabilities and characteristics of the Filipino people. It is so often seen that by innuendoes you can calumniate an entire people!"[97]

MUCH LIKE IT IS IMPOSSIBLE to pinpoint the degree to which Worcester's photographs influenced American politics, it is unclear precisely how effective the goal was of suppressing Worcester's photographs from public view. On the one hand, Martin was forced from his position as government photographer in 1914, effectively ending the Worcester-era photographic tradition of representing Filipinos, at least in official photographs of the Philippines. Amateur photographs and photographers in private practice were also pressured to change their subject matter, some of which included photographs of partially, or fully, nude Filipinos, often taken for the postcard trade. Evidence for this change in photographic practices can be found in a 1914 letter to Worcester from an unidentified individual that reads, in part: "I think I shall have to sell my camera, as with the restriction limiting the taking of pictures to persons fully clothed, there is not much left to take except a few politicians and students and no one wants their pictures anyway."[98]

On the other hand, the outbreak of World War I in 1914 helped turn American attention away from the Philippines regardless of any new standards for taking photographs. After Worcester's 1913 *National Geographic* article, no articles about the Philippines appeared in the magazine until 1930. Worcester himself felt the attention that he had been able to attract begin to slip away after the war began. A few months before the assassination of Archduke Ferdinand, Worcester had his article, "The Suppression of Involuntary Slavery in the Philippines," accepted by the prestigious weekly magazine *The Independent*. On October 23, 1914, the magazine's editor, Hamilton Holt, wrote Worcester an apologetic letter, saying that the he had hoped to publish the article at that point but that it had "been held over from week to week and now we have no idea when we can print it—probably not until the end of the war."[99] That article was to be the second of three Worcester articles published by *The Independent*. As it turned out, however, only the first, "Dangers of the Present Philippine Situation," was published, in February 1914.[100]

The only other articles that Worcester published between his return to the Philippines in 1915 and his death in 1924 were a two-page article about a bird nesting site he found on the island of Mindoro, published in the *Philippine Journal of Science* in 1919,[101] and a contribution to the popular booklet series, *The Mentor,* with its motto, "Learn One Thing At a Time." His article in *The Mentor* came with a number of photographic prints suitable for framing, including the image of General Aguinaldo and Frank Crone standing in front of corn. The article itself was a general overview of geographical and social conditions in the Philippines. It, too, contained many of Worcester's photographs, including the one of him standing next to Ibag, taken in 1901, and photographs contrasting "old style" and "new style" Bukidnon houses.[102]

When widespread American interest in the Philippines began to reemerge during World War II with the Japanese conquest of the Philippines, Worcester's photographs were turned to for republishing. Several of his photographs were used in *Peoples of the Philippines,* a 1942 report written by Herbert W. Krieger as part of the Smithsonian Institution's "War Background Studies" series. According to the anthropologist David Price, the twenty-one volumes published in the series provided "brief synopses of culture areas that were of importance during the war, written for a general, educated audience."[103] Price says that Kreiger's report provided good basic background information "for individuals who knew nothing about the Philippines."[104] However, the Worcester photographs included in Kreiger's report were nearly forty years old at that point, and nowhere does Kreiger discuss that many of the photographs may not have accurately reflected the current lives and cultures of the peoples shown. More important, Kreiger reasserted Worcester's argument about the fundamental diversity of the Philippines, as the plates included in his book include photographs of Gaddang, Tagbanua, Bontoc Igorot, Negrito, Kalinga, Tingian, Ilongot, Moro, and Bagobo individuals, along with only two photographs of Tagalogs.

The post-Philippines career of Charles Martin is another indication of Worcester's enduring influence. After his resignation as government photographer in 1914, Martin became the head of the photography lab at *National Geographic,* where he worked for more than twenty years. Worcester helped Martin secure his position at the National Geographic Society. On August 13, 1914, Worcester wrote a letter to Gilbert Grosvenor: "I have just learned that Mr. Charles Martin, the government photographer at Manila, has 'resigned' his position. From previous correspondence I am led to believe that there is little doubt that his resignation was forced." The letter continued: "The Filipinos have been after him for half a year or more because he took the pictures which I used, in part, in illustrating my Geographic Magazine article as well as many of those from which my lantern slides were made. He also made my motion picture film doing the work for me when he was on vacation leave." After assuring Grosvenor of Martin's "very exceptional ability" as a photographer," he made his pitch: "I want to do what I can to see that he obtains profitable employment as soon as possible. . . . It occurs to me that you might possibly be in a position to make some suggestions as to where a man of his exceptional ability might seek employment with a reasonable prospect of finding it."[105]

A week later, Worcester received a response from John La Gorce, the associate editor at the magazine (and the man who proclaimed in 1915 that photography was a "universal language"). La Gorce wrote: "The suggestion about Mr. Martin is a good one, and the mere fact that he took your pictures is sufficient recommendation as to his ability." Telling Worcester that Grosvenor was on a trip to Nova Scotia, he assured him that "I shall bring the matter to Mr. Grosvenor's attention just as soon as he comes back."[106] By the end of 1915, Martin was at his new job, where he remained for more than two decades.

During his long career at *National Geographic,* Martin was in a position to influence the expansion to other parts of the world of the American colonial aesthetic that he and Worcester helped to develop in the Philippines. A significant part of that aesthetic includes the bare breasts of "exotic" women. As Catherine Lutz and Jane Collins bluntly put it in their 1993 book, *Reading National Geographic:* "Nothing defines the *National Geographic* for most older American readers more than its 'naked' women."[107] More specifically: "The *Geographic* nude is first and foremost, in readers' attention, a set of breasts."[108] In other words, *National Geographic's* signature image became the "bare brown bosoms" of Nerissa Balce's analysis, "the markers of savagery [and] colonial desire"[109] that were established as a norm in the magazine through the photographs of Worcester and Martin, and then applied to other sites of exotic interest found around the world.

At the same time, Worcester's photographs continued to circulate through multiple printings of his own books and through the inclusion of his images in books by other historians. In his classic work, *Facing West: The Metaphysics of Indian Hating and Empire Building,* historian Richard Drinnon says that *The Philippines Past and Present* "became a reprinted standard reference work, and helped shape policy in the islands when Republicans came back into power in the 1920s."[110] Sullivan concurs, noting both the number of editions the book went through, and the influence of Worcester's book on other writers, including D. R. Williams, whose 1926 book, *The United States and the Philippines,* "drew heavily and uncritically on it for pronouncements on Filipino ineptitude and America's altruistically constructive role in the archipelago." Sullivan also points to a 1976 statement made by the long-serving American diplomat Lewis Gleeck that "described *Philippines Past and Present* as the 'most authoritative' work on the American regime written prior to 1914."[111]

Then, too, there were books written for popular audiences that based their material on *The Philippines Past and Present,* such as Samuel Kane's *Thirty Years with the Philippine Head-Hunters,* published in 1934. Some of the material in Kane's book was clearly "borrowed" from Worcester, and Kane included photographs taken from the Worcester archive. Worcester's photographs found their way into other books, too, including Mabel Cooke Cole and Fay-Cooper Cole's *The Story of Primitive Man,* which included some of Worcester's photographs of Negritos taken in Mariveles, Bataan, in 1901, and some of his photographs of Bagobos. The photos in their book are credited to Chicago's Field Museum, which had reproduced them from Edward Ayer's collection purchased in 1905.[112] There is also a book called *The Secret Museum of Mankind,* described by one observer as "a mystery book. It has no author or credits, no date, no page numbers, no index. . . . This was not a book published to educate (despite appearing on some public library's shelves), but to titillate (literally)—it's [*sic*] emphasis was on the female form ('Female Beauty Round the World') and fashion, and it featured as many National-Geographic-style native breasts as possible."[113] First published in 1935, this book, too, included several Worcester photographs.[114]

SOME SCHOLARS, such as Alfred McCoy, have argued that Worcester's photography amounted to little more than voyeurism, if not "outright pornography."[115] In contrast to Worcester, McCoy writes that the photographs of Albert Jenks, the author of the 1905 publication *The Bontoc Igorot,* the first volume of the Ethnological Surveys published by the Bureau of Non-Christian Tribes, were "far more humane and dignified than Worcester's racist photographs." McCoy also argues that "Jenks did more to create lasting images of the Philippines and Filipinos than any American scholar of his generation," during Jenks's long career teaching anthropology at the University of Minnesota. While Jenks may have had more influence than any other *scholar,* McCoy's interpretation of Jenks and Worcester ignores the very real role that Worcester's images had in influencing American public opinion about the Philippines. Given the reach of Worcester's articles, books, lectures, and films, he had as big a role, if not a bigger role, than Jenks did in creating "lasting images of the Philippines and Filipinos" in the American imagination.

McCoy also overstates the degree of difference between Worcester's and Jenks's ethnological photographs. While there undoubtedly are many examples of photographs in the Worcester archive that can only be classified as pornographic, such photographs are far outnumbered by Worcester's ethnological images, images that bear few stylistic differences to Jenks's or Martin's ethnological images. Recall that Jenks's 1907 review of Worcester's article in the *Philippine Journal of Science* (discussed in chapter 1) lauded Worcester's photographs. In addition, Jenks's 1905 book contained photographs from all three men, and Jenks may well have shown Worcester's and Martin's photographs alongside his own in his academic lectures.

Worcester's photographs can be understood as being more than just evidence of erotic voyeurism or colonial desire when we acknowledge the reach of his images—his illustrated government reports, his articles in *National Geographic* and elsewhere, his lecture tour, his film *Native Life in the Philippines,* and his book *The Philippines Past and Present.* The scope of his reach and the fact that Worcester presented one of his slide lectures to a U.S. Senate committee debating Philippine independence makes it apparent that Worcester's photography was recognized in his day as integral to American understandings of the Philippines. His influence is underscored by the fact that Manuel Quezon spoke out against Worcester's photographs in a speech inserted into the *Congressional Record* and that the Philippine legislature passed bills banning photographs of a type that Worcester helped make popular. Worcester's images played a central and calculated role in shaping the political debates over the relationship between the United States and the Philippines. For good or for ill, his photographs influenced American perceptions of the Philippines through much of the twentieth century. That, perhaps more than anything else, is "the truth" that Worcester's camera "can be made to tell."

Notes

Chapter One

1. "Memorandum for Use in Connection With Lecture delivered at the Grand Opera House, Manila, on January 20, 1913." (Dean C. Worcester Papers, Box 2, Bentley Historical Library, University of Michigan.)

2. The term "non-Christian" (a rough translation of the Spanish *infiel*) was used routinely by Worcester and other members of the U.S. colonial regime to refer both to Muslim Filipinos and to animist cultural minority groups found in the Philippines. See Paul A. Kramer, *The Blood of Government: Race, Empire, the United States, and the Philippines* (Chapel Hill: University of North Carolina Press, 2006), 211.

3. Kramer's book does an excellent job analyzing the intersections of race and U.S. colonialism in the Philippines.

4. A brief explanation of how the museum acquired the collection is included in "The Dean C. Worcester Photographic Collection at the U-M Museum of Anthropology," http://webapps.lsa.umich.edu/umma/exhibits/Worcester%202012/collection.html.

5. Satadru Sen, "Savage Bodies, Civilized Pleasures: M. V. Portman and the Andamanese," *American Ethnologist* 36, no. 2 (2009): 365.

6. Sen, 365.

7. Christopher Pinney, "The Parallel Histories of Anthropology and Photography," in *Anthropology and Photography,* ed. Elizabeth Edwards (New Haven: Yale University Press, 1992), 76.

8. Eleanor M. Hight and Gary D. Sampson, introduction to *Colonialist Photography: Imag(in)ing Race and Place* (New York: Routledge, 2002), 9–10.

9. "Of Scientific Interest: Results of the Menage Expedition to the Philippine Islands," *New York Times,* March 22, 1896.

10. For a biographical overview of Worcester's life, see Ralston Hayden's "Biographical Sketch" in the 1930 edition of Worcester's book, *The Philippine Past and Present.* For an account of Worcester's career in the Philippines, see Rodney Sullivan,

Exemplar of Americanism: The Philippine Career of Dean C. Worcester (Ann Arbor: University of Michigan Center for South and Southeast Asian Studies, 1991). For other analyses of Worcester, see chapter 6 of Arthur S. Pier, *American Apostles to the Philippines* (Boston: Beacon Press, 1950), chapter 20 of Richard Drinnon, *Facing West: The Metaphysics of Indian Hating and Empire Building* (New York: Schocken Books, 1990), and chapter 5 of Peter W. Stanley, ed., *Reappraising an Empire: New Perspectives on Philippine-American History* (Cambridge: Harvard University Press, 1984).

11. Dean C. Worcester and Frank S. Bourns, "Spanish Rule in the Philippines," *Cosmopolitan,* October 1897, 587–600.

12. Sullivan, 32.

13. Quoted in Sullivan, 34.

14. Dean C. Worcester, *The Philippine Islands and Their People* (New York: Macmillan, 1898), 482.

15. Worcester, *Philippine Islands,* 115.

16. According to Sullivan (36–39), the exact circumstances surrounding that meeting remain somewhat murky.

17. Dean C. Worcester to M. Douglas Flattery, November 13, 1912. (Dean C. Worcester Papers, Box 1, Bentley Historical Library, University of Michigan.)

18. Dean C. Worcester to Nanon Leas Worcester, February 11, 1899. (Dean C. Worcester Papers, Thetford Historical Society.)

19. Sullivan, 61.

20. Dean C. Worcester to Nanon Leas Worcester, February 14, 1899. (Dean C. Worcester Papers, Thetford Historical Society.)

21. Dean C. Worcester, *The Philippines Past and Present* (New York: Macmillan Company, 1914), 1.

22. Dean C. Worcester to Nanon Leas Worcester, Feb. 14, 1899.

23. Dean C. Worcester to Nanon Leas Worcester, Feb. 14, 1899.

24. Dean C. Worcester to Nanon Leas Worcester, February 16, 1899. (Dean C. Worcester Papers, Thetford Historical Society.).

25. Dean C. Worcester to Nanon Leas Worcester, February 18, 1899. (Dean C. Worcester Papers, Thetford Historical Society.).

26. Dean C. Worcester to Nanon Leas Worcester, Feb. 18, 1899.

27. Dean C. Worcester to Nanon Leas Worcester, Feb. 18, 1899.

28. Dean C. Worcester to Nanon Leas Worcester, February 23, 1899. (Dean C. Worcester Papers, Thetford Historical Society.)

29. Dean C. Worcester to Nanon Leas Worcester, Feb. 23, 1899.

30. Dean C. Worcester to Nanon Leas Worcester, Feb. 23, 1899.

31. Dean C. Worcester to Nanon Leas Worcester, March 11, 1899. (Dean C. Worcester Papers, Thetford Historical Society.)

32. Dean C. Worcester to Nanon Leas Worcester, March 17, 1899. (Dean C. Worcester Papers, Thetford Historical Society.)

33. Dean C. Worcester to Mrs. E. H. Worcester, April 17, 1899. (Dean C. Worcester Papers, Thetford Historical Society.)

34. Dean C. Worcester to Mrs. E. H. Worcester, March 8, 1899. (Dean C. Worcester Papers, Thetford Historical Society.)

35. Worcester, *Philippine Islands,* 462.

36. Worcester, *Philippine Islands,* 467.

37. Sullivan, 22.

38. Worcester, *Philippine Islands,* 501.

39. Worcester, *Philippine Islands,* 502.

40. Whenever possible, I will give the UMMA designation for specific photographs that I discuss.

41. Dean C. Worcester to Mrs. E. H. Worcester, Mar. 8, 1899.

42. Dean C. Worcester to Nanon Leas Worcester, March 11, 1899. (Dean C. Worcester Papers, Thetford Historical Society.)

43. Dean C. Worcester to Nanon Leas Worcester, March 20, 1899. (Dean C. Worcester Papers, Thetford Historical Society.)

44. Sullivan, 85.

45. Dean C. Worcester, *Some Aspects of the Philippine Question* (Chicago: Hamilton Club of Chicago Serial Publications, no. 13, 1900), 24–25.

46. For the complicated history of the use of "tribes" in the Philippine context, see Kramer, especially 211–214.

47. Dean C. Worcester to Mrs. E. H. Worcester, December 21, 1899. (Dean C. Worcester Papers, Thetford Historical Society.)

48. Sullivan, 88.

49. Dean C. Worcester, "The Native Peoples of the Philippines," *Report of the Philippine Commission,* pt. 1 (Washington: Government Printing Office, 1900), 11–12.

50. Kramer, 122–23.

51. "Prof. Worcester to Teach No More." *New York Times,* March 15, 1900.

52. Worcester, *Philippine Islands,* 75.

53. Dean C. Worcester to W. H. Holmes, June 18, 1902. (USNM/Department of Anthropology, National Anthropological Archives, Smithsonian National Museum of Natural History, Manuscript and Pamphlet File, Box 71-A, folder 767.)

54. Worcester to Holmes, June 18, 1902.

55. "Museum Notes," *American Museum Journal* 4, no. 4 (1904): 84–85.

56. Ricardo Punzalan recently completed his PhD dissertation from the University of Michigan on the possibility of virtually reunifying all of the archives, which might allow for a more complete count of the images as well as provide a methodology for identifying the overlaps and gaps between them.

57. UMMA Photography and Archive Collections website, http://www.lsa.umich.edu/umma/collections/photographyandarchivecollections.

58. Dean Worcester to Elmer E. Silver, November 11, 1914. (Dean C. Worcester Papers, Box 1, Bentley Historical Library, University of Michigan.)

59. Worcester, *Philippines Past and Present,* 13.

60. William Cameron Forbes, *Journal,* IV: 375. (W. Cameron Forbes Papers, 1900–1946 MS Am 1365, Houghton Library, Harvard University).

61. Sullivan, 98.

62. Dean C. Worcester, "Report of the Secretary of the Interior," *Report of the Philippine Commission, 1901* (Washington, D.C.: Government Printing Office, 1902), 35–36.

63. David P. Barrows, *Instructions for Volunteer Field Workers* (Manila: Bureau of Non-Christian Tribes for the Philippine Islands, 1901), 3.

64. Barrows, 3.

65. Mary Jane B. Rodriguez, "Reading a Colonial Bureau: The Politics of Cultural Investigation of the Non-Christian Filipinos," *Social Science Diliman* 6, no. 1 (2010): 8. In his 1911 article in *National Geographic Magazine,* Worcester repudiated Blumen-

tritt's "extraordinarily incorrect statements relative to the non-Christian people of" the Philippines, particularly in regards to how many "tribes" there were in northern Luzon (215).

66. Barrows, 12.

67. Rodriguez, 11.

68. Paul C. Freer, "Report of the Superintendent of Government Laboratories for the Year Ending August 31, 1902," *Report of the Philippine Commission, 1902* (Washington, D.C.: Government Printing Office, 1903), 546.

69. Freer, 582.

70. David P. Barrows, "Report of the Chief of the Bureau of Nonchristian Tribes for the Year Ending August 31, 1902," *Report of the Philippine Commission, 1902* (Washington, D.C.: Government Printing Office, 1903), 687.

71. Paul C. Freer, *Description of the New Buildings of the Bureau of Government Laboratories* (Manila: Bureau of Public Printing, 1905), 26.

72. Karl L. Hutterer, "Dean C. Worcester and Philippine Anthropology," *Philippine Quarterly of Culture and Society* 6 (1978): 147.

73. Dean C. Worcester, "Report of the Secretary of the Interior," *Report of the Philippine Commission, 1904,* pt. 2 (Washington, D.C.: Government Printing Office, 1905), 56.

74. Dean C. Worcester, "The Non-Christian Tribes of Northern Luzon," *Philippine Journal of Science* 1, no. 8 (1906): 801.

75. Hutterer, 145–46.

76. Forbes *Journal,* I: 320–22.

77. Hutterer, 146.

78. Dean C. Worcester, "Report of the Secretary of the Interior," *Report of the Philippine Commission, 1907,* pt. 2 (Washington, D.C.: Government Printing Office, 1908), 3.

79. Hutterer, 147.

80. Charles C. Lockwood, *The Life of Edward E. Ayer* (Chicago: A.C. McClurg and Co., 1929), 87.

81. Lockwood, 86. According to Lockwood, "Mr. Worcester had been [in the Philippines] more than ten years" when Ayer visited him (86). This appears to have been a mistake, as other evidence clearly reveals that Worcester sold Ayer the photographs in 1905, just six years after Worcester was appointed to the Schurman Commission.

82. Lockwood, 86–87.

83. Paul C. Freer, "Report of the Director, Bureau of Science," *Report of the Philippine Commission, 1907,* pt. 2 (Washington, D.C.: Government Printing Office, 1908), 178.

84. David P. Barrows, "Second Annual Report of the Chief of the Ethnological Survey for the Philippine Islands," *Report of the Philippine Commission, 1903,* pt. 2 (Washington, D.C.: Government Printing Office, 1904), 789.

85. Dean C. Worcester, *Index to Philippine Photographs,* 1. (Dean C. Worcester Collection of Philippine Photographs, Newberry Library.)

86. Worcester, *Index,* 41.

87. Worcester, *Index,* 55.

88. Worcester, *Index,* 167–68.

89. Worcester, *Index,* 258.

90. Worcester, *Index,* 350.

91. Worcester, *Index,* 360.

92. Paul C. Freer, "Report of the Director, Bureau of Science," *Report of the Philippine Commission, 1906,* pt. 2 (Washington, D.C.: Government Printing Office, 1907), 123.

93. Dean C. Worcester, "Report of the Secretary of the Interior," *Report of the Philippine Commission, 1906,* pt. 2 (Washington, D.C.: Government Printing Office, 1907), 29–30.

94. F. W. Putnam to William Cameron Forbes, May 17, 1905. (Accession File 12–61A, Peabody Museum of Archaeology, Harvard University.)

95. Forbes, *Journal,* II: 121.

96. For more information on the Worcester photographs in this collection, see Jutta Beate Englehard and Stefan Rohde-Enslin, "Kolonialzeitliche Photographien von den Philippinen," *Kölner Museums Bulletin* (April 1997): 34–46.

97. R. S. Offley, "Report of the Governor of Mindoro," *Report of the Philippine Commission, 1907,* pt. 1 (Washington, D.C.: Government Printing Office, 1908), 356.

98. Worcester, "Non-Christian Tribes," 863.

99. Albert Ernest Jenks, review of "The Non-Christian Tribes of the Northern Luzon," by Dean C. Worcester (1906). *American Anthropologist* 9, no. 3 (1907): 587.

100. Jenks, 588.

101. Jenks, 592.

102. Christopher Pinney, *Photography and Anthropology* (London: Reaktion Books, 2011), 28–29.

103. Pinney, 29.

104. Jenks, 592.

105. For more on Worcester's commercial interests in the Philippines, see Sullivan, chapters 8 and 9.

Chapter Two

1. William Cameron Forbes, *Journal,* III: 120. (W. Cameron Forbes Papers, 1900–1946 MS Am 1365, Houghton Library, Harvard University).

2. Forbes, *Journal,* IV: 84.

3. My thanks to Mike Price for bringing this to my attention.

4. In the UMMA archive, this photograph is 01-A-002, with 01-A-001 being a photograph of Ibag posed in the same spot but without Worcester standing next to him.

5. Dean C. Worcester, *Index to Philippine Photographs,* 7. (Dean C. Worcester Collection of Philippine Photographs, Newberry Library.)

6. Vernadette Vicuña Gonzalez, "Headhunter Itineraries: The Philippines as America's Dream Jungle," *Global South* 3, no. 2 (2009): 150.

7. Bonnie M. Miller, *From Liberation to Conquest: The Visual and Popular Cultures of the Spanish-American War of 1898* (Amherst: University of Massachusetts Press, 2011), 213.

8. "Uncle Sam's Ape-Men," *Sunday News (Charleston S.C.),* June 14, 1900, 11.

9. Paul A. Kramer, *The Blood of Government: Race, Empire, the United States, and the Philippines* (Chapel Hill: University of North Carolina Press, 2006), 272.

10. Laura Wexler, *Tender Violence: Domestic Visions in an Age of U.S. Imperialism* (Chapel Hill: University of North Carolina Press, 2000), 270.

11. John F. Kasson, *Houdini, Tarzan, and the Perfect Man: The White Male Body and the Challenge of Modernity in America* (New York: Hill and Wang, 2001), 30.

12. Dean C. Worcester, "Notes and Documents, 1901 January 1–June 30," 79. (Worcester Philippine History Collection, Special Collections Library, University of Michigan.) "Semilla" most likely refers to Valentin Semilla, a local councilman in Mariveles who also accompanied the Negrito delegation to the World's Fair in St. Louis.

13. Worcester, "Notes," 80.

14. Worcester, "Notes," 80–81.

15. Worcester, "Notes," 81.

16. Philippa Levine, "States of Undress: Nakedness and the Colonial Imagination," *Victorian Studies* 50, no. 2 (2008): 194.

17. Levine, 195–96.

18. Worcester, *Index,* 11.

19. Levine, 206.

20. Ruth Barcan, *Nudity: A Cultural Anatomy (Dress, Body, Culture)* (Oxford: Berg, 2004), 143.

21. William A. Ewing, *The Body: Photographs of the Human Form* (San Francisco: Chronicle, 1994), 15.

22. Alison Griffiths, *Wondrous Difference: Cinema, Anthropology, and Turn-of-the-Century Visual Culture* (New York: Columbia University Press, 2002), xx.

23. Elizabeth Mary Holt, *Colonizing Filipinas: Nineteenth Century Representations of the Philippines in Western Historiography* (Manila: Ateneo de Manila University Press, 2002), 111.

24. Nerissa S. Balce, "The Filipina's Breast: Savagery, Docility, and the Erotics of the American Empire," *Social Text* 87 (2006): 89.

25. Balce, 101.

26. Balce, 103.

27. Barcan, 163.

28. Vicente L. Rafael, *White Love and Other Events in Filipino History* (Durham, N.C.: Duke University Press, 2000), 77.

29. Barcan, 17.

30. Dean Worcester, "The Non-Christian Tribes of Northern Luzon," *Philippine Journal of Science* 1, no. 8 (1906): 805.

31. Worcester, "Non-Christian Tribes," 805.

32. Barcan, 138.

33. Worcester, "Non-Christian Tribes," 807.

34. The perception that colonial subjects were "inappropriately" dressed sometimes resulted in discomfort for Europeans (and Americans). See Barcan, 202, note 15.

35. Worcester, "Non-Christian Tribes," 869.

36. Worcester, "Non-Christian Tribes," 820.

37. Worcester, "Notes," 84–85.

38. Worcester, "Notes," 113.

39. List of Photographs Donated by Dean C. Worcester, 1902, Box 71-A, folder 767, USNM/Department of Anthropology, Manuscript and Pamphlet File.

40. Dean Worcester, *The Philippine Islands and Their People* (New York: Macmillan, 1898), 34.

41. In the list of photographs that Worcester sent to Holmes in 1902, Worcester mentions a series of photographs of naked Tagalog men previously sent by Penoyer

L. Sherman, Worcester's former secretary. Those photographs are included in the National Anthropological Archives.

42. Worcester did not sell these photographs to Ayers, and they are not listed in the 1905 *Index*. Somewhat curiously, the photographs are included in the list of photographs Worcester sold to Forbes, but the photographs are not in the collection at the Harvard Peabody Museum. It is unknown whether they ever entered the collection.

43. Worcester, "Notes," 16.

44. It is possible that Worcester believed that the German man would be sympathetic to photographs of naked girls. Included in the UMMA collection is a series of photographs taken of pages torn from a German book, *Archiv für Anthropologie,* that show fully nude girls and young women in poses similar to Worcester's photographs of nude Tagalogs.

45. Albert Ernest Jenks, *The Bontoc Igorot* (Manila: Bureau of Public Printing, 1905), 122.

46. Mertin L. Miller, "Report of the Acting Chief of the Ethnological Survey," *Report of the Philippine Commission, 1904,* pt. 2 (Washington, D.C.: Government Printing Office, 1905), 561.

47. Robert W. Rydell, *All the World's a Fair: Visions of Empire at American International Expositions, 1876–1916* (Chicago: University of Chicago Press, 1984), 172.

48. Miller, 569.

49. Worcester, *Index,* 176.

50. Worcester, *Index,* 170.

51. List of Photographs Donated by Dean C. Worcester, 1902, Box 71-A, folder 767, USNM/Department of Anthropology, Manuscript and Pamphlet File.

52. Worcester, *Index,* 625.

53. Rodney J. Sullivan, *Exemplar of Americanism: The Philippine Career of Dean C. Worcester* (Ann Arbor: University of Michigan Center for South and Southeast Asian Studies, 1991), 231.

54. Dean C. Worcester, "Report of the Secretary of the Interior," *Report of the Philippine Commission, 1910* (Washington, D.C.: Government Printing Office, 1911), 76.

55. Frederick Chamberlin, *The Philippine Problem, 1898–1913* (Boston: Little, Brown, and Company, 1913), opposite page 160.

56. Benito M. Vergara Jr., *Displaying Filipinos: Photography and Colonialism in Early 20th Century Philippines* (Manila: University of the Philippines Press, 1995), 104.

57. Vergara, 106.

58. Eric Breitbart, *A World on Display: Photographs from the St. Louis World's Fair* (Albuquerque: University of New Mexico Press, 1997), 25.

59. Wexler, 271.

60. Rafael, 83.

61. Rafael, 84.

62. Kramer, 320.

63. Worcester, "Notes," 105.

64. Filomeno V. Aguilar Jr., "Tracing Origins: *Ilustrado* Nationalism and the Racial Science of Migration Waves," *Journal of Asian Studies* 64, no. 3 (2005): 614.

65. Kramer, 248–49.

66. Kramer, 72.

67. Jenks, 41–42.

68. Worcester, "Notes," 106.

69. For additional photographs of Muro, see Mark Rice, "His Name Was Don Francisco Muro: Reconstructing an Image of American Imperialism," *American Quarterly* 62, no. 1 (2010): 49–76.

70. Worcester, "Notes," 107.

71. Worcester, "Notes," 108.

72. Worcester, "Notes," 416.

73. Worcester, "Notes," 451.

74. Worcester, "Notes," 462.

75. Worcester, "Notes," 466.

76. Dean C. Worcester, *The Philippines Past and Present* (New York: The Macmillan Company, 1914), 344.

77. The staff at the UMMA has recently digitally overlaid the three photographs in the Igorot sequence. The result makes a compelling argument in favor of all three photographs showing Muro.

78. *Index*, 625.

79. According to the *Index* Worcester prepared for Ayer, by 1905 Muro had "retired from public life." *Index*, 184.

Chapter Three

1. Benito M. Vergara Jr. *Displaying Filipinos: Photography and Colonialism in Early 20th Century Philippines* (Manila: University of the Philippines Press, 1995), 84.

2. Dean C. Worcester, "The Non-Christian Tribes of Northern Luzon," *Philippine Journal of Science* 1, no. 8 (1906): 868.

3. Dean C. Worcester, "The Non-Christian Peoples of the Philippine Islands: With an Account of What Has Been Done to Them Under American Rule," *National Geographic Magazine*, November 1913, 1229.

4. Julie A. Tuason, "The Ideology of Empire in *National Geographic Magazine*'s Coverage of the Philippines, 1898–1908," *Geographical Review* 89, no. 1 (1999): 35.

5. Tuason, 50.

6. Vernadette Vicuña Gonzalez, "Headhunter Itineraries: The Philippines as America's Dream Jungle," *Global South* 3, no. 2 (2009): 155.

7. For more on this, see Paul A. Kramer, *The Blood of Government: Race, Empire, the United States, and the Philippines* (Chapel Hill: University of North Carolina Press, 2006).

8. Richard Ohmann, *Selling Culture: Magazines, Markets, and Class at the Turn of the Century* (New York: Verso, 1998), 29.

9. Matthew Schneirov, *The Dream of a New Social Order: Popular Magazines in America, 1893–1914* (New York: Columbia University Press, 1994), 4.

10. Schneirov, 185.

11. Ohmann, 278.

12. Tamar Y. Rothenberg, *Presenting America's World: Strategies of Innocence in "National Geographic Magazine," 1888–1945* (Burlington, Vt.: Ashgate, 2007), 30

13. Rothenberg, 54.

14. Dean C. Worcester, "Notes on Some Primitive Philippine Tribes," *National Geographic Magazine*, June 1898, 284. Subsequent references will be noted in-text by page number.

15. For a discussion of imperialist nostalgia, see Renato Rosaldo, "Imperialist Nostalgia," *Representations* 26 (1989): 107–22.

16. Gilbert Grosvenor, *The National Geographic Society and Its Magazine* (Washington: National Geographic Society, 1957), 37.

17. Quoted in Grosvenor, 39.

18. Howard S. Abramson. *"National Geographic": Behind America's Lens on the World* (New York: Crown, 1988), 131.

19. Quoted in Catherine A. Lutz and Jane L. Collins, *Reading "National Geographic"* (Chicago: University of Chicago Press, 1993), 28.

20. Dean C. Worcester, *Index to Philippine Photographs,* 75. (Dean C. Worcester Collection of Philippine Photographs, Newberry Library.)

21. "American Development in the Philippines," *National Geographic Magazine,* May 1903, 202.

22. "Benguet—The Garden of the Philippines," *National Geographic Magazine,* May 1903, 209.

23. Grosvenor, 39.

24. Lutz and Collins, 114.

25. Grosvenor, 37.

26. Rothenberg, 57.

27. Kramer, 357. Subscriptions grew from thirty-four hundred to around eleven thousand in 1905. Some historians credit the January 1905 issue, with its eleven pages of photographs taken in Lhasa, Tibet, as being the more important issue in the magazine's adoption of photography.

28. Gonzalez, 154.

29. Vergara, 39.

30. United States Bureau of the Census, *Census of the Philippine Islands,* vol. 2 (Washington, D.C.: Government Printing Office, 1905), 14–15.

31. Vergara, 50.

32. Vergara, 54–55.

33. Quoted in Melissa Banta, "Photographic Encounters in the Philippines, 1898–1910," *IIAS Newsletter* 44 (2007): 14.

34. Vergara, 62.

35. Gilbert H. Grosvenor, ed., preface to *Scenes from Every Land* (Washington: National Geographic Society, 1907), not paginated.

36. Tuason, 39.

37. See Rodney J. Sullivan, *Exemplar of Americanism: The Philippine Career of Dean C. Worcester* (Ann Arbor: Center for South and Southeast Asian Studies, University of Michigan, 1991), especially chapters 8 and 9.

38. H. W. Brands, *Bound to Empire: The United States and the Philippines* (New York: Oxford University Press, 1992), 102.

39. Kramer, 344–45.

40. Charles Martin to Dean Conant Worcester, April 17, 1911. (Dean C. Worcester Papers, Box 1, Bentley Historical Library, University of Michigan.)

41. Charles Martin to Dean Conant Worcester, April 24, 1911. (Dean C. Worcester Papers, Box 1, Bentley Historical Library, University of Michigan.)

42. Dean C. Worcester, "Field Sports Among the Wild Men of Northern Luzon," *National Geographic Magazine,* March 1911, 215. Subsequent references will be noted in-text by page number.

43. Peter W. Stanley, "'The Voice of Worcester Is the Voice of God': How One American Found Fulfillment in the Philippines," in *Reappraising an Empire: New Perspectives on Philippine-American History*, ed. Peter W. Stanley (Cambridge: Harvard University Press, 1984), 141.

44. The photograph included in the *National Geographic* article is not in the UMMA archive, but other photographs from the series are.

45. Vergara, 84.

46. Gonzalez, 155.

47. Gonzalez, 156.

48. Vergara, 8.

49. Dean C. Worcester, "Head-Hunters of Northern Luzon," *National Geographic Magazine*, September 1912, 833. Subsequent references will be noted in-text by page number.

50. *Index*, 85.

51. Gonzalez, 156.

52. Dean Worcester to Edmund Felder, November 14, 1912. (Dean C. Worcester Papers, Box 1, Bentley Historical Library, University of Michigan.)

53. Worcester to Felder, Nov. 14.

54. Dean C. Worcester, "Non-Christian Peoples of the Philippine Islands," 1157. Subsequent references will be noted in-text by page number.

55. Worcester, "Non-Christian Tribes of Northern Luzon," 820.

56. Dean Worcester to Gilbert Grosvenor, November 26, 1913. (Dean C. Worcester Papers, Box 1, Bentley Historical Library, University of Michigan.)

57. Gilbert Grosvenor to Edward H. Fallows, November 19, 1913. (Dean C. Worcester Papers, Box 1, Bentley Historical Library, University of Michigan.)

Chapter Four

1. Paul A. Kramer, *The Blood of Government: Race, Empire, the United States, and the Philippines* (Chapel Hill: University of North Carolina Press, 2006), 368.

2. Rodney J. Sullivan, *Exemplar of Americanism: The Philippine Career of Dean C. Worcester* (Ann Arbor: Center for South and Southeast Asian Studies, University of Michigan, 1991), 169.

3. "Worcester Gives Up Philippines Post," *New York Times*, September 7, 1913.

4. Quoted in Sullivan, 169.

5. "Worcester Gives Up Philippines Post."

6. Dean C. Worcester to Edmund A. Felder, November 14, 1912. (Dean C. Worcester Papers, Box 1, Bentley Historical Library, University of Michigan.)

7. Worcester to Felder, Nov. 14, 1912.

8. Worcester to Felder, Nov. 14, 1912.

9. Worcester to Felder, Nov. 14, 1912.

10. Edmund A. Felder to Dean C. Worcester, February 11, 1913. (Dean C. Worcester Papers, Box 1, Bentley Historical Library, University of Michigan.)

11. Felder to Worcester, Feb. 11, 1913.

12. Dean C. Worcester to M. Douglas Flattery, November 13, 1912. (Dean C. Worcester Papers, Box 1, Bentley Historical Library, University of Michigan.)

13. Worcester to Flattery, Nov. 13, 1912.

14. M. Douglas Flattery to Dean C. Worcester, March 8, 1913. (Dean C. Worcester Papers, Box 1, Bentley Historical Library, University of Michigan.)

15. Flattery to Worcester, March 8, 1913.

16. Dean C. Worcester to M. Douglas Flattery, September 21, 1913. (Dean C. Worcester Papers, Box 1, Bentley Historical Library, University of Michigan).

17. Worcester to Flattery, Sept. 21, 1913.

18. Worcester to Felder, Nov 14, 1912.

19. "Memorandum for Use in Connection With Lecture delivered at the Grand Opera House, Manila, on January 20, 1913." (Dean C. Worcester Papers, Box 2, Bentley Historical Library, University of Michigan.)

20. Michael Salman, *The Embarrassment of Slavery: Controversies over Bondage and Nationalism in the American Colonial Philippines* (Berkeley: University of California Press, 2001), 201.

21. Dean C. Worcester, "The Non-Christian Tribes of the Philippine Islands and What the United States Has Done for Them," 1. (Dean C. Worcester Papers, Thetford Historical Society.)

22. Dean C. Worcester, *The Philippines Past and Present* (New York: Macmillan Company, 1914), 652.

23. Dean C. Worcester, "Memorandum for the Governor-General," October 31, 1910. (Dean C. Worcester Papers, Thetford Historical Society.)

24. Worcester, "Non-Christian Tribes," 15.

25. Worcester, "Non-Christian Tribes," 10.

26. Worcester, "Non-Christian Tribes," 21.

27. "Filipinos Incapable of Ruling," *Manila Times*, October 11, 1910, 1–2. For more on the response to Worcester's YMCA lectures, see Kramer, 342–44. See also Worcester, *Philippines Past and Present*, 652–53, and James Blount, *The American Occupation of the Philippines, 1898–1912* (New York: Knickerbocker Press, 1912), 583–85.

28. "Memorandum for Use."

29. "A Man of Controversy," *Chicago Evening Post*, July 17, 1913. (Clipping found in Worcester Philippine History Collection, Volume 18, folder 2, Special Collections Library, University of Michigan.)

30. William Dinwiddie to Dean C. Worcester, June 21, 1911. (Dean C. Worcester Papers, Box 1, Bentley Historical Library, University of Michigan.).

31. Dinwiddie to Worcester, June 21, 1911.

32. Dean C. Worcester to William Dinwiddie, April 22, 1911. (Dean C. Worcester Papers, Box 1, Bentley Historical Library, University of Michigan.)

33. "Legislation," *Annual Report of the Philippine Commission to the Secretary of War, 1913* (Washington, D.C.: Government Printing Office, 1914), 5.

34. "Man of Controversy."

35. Worcester to Dinwiddie, Apr. 22, 1911.

36. Charles Martin to Dean C. Worcester, April 17, 1911. (Dean C. Worcester Papers, Box 1, Bentley Historical Library, University of Michigan.)

37. Martin to Worcester, Apr. 17, 1911.

38. Charles Martin to Dean C. Worcester, April 24, 1911. (Dean C. Worcester Papers, Box 1, Bentley Historical Library, University of Michigan.)

39. Dean C. Worcester to William Dinwiddie, November 28, 1911. (Dean C. Worcester Papers, Box 1, Bentley Historical Library, University of Michigan.)

40. Worcester to Dinwiddie, Nov. 28, 1911.

41. Worcester to Dinwiddie, Nov. 28, 1911.

42. See Alison Griffiths, *Wondrous Difference: Cinema, Anthropology, and Turn-of-the-Century Visual Culture* (New York: Columbia University Press, 2002), for more on this.

43. Worcester to Dinwiddie, Nov. 28, 1911.

44. Worcester to Dinwiddie, Nov. 28, 1911.

45. George Magie to William Dinwiddie, June 23, 1911. (Dean C. Worcester Papers, Box 1, Bentley Historical Library, University of Michigan.)

46. William Dinwiddie to John N. Blair, April 15, 1913. (Dean C. Worcester Papers, Box 1, Bentley Historical Library, University of Michigan.).

47. Dinwiddie to Blair, Apr. 15, 1913.

48. John N. Blair to William Dinwiddie, April 16, 1913. (Dean C. Worcester Papers, Box 1, Bentley Historical Library, University of Michigan.)

49. John N. Blair to Dean C. Worcester, April 16, 1913. (Dean C. Worcester Papers, Box 1, Bentley Historical Library, University of Michigan.)

50. Charles Martin to Dean C. Worcester, April 2, 1914. (Dean C. Worcester Papers, Box 1, Bentley Historical Library, University of Michigan.)

51. Martin to Worcester, Apr. 2, 1914.

52. George Byron Gordon to Charles Martin, September 30, 1914. (George B. Gordon Director's Office Records, Penn Museum Archives.)

53. Gordon to Martin, Sept. 30, 1914.

54. Charles Martin to George Byron Gordon, November 7, 1914. (George B. Gordon Director's Office Records, Penn Museum Archives.)

55. Charles Martin to George Byron Gordon, September 11, 1915. (George B. Gordon Director's Office Records, Penn Museum Archives.)

56. Charles Martin to George Byron Gordon, September 25, 1915. (George B. Gordon Director's Office Records, Penn Museum Archives.)

57. Some of the footage, under the title "Native Life in the Philippines," can be streamed at http://archive.org/details/upenn-f16–550_Bontoc_Igorot_A.

58. Dean C. Worcester, "Report of the Secretary of the Interior," *Report of the Philippine Commission, 1912,* vol. IV (Washington, D.C.: Government Printing Office, 1913), 77.

59. Cornélis De Witt Willcox, *The Head Hunters of Northern Luzon: From Ifugao to Kalinga, a Ride Through the Mountains of Northern Luzon* (Kansas City, Mo.: Franklin Hudson Publishing Co., 1912), footnote on 242.

60. Griffiths, 234.

61. Emilie de Brigard, "The History of Ethnographic Film," in *Principles of Visual Anthropology, ed. Paul Hockings* (The Hague: Mouton Publishers, 1975), 19–20.

62. Leonard Donaldson, *The Cinematograph and Natural Science* (London: Ganes, Limited, 1912), 46–47.

63. Dean C. Worcester, "Report of the Secretary of the Interior," *Report of the Philippine Commission, 1910* (Washington, D.C.: Government Printing Office, 1911), 78.

64. Worcester, "1910 Report," 92–93.

65. Nick Deocampo, *Film: American Influences on Philippine Cinema* (Manila: Anvil Publishing, 2011), 279.

66. "Pictures in the Philippines," *Motography,* July 1911, 22.

67. "Memorandum of Moving Picture Films," 1–5. (Dean C. Worcester Papers, Box 1, Bentley Historical Library, University of Michigan.)

68. "Memorandum of Moving Picture Films," 6–12.

69. Griffiths, xxxiii.

70. "Memorandum of Moving Picture Films," 13.

71. "Memorandum of Moving Picture Films," 6.

72. Cablegram to Philippine Lyceum Bureau, July 18, 1913. (Dean C. Worcester Papers, Box 1, Bentley Historical Library, University of Michigan.)

73. "Our New Policy in Philippines is Attacked," *New York Times,* November 18, 1913.

74. Kramer, 368.

75. Quoted in Kramer, 358.

76. "Dean Worcester's Lectures," *New York Times,* December 29, 1913.

77. Griffiths, 267.

78. The head may not be real. It is known that Worcester staged headhunting scenes for his films, using papier mâché heads. In addition, this particular photograph is not in the UMMA archive, nor does it resemble any other known Worcester or Martin photograph.

79. "The Philippines: Lectures by Hon. Dean C. Worcester," 2. (Dean C. Worcester Papers, Box 2, Bentley Historical Library, University of Michigan.)

80. Gilbert Grosvenor to Edward H. Fallows, November 19, 1913. (Dean C. Worcester Papers, Box 1, Bentley Historical Library, University of Michigan.)

81. Grosvenor to Fallows, Nov. 19, 1913.

82. Tamar Y. Rothenberg, *Presenting America's World: Strategies of Innocence in "National Geographic Magazine," 1888–1945* (Burlington, Vt.: Ashgate, 2007), 54.

83. Rothenberg, 56–57. Grosvenor's letter to his mother is quoted in footnote 75.

84. Grosvenor to Fallows, Nov. 19, 1913.

85. Dean Worcester, "Notes for National Geographic Society Lecture, Dec. 5, 1913," 8–9. (Dean C. Worcester Papers, Box 2, Bentley Historical Library, University of Michigan.)

86. Worcester, "Notes for National Geographic Society Lecture," 1.

87. Worcester, "Notes for National Geographic Society Lecture," 2.

88. Worcester, "Notes for National Geographic Society Lecture," 7–8.

89. "Dean Worcester's Lectures," *New York Times,* December 29, 1913.

90. "Calls Wild Men our Wards," *New York Times,* December 31, 1913.

91. Description of Carnegie Hall Lecture, 1 [three-page typescript]. (Dean C. Worcester Papers, Box 2, Bentley Historical Library, University of Michigan.)

92. Benito M. Vergara Jr., *Displaying Filipinos: Photography and Colonialism in Early 20th Century Philippines* (Manila: University of Philippines Press, 1995), 62.

93. Description of Carnegie Hall Lecture.

94. "Worcester Pleads for the Filipinos," *New York Sun,* December 31, 1913.

95. "Calls Wild Men."

96. Quoted in Kramer, 369.

97. Typescript lecture schedule. (Dean C. Worcester Papers, Box 2, Bentley Historical Library, University of Michigan.)

98. Dean C. Worcester to W. H. Demarest, January 7, 1914. (Dean C. Worcester Papers, Box 1, Bentley Historical Library, University of Michigan.)

99. "Synopsis of lecture at Brooklyn Academy of Arts." (Dean C. Worcester Papers, Box 2, Bentley Historical Library, University of Michigan.)

100. "Wild Tribes Drop the Bolo for Baseball," *Wilmington Journal,* January 23, 1914.

101. "Wild Tribes Drop the Bolo for Baseball."

102. "Would Hold Philippines," *Baltimore Sun,* January 24, 1914.

103. Dean Conant Worcester to Gilbert H. Grosvenor, February 17, 1914. (Dean C.

Worcester Papers, Box 1, Bentley Historical Library, University of Michigan.) The list of photographs that Worcester sent Grosvenor is not included with the letter.

104. Gilbert H. Grosvenor to Dean Conant Worcester, February 19, 1914. (Dean C. Worcester Papers, Box 1, Bentley Historical Library, University of Michigan.)

105. My thanks to Nick Deocampo for bringing this advertisement to my attention.

106. W. Stephen Bush, "Native Life in the Philippines," *Moving Picture World,* April 18, 1914, 365.

107. Deocampo, 279.

108. Bush, 365.

Chapter Five

1. Rodney J. Sullivan, *Exemplar of Americanism: The Philippine Career of Dean C. Worcester* (Ann Arbor: University of Michigan Center for South and Southeast Asian Studies, 1991), 166.

2. James H. Blount, *The American Occupation of the Philippines, 1898–1912* (New York: Knickerbocker Press, 1912), v–vi.

3. Sullivan, 184.

4. "The Philippines," *New York Times,* August 25, 1912. The quote from Blount's book is found on page 571.

5. "The Philippines," *New York Times,* September 1, 1912.

6. Blount, 543.

7. Blount, 571.

8. Blount, 573.

9. Blount, 575.

10. Blount, 575–76.

11. Blount, 578.

12. James A. Smith, "The Philippines As I Saw Them," *Sunset,* August 1910, 127.

13. Blount, 579.

14. Blount, 579–80.

15. Sullivan, 162.

16. Paul A. Kramer, *The Blood of Government: Race, Empire, the United States, and the Philippines* (Chapel Hill: University of North Carolina Press, 2006), 366.

17. Dean C. Worcester, *The Philippines Past and Present* (New York: Macmillan Company, 1914), 14.

18. "Mr. Worcester's Defense of American Policy in the Philippines," *American Review of Reviews,* March 1914, 448.

19. Sullivan, 162.

20. Alfred W. McCoy, "Orientalism of the Philippine Photograph: America Discovers the Philippine Islands," http://uwdc.library.wisc.edu/collections/seait/philmatclass#board2, accessed August 5, 2012.

21. Worcester, *Philippines Past and Present,* frontispiece to vol. 1.

22. Benito M. Vergara Jr. *Displaying Filipinos: Photography and Colonialism in Early 20th Century Philippines* (Manila: University of the Philippines Press, 1995), 139.

23. Worcester, *Philippines Past and Present,* frontispiece to vol. 2.

24. Vergara, 154.

25. Dean C. Worcester, *Index to Philippine Photographs,* 174. (Dean C. Worcester Collection of Philippine Photographs, Newberry Library.)

26. Vergara, 157. See Vergara, 151–59, for a lengthy discussion of these two photographs.

27. Worcester, *Philippines Past and Present*, 464.

28. Worcester, *Philippines Past and Present*, 466.

29. Vergara, 137.

30. Vergara, 138.

31. Worcester, *Philippines Past and Present*, facing 464.

32. Vergara, 84.

33. Samuel E. Kane, *Thirty Years with the Philippine Head-Hunters* (London: Jarrolds, 1934), 226.

34. Worcester, *Philippines Past and Present*, 541.

35. Worcester, *Philippines Past and Present*, 544.

36. Worcester, *Philippines Past and Present*, 540–44, and Kane, 229–33, tell different versions of the same story. It is clear that Kane based much of his writing on Worcester's book, but changed some of the details.

37. Worcester, *Philippines Past and Present*, 543.

38. Worcester, *Philippines Past and Present*, facing 418.

39. Kane, 234.

40. Worcester, *Philippines Past and Present*, 543.

41. Worcester, *Philippines Past and Present*, opposite 664.

42. Worcester, *Philippines Past and Present*, 623.

43. Worcester, *Philippines Past and Present*, 624.

44. Kramer, 367.

45. Dean C. Worcester, "Lecture to Accompany Film and Slides Illustrating 'Native Life in the Philippines,'" 3. (Dean C. Worcester Papers, Box 2, Bentley Historical Library, University of Michigan.)

46. Dean C. Worcester, "Head-Hunters of Northern Luzon," *National Geographic Magazine*, September 1912, 886–89.

47. Dean C. Worcester to Elmer E. Silver, November 11, 1914. (Dean C. Worcester Papers, Box 1, Bentley Historical Library, University of Michigan.)

48. Worcester to Silver, Nov. 11, 1914.

49. Kramer, 354.

50. Gilbert Hitchcock to Dean Worcester, December 11, 1914. (Worcester Philippine History Collection, Special Collections Library, University of Michigan.)

51. Dean Conant Worcester to Gilbert Hitchcock, December 12, 1914. (Worcester Philippine History Collection, Special Collections Library, University of Michigan.)

52. Worcester to Hitchcock, Dec. 12, 1914.

53. U.S. Congress, Senate, *An Act to Declare the Purpose of the People of the United States as to the Future Political Status of the People of the Philippine Islands and to Provide a More Autonomous Government for the Islands: Hearings Before the Senate Committee on the Philippines on H.R. 18459*. 63rd Cong., 3rd sess. (1914), 44. Hereinafter referred to as *Hearings*.

54. Clarence B. Miller to Dean C. Worcester, December 26, 1914. (Worcester Philippine History Collection, Special Collections Library, University of Michigan.)

55. *Hearings*, 59.

56. *Hearings*, 264–65.

57. *Hearings*, 269.

58. *Hearings,* 269.

59. *Hearings,* 271.

60. *Index,* 150.

61. "Head-Hunters," 894.

62. "Head-Hunters," 889.

63. "Hon. Dean C. Worcester's Lecture on 'The Philippines,'" *Bulletin of the Brooklyn Institute of Arts and Sciences,* January 10, 1914, 7.

64. Smith, 131.

65. *Index,* 146.

66. *Hearings,* 272. Bracketed word in the original.

67. *Hearings,* 272.

68. *Hearings,* 272–73.

69. *Hearings,* 292.

70. *Hearings,* 292.

71. *Hearings,* 294.

72. Sullivan, 215–16.

73. *Hearings,* 294.

74. *Hearings,* 295.

75. *Hearings,* 302.

76. *Hearings,* 310.

77. Douglas O. Morgan to Dean C. Worcester, January 13, 1915. (Worcester Philippine History Collection, Special Collections Library, University of Michigan.)

78. Dean C. Worcester to Douglas O. Morgan, January 14, 1915. (Worcester Philippine History Collection, Special Collections Library, University of Michigan.)

79. J. R. Wilson to Dean C. Worcester, February 15, 1915. (Worcester Philippine History Collection, Special Collections Library, University of Michigan.)

80. Wilson to Worcester, Feb. 15, 1915.

81. Sullivan, 182.

82. *Hearings,* 38–39.

83. *Hearings,* 39–40.

84. *Hearings,* 120.

85. Sullivan, 156.

86. *Manuel L. Quezon's speech on the new freedom in the Philippines: Speech of Hon. Clyde H. Tavenner of Illinois in the House of Representatives, July 11, 1914* (Washington, D.C.: Government Printing Office, 1914), 6.

87. "Nude and Semi-Nude to be Taboo," *Cablenews,* October 13, 1913. (Worcester Philippine History Collection, Special Collections Library, University of Michigan.)

88. Newspaper fragment attributed to *Bulletin,* December 2, 1913. (Worcester Philippine History Collection, Special Collections Library, University of Michigan.)

89. "Photographing of Igorots and Negritos Taboo," *Cablenews,* February 26, 1914. (Worcester Philippine History Collection, Special Collections Library, University of Michigan.)

90. *Bulletin,* February 24, 1914. (Worcester Philippine History Collection, Special Collections Library, University of Michigan.)

91. *Hearings,* 350.

92. *Hearings,* 350.

93. Wilfred T. Denison, "Report of the Secretary of the Interior," *Annual Report of the Philippine Commission, 1914* (Washington, D.C.: Government Printing Office, 1915), 105.

94. Denison, 104.

95. Kramer, 378–79.

96. Maximo M. Kalaw, *The Case for the Filipinos* (New York: Century Co., 1916), 159–60.

97. Kalaw, 165.

98. The folder containing this letter at the Special Collections Library at the University of Michigan indicates that Charles Martin wrote it. However, the signature on the letter does not match Martin's signature on another letter that he definitively wrote. (Worcester Philippine History Collection, Special Collections Library, University of Michigan.)

99. Hamilton Holt to Dean C. Worcester, October 23, 1914. (Dean C. Worcester Papers, Box 1, Bentley Historical Library, University of Michigan.)

100. Dean C. Worcester, "Dangers of the Present Philippine Situation," *Independent,* February 23, 1914, 263–65.

101. Dean C. Worcester, "A Nesting Place of *Micropus Subfurcatus* in Mindoro," *Philippine Journal of Science* 15, no. 6 (1919): 533–34.

102. Dean C. Worcester, "The Philippine Islands," *Mentor,* August 16, 1915.

103. David H. Price. *Anthropological Intelligence: The Deployment and Neglect of American Anthropology in the Second World War* (Durham, N.C.: Duke University Press, 2008), 96.

104. Price, 97.

105. Dean C. Worcester to Gilbert Grosvenor, August 13, 1914. (Dean C. Worcester Papers, Box 1, Bentley Historical Library, University of Michigan.)

106. John O. LaGorce to Dean C. Worcester, August 20, 1914. (Dean C. Worcester Papers, Box 1, Bentley Historical Library, University of Michigan.)

107. Catherine A. Lutz and Jane L. Collins, *Reading "National Geographic"* (Chicago: University of Chicago Press, 1993), 115.

108. Lutz and Collins, 175.

109. Nerissa S. Balce, "The Filipina's Breast: Savagery, Docility, and the Erotics of the American Empire," *Social Text 87* (2006): 89.

110. Richard Drinnon, *Facing West: The Metaphysics of Indian Hating and Empire Building* (1980; New York: Schocken Books 1990), 301.

111. Sullivan, 177–78.

112. Mabel Cook Cole and Fay-Cooper Cole, *The Story of Primitive Man: His Earliest Appearance and Development* (Chicago: University of Knowledge, 1940).

113. "The Secret Museum of Mankind," http://ian.macky.net/secretmuseum/. Accessed June 12, 2012.

114. *The Secret Museum of Mankind* (New York: Manhattan Books, no date [1935]).

115. McCoy.

Bibliography

Archival Sources

Forbes, W. Cameron, Papers. Houghton Library, Harvard University.

Gordon, George B., Director's Office Records, Penn Museum Archives.

Historic Photo Archive, Rautenstrach-Joest Museum, Köln, Germany.

National Anthropological Archives, Smithsonian Institution.

Peabody Museum of Archaeology, Harvard University.

Photo Archives—Philippine Collections, Field Museum, Chicago.

Worcester, Dean C., Collection of Philippine Photographs. Newberry Library, Chicago.

Worcester, Dean C., Papers. Bentley Historical Library, University of Michigan.

Worcester, Dean C., Papers. Thetford (Vermont) Historical Society.

Worcester, Dean C., Photographic Collection at the University of Michigan Museum of Anthropology.

Worcester Philippine History Collection, Special Collections Library, University of Michigan.

Newspapers

Baltimore Sun
Cablenews
Chicago Evening Post
Manila Times
New York Sun
New York Times
Sunday News (Charleston, S.C.)
Wilmington Journal

Works by Dean C. Worcester

Worcester, Dean C. "Dangers of the Present Philippine Situation." *Independent,* February 23, 1914, 263–65.

Worcester, Dean C. "Field Sports Among the Wild Men of Northern Luzon." *National Geographic Magazine,* March 1911, 215–67.

Worcester, Dean C. "Head-Hunters of Northern Luzon." *National Geographic Magazine,* September 1912, 833–930.

Worcester, Dean C., dir. *Native Life in the Philippines.* 1913.

Worcester, Dean C. "The Native Peoples of the Philippines." *Report of the Philippine Commission,* part 1. Washington, D.C.: Government Printing Office, 1900.

Worcester, Dean C. "A Nesting Place of *Micropus Subfurcatus* in Mindoro." *Philippine Journal of Science* 15, no. 6 (1919): 533–34.

Worcester, Dean C. "The Non-Christian Peoples of the Philippine Islands: With an Account of What Has Been Done for Them Under American Rule." *National Geographic Magazine,* November 1913, 1157–1256.

Worcester, Dean C. "The Non-Christian Tribes of Northern Luzon." *Philippine Journal of Science* 1, no. 8 (1906): 791–875.

Worcester, Dean C. "Notes on Some Primitive Philippine Tribes." *National Geographic Magazine,* June 1898, 284–301.

Worcester, Dean C. "The Philippine Islands." *Mentor,* August 16, 1915.

Worcester, Dean C. *The Philippine Islands and Their People.* New York: Macmillan Company, 1898.

Worcester, Dean C. *The Philippines Past and Present.* New York: Macmillan Company, 1914.

Worcester, Dean C. "Report of the Secretary of the Interior." *Report of the Philippine Commission, 1901.* Washington, D.C.: Government Printing Office, 1902.

Worcester, Dean C. "Report of the Secretary of the Interior." *Report of the Philippine Commission, 1904.* Washington, D.C.: Government Printing Office, 1905.

Worcester, Dean C. "Report of the Secretary of the Interior." *Report of the Philippine Commission, 1906.* Washington, D.C.: Government Printing Office, 1907.

Worcester, Dean C. "Report of the Secretary of the Interior." *Report of the Philippine Commission, 1907.* Washington, D.C.: Government Printing Office, 1908.

Worcester, Dean C. "Report of the Secretary of the Interior." *Report of the Philippine Commission, 1910.* Washington, D.C.: Government Printing Office, 1911.

Worcester, Dean C. "Report of the Secretary of the Interior." *Report of the Philippine Commission, 1912.* Washington, D.C.: Government Printing Office, 1913.

Worcester, Dean C. *Some Aspects of the Philippine Question.* Chicago: Hamilton Club of Chicago Serial Publications, no. 13, 1900.

Worcester, Dean C., and Frank S. Bourns. "Spanish Rule in the Philippines." *Cosmopolitan,* October 1897, 587–600.

Other Government Documents

Barrows, David P. *Instructions for Volunteer Field Workers.* Manila: Bureau of Non-Christian Tribes for the Philippine Islands, 1901.

Barrows, David P. "Report of the Chief of the Bureau of Nonchristian Tribes for the Year Ending August 31, 1902." *Report of the Philippine Commission, 1902.* Washington, D.C.: Government Printing Office, 1903.

Barrows, David P. "Second Annual Report of the Chief of the Ethnological Survey for the Philippine Islands." *Report of the Philippine Commission, 1903.* Washington, D.C.: Government Printing Office, 1904.

Denison, Wilfred T. "Report of the Secretary of the Interior." *Annual Report of the Philippine Commission, 1914.* Washington, D.C.: Government Printing Office, 1915.

Freer, Paul C. *Description of the New Buildings of the Bureau of Government Laboratories.* Manila: Bureau of Public Printing, 1905.

Freer, Paul C. "Report of the Director, Bureau of Science." *Report of the Philippine Commission, 1906.* Washington, D.C.: Government Printing Office, 1907.

Freer, Paul C. "Report of the Director, Bureau of Science." *Report of the Philippine Commission, 1907.* Washington, D.C.: Government Printing Office, 1908.

Freer, Paul C. "Report of the Superintendent of Government Laboratories for the Year Ending August 31, 1902." *Report of the Philippine Commission, 1902.* Washington, D.C.: Government Printing Office, 1903.

Jenks, Albert Ernest. *The Bontoc Igorot.* Manila: Bureau of Public Printing, 1905.

"Legislation." *Annual Report of the Philippine Commission to the Secretary of War, 1913.* Washington, D.C.: Government Printing Office, 1914.

Miller, Mertin L. "Report of the Acting Chief of the Ethnological Survey." *Report of the Philippine Commission, 1904.* Washington, D.C.: Government Printing Office, 1905.

Offley, R. S. "Report of the Governor of Mindoro." *Report of the Philippine Commission, 1907.* Washington, D.C.: Government Printing Office, 1908.

Quezon, Manuel L. *Manuel L. Quezon's Speech on the New Freedom in the Philippines: Speech of Hon. Clyde H. Tavenner of Illinois in the House of Representatives, July 11, 1914.* Washington, D.C.: Government Printing Office, 1914.

United States Bureau of the Census. *Census of the Philippines.* Washington, D.C.: Government Printing Office, 1905.

U.S. Congress. Senate. *An Act to Declare the Purpose of the People of the United States as to the Future Political Status of the People of the Philippine Islands and to Provide a More Autonomous Government for the Islands: Hearings Before the Senate Committee on the Philippines on H.R. 18459.* Sixty-third Congress, third session, 1914.

Other Sources

Abramson, Howard S. *"National Geographic": Behind America's Lens on the World.* New York: Crown, 1988.

Aguilar, Filomeno V., Jr. "Tracing Origins: *Ilustrado* Nationalism and the Racial Science of Migration Waves." *Journal of Asian Studies* 6, no. 3 (2005): 605–37.

"American Development in the Philippines." *National Geographic Magazine,* May 1903, 197–203.

Balce, Nerissa S. "The Filipina's Breast: Savagery, Docility, and the Erotics of the American Empire." *Social Text 87* (2006): 89–110.

Banta, Melissa. "Photographic Encounters in the Philippines, 1898–1910." *IIAS Newsletter* 44 (2007): 14–15.

Barcan, Ruth. *Nudity: A Cultural Anatomy (Dress, Body, Culture).* Oxford: Berg, 2004.

"Benguet—The Garden of the Philippines." *National Geographic Magazine,* May 1903, 203–10.

Blount, James H. *The American Occupation of the Philippines, 1898–1912.* New York: Knickerbocker Press, 1912.

Brands, H. W. *Bound to Empire: The United States and the Philippines*. New York: Oxford University Press, 1992.

Breitbart, Eric. *A World on Display: Photographs from the St. Louis World's Fair*. Albuquerque: University of New Mexico Press, 1997.

Bush, W. Stephen. "Native Life in the Philippines." *The Moving Picture World*, April 18, 1914, 365.

Chamberlin, Frederick. *The Philippine Problem, 1898–1913*. Boston: Little, Brown, and Company, 1913.

Cole, Mabel Cook, and Fay-Cooper Cole. *The Story of Primitive Man: His Earliest Appearance and Development*. Chicago: University of Knowledge, 1940.

de Brigard, Emilie. "The History of Ethnographic Film." In *Principles of Visual Anthropology*, edited by Paul Hockings, 13–43. The Hague: Mouton Publishers, 1975.

Deocampo, Nick. *Film: American Influences on Philippine Cinema*. Manila: Anvil Publishing, 2011.

Donaldson, Leonard. *The Cinematograph and Natural Science*. London: Ganes, Limited, 1912.

Drinnon, Richard. *Facing West: The Metaphysics of Indian Hating and Empire Building* 1980. New York: Schocken Books, 1990.

Englehard, Jutta Beate, and Stefan Rohde-Enslin. "Kolonialzeitliche Photographien von den Philippinen." *Kölner Museums Bulletin* (April 1997): 34–46.

Ewing, William A. *The Body: Photographs of the Human Form*. San Francisco: Chronicle, 1994.

Gonzalez, Vernadette Vicuña. "Headhunter Itineraries: The Philippines as America's Dream Jungle." *Global South* 3, no. 2 (2009): 144–72.

Griffiths, Alison. *Wondrous Difference: Cinema, Anthropology, and Turn-of-the-Century Visual Culture*. New York: Columbia University Press, 2002.

Grosvenor, Gilbert. *The National Geographic Society and Its Magazine*. Washington, D.C.: National Geographic Society, 1957.

Grosvenor, Gilbert, ed. *Scenes from Every Land*. Washington, D.C.: National Geographic Society, 1907.

Hayden, Ralston. "Biographical Sketch." In *Philippines Past and Present*, by Dean C. Worcester, 3–79. New York: Macmillan Company, 1930.

Hight, Eleanor M., and Gary D. Sampson. "Introduction: Photography, 'Race,' and Post-colonial Theory." In *Colonialist Photography: Imag(in)ing Race and Place*, edited by Eleanor M. Hight and Gary D. Sampson, 1–19. New York: Routledge, 2002.

Holt, Elizabeth Mary. *Colonizing Filipinas: Nineteenth Century Representations of the Philippines in Western Historiography*. Manila: Ateneo de Manila University Press, 2002.

"Hon. Dean C. Worcester's Lecture on 'The Philippines.'" *Bulletin of the Brooklyn Institute of Arts and Sciences,* January 10, 1914.

Hutterer, Karl L. "Dean C. Worcester and Philippine Anthropology." *Philippine Quarterly of Culture and Society* 6 (1978): 125–56.

Jenks, Albert Ernest. Review of "The Non-Christian Tribes of Northern Luzon," by Dean C. Worcester. *American Anthropologist* 9, no. 3 (1907): 587–93.

Kalaw, Maximo M. *The Case for the Filipinos*. New York: Century Company, 1916.

Kane, Samuel E. *Thirty Years with the Philippine Head-Hunters*. London: Jarrolds, 1934.

Kasson, John F. *Houdini, Tarzan, and the Perfect Man: The White Male Body and the Challenge of Modernity in America*. New York: Hill and Wang, 2001.

Kramer, Paul A. *The Blood of Government: Race, Empire, the United States, and the Philippines*. Chapel Hill: University of North Carolina Press, 2006.

Levine, Philippa. "States of Undress: Nakedness and the Colonial Imagination." *Victorian Studies* 50, no. 2 (2008): 189–219.

Lockwood, Charles C. *The Life of Edward E. Ayer.* Chicago: A.C. McClurg and Co., 1929.

Lutz, Catherine A. and Jane L. Collins, *Reading "National Geographic".* Chicago: University of Chicago Press, 1993.

McCoy, Alfred. "Orientalism of the Philippine Photograph: America Discovers the Philippine Islands," http://uwdc.library.wisc.edu/collections/seait/philmatclass#board2. Accessed August 5, 2012.

Miller, Bonnie M. *From Liberation to Conquest: The Visual and Popular Cultures of the Spanish-American War of 1898.* Amherst: University of Massachusetts Press, 2011.

"Mr. Worcester's Defense of American Policy in the Philippines." *American Review of Reviews,* March 1914, 447–48.

Ohmann, Richard. *Selling Culture: Magazines, Markets, and Class at the Turn of the Century.* New York: Verso, 1998.

"Pictures in the Philippines." *Motography,* July 1911, 22.

Pier, Arthur S. *American Apostles to the Philippines.* Boston: Beacon Press, 1950.

Pinney, Christopher. "The Parallel Histories of Anthropology and Photography." In *Anthropology and Photography,* edited by Elizabeth Edwards, 74–95. New Haven: Yale University Press, 1992.

Pinney, Christopher. *Photography and Anthropology.* London: Reaktion Books, 2011.

Price, David H. *Anthropological Intelligence: The Deployment and Neglect of American Anthropology in the Second World War.* Durham, N.C.: Duke University Press, 2008.

Rafael, Vicente L. *White Love and Other Events in Filipino History.* Durham, N.C.: Duke University Press, 2000.

Rice, Mark. "His Name Was Don Francisco Muro: Reconstructing an Image of American Imperialism." *American Quarterly* 62, no. 1 (2010): 49–76.

Rodriguez, Mary Jane B. "Reading a Colonial Bureau: The Politics of Cultural Investigation of the Non-Christian Filipinos." *Social Science Diliman* 6, no. 1 (2010): 1–27.

Rosaldo, Renato. "Imperialist Nostalgia." *Representations* 26 (1989): 107–22.

Rothenberg, Tamar Y. *Presenting America's World: Strategies of Innocence in "National Geographic Magazine," 1888–1945.* Burlington, Vt.: Ashgate: 2007.

Rydell, Robert. *All the World's a Fair: Visions of Empire at American International Expositions, 1876–1916.* Chicago: University of Chicago Press, 1984.

Salman, Michael. *The Embarrassment of Slavery: Controversies over Bondage and Nationalism in the American Colonial Philippines.* Berkeley: University of California Press, 2001.

Schneirov, Matthew. *The Dream of a New Social Order: Popular Magazines in America, 1893–1914.* New York: Columbia University Press, 1994.

The Secret Museum of Mankind. New York: Manhattan Books, no date [1935].

Sen, Satadru. "Savage Bodies, Civilized Pleasures: M. V. Portman and the Andamanese." *American Ethnologist* 36, no. 2 (2009): 364–79.

Smith, James F. "The Philippines As I Saw Them." *Sunset,* August 1910, 127–38, 223–25.

Stanley, Peter W. "'The Voice of Worcester Is the Voice of God': How One American Found Fulfillment in the Philippines." In *Reappraising an Empire: New Perspectives on Philippine-American History,* edited by Peter W. Stanley, 117–41. Cambridge: Harvard University Press, 1984.

Sullivan, Rodney J. *Exemplar of Americanism: The Philippine Career of Dean C. Worcester.* Ann Arbor: University of Michigan Center for South and Southeast Asian Studies, 1991.

Tuason, Julie A. "The Ideology of Empire in *National Geographic Magazine*'s Coverage of the Philippines, 1898–1908." *Geographical Review* 89, no. 1 (1999): 34–53.

Vergara, Benito M., Jr. *Displaying Filipinos: Photography and Colonialism in Early 20th Century Philippines*. Manila: University of the Philippines Press, 1995.

Wexler, Laura. *Tender Violence: Domestic Visions in an Age of U.S. Imperialism*. Chapel Hill: University of North Carolina Press, 2000.

Willcox, Cornélis De Witt. *The Head Hunters of Northern Luzon: From Ifugao to Kalinga, a Ride Through the Mountains of Northern Luzon*. Kansas City, Mo.: Franklin Hudson Publishing Co., 1912.

Index

American Occupation of the Philippines, The (Blount), 156–71, 176, 182

American-Philippine Company, 118, 120, 123, 124, 134, 141, 171, 179–81

anthropometric photography, 26, 38, 87

archives of Dean Worcester photographs
classification of Philippine "tribes" in, 7, 14–16, 20, 22, 26–27, 29, 30–35, 42, 95, 99, 107
creation of, 2–4, 21, 25, 28–29, 30, 39, 42, 187
disseminating, 19–21, 30–36, 58, 62–63, 84
locations of, 3, 20–21
nakedness and nudity in, 48, 50–57, 58–63, 71, 191–92

Ayer, Edward E. (Newberry Library/ Field Museum), 31–35, 36, 42, 55, 56, 58–59, 62, 65, 100, 110, 176, 191

Barrows, David P. (Bureau of Non-Christian Tribes), 24–26, 33, 51

Blount, James, 156–61, 176, 182

Blumentritt, Ferdinand, 24, 99

Bourns, Frank, 3–6, 13, 19, 86, 87

Bureau of Non-Christian Tribes, 24–27, 41, 47

census of the Philippine Islands (1903)
classifications of Philippine "tribes" in, 29, 92, 99, 112, 146
Dean Worcester's photographs and, 86, 93–96, 148

colonial photography, 3, 50–51, 62, 80, 161, 164

Dinwiddie, William, 127–35, 140

ethnographic film, 137–38, 140

ethnographic photography, 4, 38, 60, 62, 87, 106, 159, 177

Ethnological Survey (Bureau of Non-Christian Tribes), 24, 28, 30–31, 36, 51, 58–62, 106, 186–87, 191

Fallows, Edward, 116, 124, 141, 143–47

Felder, Edmund, 112, 117, 120–23, 125, 127

Flattery, Douglas, 7, 122–24, 127, 128

Forbes, William Cameron, 21, 30, 40–42, 47, 125, 157, 163
purchases Dean Worcester's photographs, 35–36, 55, 58

Freer, Paul (Bureau of Government Laboratories), 25, 26, 32–33, 35

Gordon, George Byron, 134–36
Grosvenor, Gilbert, 84, 89, 92–93, 96–
    96, 112, 115–16, 144–46, 152–53,
    190

Holmes, William Henry, 19–20, 55–56,
    64–65

Ibag (Negrito), 42, 44, 45, 92, 108, 130,
    142, 177, 189
"Igorot sequence" (Don Francisco
    Muro), 63–71, 73–75, 78, 80,
    149

Jenks, Albert, 3, 26, 36–38, 58, 70,
    191–92
Jones bill, 97, 117, 155, 168, 169, 173,
    182
    Dean Worcester's testimony and, 171–
    72, 179–80

Kalaw, Maximo, 187–88
Kipling, Rudyard, 18, 97, 147
Küppers-Loosen, Georg, 35–36, 55–56,
    58

Martin, Charles
    accuses Dean Worcester of cheating
        him, 134–35
    contributions to the Worcester
        archive, 3, 28–29, 32–33, 37–38,
        93, 98–99, 107, 162, 186, 192
    filmmaking activities, 120–21, 127–
        33, 136, 140
    goes to work for the National Geo-
        graphic Society, 136, 189–90
    hired as government photographer,
        35–36
    leaves his position as government
        photographer, 134, 186, 188
McKinley, William, 6, 8, 157
Menage Expedition, 5–6, 12–13, 86, 87
Muro, Don Francisco (Bontoc Igorot),
    69–79, 139, 178

nakedness and nudity
    in Dean Worcester's photographs,
        48, 50–57, 58–63, 71, 184–86,
        191–92

theories of, 41, 47–50, 52, 55, 56, 93,
    182
National Geographic Magazine
    Dean Worcester's articles in (see
        Worcester, Dean C., articles in
        National Geographic Magazine)
    nudity in, 88, 90–93, 190
    rise of monthly magazines and, 84–86
    rise of photography in, 88–90, 93–95
National Geographic Society, 83, 89, 93,
    96, 136, 189
    Dean Worcester's lectures before, 18–
    19, 116, 143–48
Native Life in the Philippines (motion
    picture), 2, 139–40, 142, 153–55,
    156, 170, 185, 192
Newberry Library, 21, 31, 44, 58, 62,
    81, 90, 94–95, 101, 106, 110–11,
    175–76

Peabody Museum (Harvard University),
    21, 35–36
Penn Museum, 134–36
Philippine-American War, 3, 8–13, 16,
    44, 147, 157, 163, 164
Philippine "tribes" in Dean Worcester's
    films
    Ifugaos, 125, 126, 129, 140, 170
    Igorots (Bontoc), 125, 126, 129, 140,
        151
    Igorots (Lepanto), 140
    Ilongots, 129, 140
    Kalingas, 140
    Negritos, 125, 139, 146, 147
    Tingians, 125, 126, 129, 140
Philippine "tribes" in Dean Worcester's
    photographic archives
    Atás, 20, 26, 34, 95, 113
    Bagobos, 34, 95, 114, 189, 191
    Bilanes, 20, 34, 95, 114
    Bukidnons, 95, 114, 149, 166–68,
        178–79, 187, 189
    Gaddans, 20, 34, 95, 189
    Guíangas, 20, 34
    Ifugaos, 1, 29, 37–39, 99, 105, 107,
        109, 110, 125
    Igorots (Benguet), 29, 32, 34, 37, 65,
        73, 99, 100, 107, 114, 126
    Igorots (Bontoc), 1, 33, 34, 58–63,

64–75, 78, 99, 104, 106, 107, 109–10, 113–15, 125, 162–63, 177–78, 189
Ilocanos, 29
Ilongots, 33, 38, 52, 80–82, 99, 108, 185, 189
Kalaganes, 20, 34
Kalingas, 20, 34, 37–38, 52–53, 80, 95, 99, 107–10, 113–14, 165–66, 189
Mangyans, 6, 33, 36, 86, 88, 90, 92, 114
Moros, 6, 20, 189
Negritos, 20, 22–23, 26, 29, 32–34, 38, 42–49, 52–55, 69, 87, 91–92, 96, 108, 114, 142–43, 148, 177, 189, 191
Pampangans, 29
Pangasinans, 29
Remontado, 26, 34, 95
Samales, 20, 34
Subanos, 33
Tagacaoles (Tagakaoles), 20, 34
Tagalogs, 15–17, 20, 29, 32–34, 56–58, 87, 189
Tagbanúas, 6, 20, 26–27, 34, 86–88, 90–92, 95, 189
Tingians (Tinguianes), 20, 34, 37–39, 126, 185, 189
Tirurayes, 20, 34, 113
Visayans, 29, 34, 87, 161
Zamboanguenos, 29
Pit-a-pit (Bontoc Igorot), 162–63

Quezon, Manuel, 97, 173–75, 183–84, 192

Rautenstrauch-Jost Museum, 21, 36, 58
Roosevelt, Theodore, 93, 157

Saking (Kalinga), 165–67
Schurman, Jacob, 6, 10, 11
Schurman Commission, 6, 8–19, 24, 156, 163
Spanish-American War, 5, 8, 44, 127, 163
St. Louis World's Fair, 45–46, 59, 60, 62, 67, 69, 75, 78

Taft, William Howard, 73, 86, 145, 157, 171, 181
Taft Commission, 19, 157, 158, 163

United States National Museum, 19–20, 55–56, 64–65
University of Michigan Museum of Anthropology (UMMA), 3, 7, 14–16, 21–22, 26, 29–30, 34, 47–48, 55–58, 60, 68, 70, 74–75, 78, 95, 99, 105

Wilson, Woodrow, 1, 97, 116, 142, 145–46, 156, 184
Worcester, Dean C.
  accusations of dishonesty leveled at
    by William Dinwiddie, 133–34
    by Charles Martin, 134–36
  annual inspection trips as secretary of the interior, 21–22, 28, 41–42, 102, 107, 115, 124, 130, 165
  annual reports as secretary of the interior, 24, 28–30, 63–67, 69, 84, 102, 136, 138, 139
  articles in *National Geographic Magazine* (chronological order)
    "Notes on Some Primitive Philippine Tribes" (1898), 86–88, 90, 92, 97, 100, 113
    "Field Sports Among the Wild Men of Northern Luzon" (1911), 83, 99–106, 174
    "Head-Hunters of Northern Luzon" (1912), 84, 106–12, 160, 170, 175–76, 187–88
    "The Non-Christian Peoples of the Philippine Islands" (1913), 84, 112–15, 118, 200
  articles (other, chronological order)
    "Spanish Rule in the Philippines" (1897), 5
    "The Non-Christian Tribes of Northern Luzon" (1906), 29, 36–39, 42, 51, 114, 192
    "Dangers of the Present Philippine Situation" (1914), 188
  books
    The Philippine Islands and Their

Worcester, Dean C. (*continued*)
   People (1898), 5–6, 13–14, 19,
      56, 86–87, 156
   The Philippines Past and Present
      (1914), 2, 8, 12, 21, 63, 80,
      155, 156, 160–70, 172, 174,
      177, 185, 190–91, 192
   business interests in the Philippines,
      19, 39, 118, 120, 123–24, 141,
      170, 179, 182, 187
   contemporary criticisms of, 4, 21–22,
      30, 42, 156–61, 182, 183–88
   development as a photographer, 4–5,
      7–8, 9–16, 22, 70–71
   filmmaking activities, 98, 120–
      25, 126–35, 136–37, 139–
      40
   influence of photographs of, 82, 84,
      105, 117, 124, 155, 159–60, 182,
      183–84, 188–89, 191–92
   lectures, 1–2, 17–20, 42, 47–48, 63,
      79, 80, 116–17, 118–26, 141–55,
      156, 160, 170–79, 182, 185, 187,
      192
   testimony before U.S. Senate com-
      mittee (1914), 63, 155, 171–72,
      174–76, 179–86
Worcester, Nanon Leas, 7–12, 15

Printed and bound by CPI Group (UK) Ltd, Croydon, CR0 4YY

09/06/2025